"Scott Giacomucci's book brings an intersection of the macro-vision of healing to the micro-version of healing trauma in the person and group and society. A profoundly skillful presentation awaits you. Jump in and swim in this collection of brilliance and wisdom about the world, our friends, and our lives."

Ed Schreiber, *DD, Ed.M, MSW, TEP, Director of the Zerka T. Moreno Foundation; Adjunct Professor, Lesley University Drama Therapy Program; Co-Editor of the* Autobiography of a Genius *by Jacob Moreno,* The Quintessential Zerka *and* To Dream Again *by Zerka Moreno*

"Giacomucci's work contributes meaningfully to the growing literature on trauma-informed practice. His integration of psychodrama with clinical treatment for complex PTSD is both timely and valuable."

Natan P.F. Kellermann, *PhD, Clinical psychologist, psychodramatist (retired); author of* Focus on Psychodrama *(1992),* Holocaust Trauma *(2009),* Sociodrama and Collective Trauma *(2007), and co-editor of* Psychodrama with Trauma Survivors *(2000)*

"Scott's careful investigation of the intricacies of psychodramatic interventions and their limitations is, at the very least, a breakthrough in the field and demands careful study."

Jonathan D. Moreno, *PhD, David and Lyn Silfen University Professor Emeritus, University of Pennsylvania; Author of* Impromptu Man *(2014) and* Absolutely Essential *(2025)*

"*Trauma-Focused Psychodrama* by Scott Giacomucci is a meticulously crafted and thoughtfully organized guidebook. It offers essential knowledge and clinical wisdom for psychodrama group psychotherapists working with complex trauma, supporting the safer and more effective use of the method. This book stands out as an invaluable resource not only for psychodramatists but for all professionals working in the field of trauma."

Deniz Altınay, *MA, President of Istanbul Psychodrama Institute; Chair of Psychodrama Section, Co-Chair of the Social and Collective Traumas Committee of the International Association of Group Psychotherapy (IAGP)*

"Scott Giacomucci's *Trauma-Focused Psychodrama* is more than a training manual – it is a master class in integrating theory, research, and action. Drawing on EMDR, Somatic Experiencing, neurobiology, and the Adaptive Information Processing model, he makes explicit links between psychodrama and contemporary trauma therapies, weaving in concepts such as memory reconsolidation, posttraumatic growth, and role training for recovery. This theoretical clarity, combined with generous practical examples and links to live demonstrations, shows readers not only what to do but why it matters. Scott also addresses psychodrama's historical reputation for catharsis and powerfully reframes it – shifting 'Do, Undo, Redo' to 'Resource, Undo, Redo' – placing resourcing and integration at the heart of trauma-focused action methods. For students and practitioners alike, this book models the thoughtful, ethically attuned, and evidence-informed psychodrama our field most needs."

Catherine D. Nugent, *LCPC, TEP, Executive Director/Principal Trainer, Laurel Psychodrama Training Institute; Former Chief, Workforce Development Branch, Substance Abuse and Mental Health Services Administration*

"Long ago I had decades of experience with the power of psychodrama in bringing about change with our patients who now would be diagnosed with complex PTSD although that terminology had not yet evolved. Nothing was as effective as a therapeutic tool that could compare to psychodrama. But like any other power tool, it must be developed in the hands of competent, responsible and safe practitioners. This is why I am so pleased that Scott Giacomucci is extending his important work with a special focus on these patients. I am truly gratified that finally, psychodrama is getting the attention it deserves and that is long overdue."

Sandra L. Bloom, *MD, Founder of Creating Presence; Author of* Creating Sanctuary: Toward the Evolution of Sane Societies*; Chief Editor of* The Oxford Handbook of Trauma-Informed Social Health*; Associate Professor of Health Management and Policy, Dornsife School of Public Health, Drexel University*

"This authoritative, careful, systematic, and remarkably international guide offers an unprecedented look into the theory and application of psychodramatic techniques across diverse settings. It is an important addition for education professionals worldwide, presenting scientifically reflected, intercontinental applications and numerous role models for enhancing one's own educational practice."

Dan Tomasulo, *PhD, TEP, MFA, MAPP, Professor of Education, Academic Director, Spirituality Mind Body Institute, Teachers College, Columbia University*

"Human services fields must meet the changing needs of people who are experiencing increasing complex effects of multiple challenges. Dr. Scott Giacomucci has an instinct for healing-focused orientations and interventions that not only consider trauma's impacts but also trauma's possibilities. In this practical and hopeful book, Dr. Giacomucci leads us through what is needed to co-create spaces of deep resilience. Not the ability to return to a pre-trauma shape but the potent welcome of tenacious integrative transformation."

Leticia Nieto, *PsyD, LMFT, TEP, Leadership coach, psychotherapist, and educator; Author of* Beyond Inclusion, Beyond Empowerment: A Developmental Strategy to Liberate Everyone; *former Professor of Counseling, Saint Martin's University*

"Dr. Scott Giacomucci's *Trauma-Focused Psychodrama: Experiential Therapy for Complex PTSD* is a groundbreaking and essential contribution to the literature on psychodrama and trauma treatment. This book offers not only a deep exploration of trauma, PTSD, and CPTSD through the lens of psychodrama but also provides practical, experiential guidance for clinicians and trainees alike. As an international trainer, I see this work as a vital resource for psychodramatists, social workers, and mental health professionals across the globe, and I believe it will become a cornerstone text for training programs and certification preparation worldwide."

Daniela Simmons, *PhD, TEP, Creator of Tele'Drama; International Trainer, Educator, and Supervisor in Psychodrama, Sociometry, and Group Psychotherapy; Leadership and Organizational Consultant*

"In his new book, *Trauma-Focused Psychodrama: Experiential Therapy for Complex PTSD*, Dr. Scott Giacomucci builds on the foundation of his previous work to make the case for the use of psychodrama as a primary modality for the treatment of complex trauma. As before, Dr. Giacomucci emphasizes the need for practitioner training and the safety and the safeguarding of clients as essential bases of this powerful technique that is both trauma-informed and trauma-responsive. I highly recommend this text."

Christine A. Courtois, *PhD, ABPP, Consultant/Trainer, Trauma Psychology and Trauma Treatment; Author of* Healing the Incest Wound: Adult Survivors in Therapy *(1988; 2010); Co-editor of* Treating Complex Traumatic Stress Disorders in Adults *(2009; 2020), Author of* It's Not You, It's What Happened to You *(2014; 2020)*

"Scott Giacomucci articulates innovative approaches to experiential group treatment grounded in theory and refined through extensive clinical practice. His book effectively addresses complex trauma reactions within a cost-efficient group format, while maintaining the highest standards for participant safety."

Jacqueline Corcoran, *PhD, LCSW, Professor and Faculty Director, DSW Program, School of Social Policy & Practice, University of Pennsylvania*

Trauma-Focused Psychodrama

This book presents trauma-focused psychodrama as an effective treatment for trauma, posttraumatic stress disorder (PTSD), and complex PTSD.

Chapters focus on common themes and psychodrama enactments related to trauma, including strengths-based scenes, working with defenses, parts of self, traumatic loss, inner child work, perpetrator work, embodying posttraumatic growth, and vicarious trauma. Psychodrama's interventions, history, theory, and research for the treatment of trauma and trauma-related conditions in group therapy settings are outlined. Trauma-informed principles, risks of retraumatization, sociometry, and psychodrama-like interventions will be covered. Each chapter contains various examples and depictions of interventions and experiences from the author's practice in both inpatient and outpatient settings.

Trauma-Focused Psychodrama provides psychodramatists and other group practitioners with essential teaching related to trauma-informed practice and trauma-focused psychodrama. Psychotherapists and psychodrama trainees will find this book useful to guide and support their learning and clinical practice.

Scott Giacomucci is Director/Founder of the Phoenix Center for Experiential Trauma Therapy in Pennsylvania and a Visiting Assistant Professor at Bryn Mawr College Graduate School of Social Work and Social Research.

Trauma-Focused Psychodrama

Experiential Therapy for Complex PTSD

Scott Giacomucci

Routledge
Taylor & Francis Group
NEW YORK AND LONDON

Designed cover image: Getty Images

First published 2026
by Routledge
605 Third Avenue, New York, NY 10158

and by Routledge
4 Park Square, Milton Park, Abingdon, Oxon, OX14 4RN

Routledge is an imprint of the Taylor & Francis Group, an informa business

ISBN: 978-1-041-07242-3 (hbk)
ISBN: 978-1-041-07241-6 (pbk)
ISBN: 978-1-003-63949-7 (ebk)

DOI: 10.4324/9781003639497

Typeset in Times New Roman by Apex CoVantage, LLC

For Product Safety Concerns and Information please contact our EU representative:
GPSR@taylorandfrancis.com
Taylor & Francis Verlag GmbH, Kaufingerstraße 24, 80331 München, Germany.

To everyone suffering from trauma
around the world,
and all of the brave helpers
doing something about it.

Contents

Figures

About the Author

Scott Giacomucci is Director/Founder of the Phoenix Center for Experiential Trauma Therapy in Media, Pennsylvania, and Director of Trauma Services at Mirmont Treatment Center. He is Research Associate and Visiting Assistant Professor at Bryn Mawr College's Graduate School of Social Work and Social Research, teaching a course on trauma-focused psychodrama. He presents regularly at local and global events and offers trauma-focused psychodrama training at the Phoenix Center in Pennsylvania. Scott completed his Doctorate in Clinical Social Work from the University of Pennsylvania and is recognized as a board-certified diplomate of clinical social work. He is also Fellow of the American Academy of Experts in Traumatic Stress, Fellow of the American Society of Group Psychotherapy and Psychodrama (ASGPP), Certified Eye Movement Desensitization and Reprocessing Consultant, Certified Group Psychotherapist, and Board-Certified Trainer, Educator & Practitioner in Sociometry, Psychodrama, and Group Psychotherapy. His open-access book, *Social Work, Sociometry, & Psychodrama* (2021, Springer Nature), has been downloaded over 600,000 times and received multiple awards. He is also the author of *Trauma-Informed Principles in Group Therapy, Psychodrama, & Organizations: Action Methods for Leadership* (2023, Routledge).

He served two elected terms on the Executive Council of the ASGPP. He is co-chair of ASGPP's research committee, was a founding member of ASGPP's Sociatry and Social Justice Committee, and is Co-Chief-Editor of the *Journal of Psychodrama, Sociometry, and Group Psychotherapy*. Scott currently serves on the board of the Philadelphia Area Group Psychotherapy Society and the Social and Collective Trauma Committee of the International Association of Group Psychotherapy & Group Processes.

He has published over two dozen peer-reviewed articles or book chapters, including an ongoing line of mixed-methods research on trauma-focused psychodrama. His YouTube channel reaches a few thousand people each day and has over 600 videos on trauma, group therapy, and psychodrama. Scott is the recipient of various awards, including the first recipient of the National Association of Social Workers' Emerging Social Work Leader Award, the 2019 Group Practice Award from ACA's Association of Specialists in Group Work, the 2022 ASGPP David Kipper Scholar Award, and the 2024 ASGPP Innovator's Award. He co-edited the books *Psychodrama in Education* (2024) and *Autobiography of a Genius* (2019), written by psychodrama's founder, Jacob Moreno, MD. Scott also serves as a co-editor of the first international psychodrama book series by Springer Nature titled *Psychodrama in Counselling, Coaching, and Education.*

Dr. Scott Giacomucci,
DSW, LCSW, BCD, CGP, FAAETS, TEP

Foreword

As a sympathetic observer of psychodrama for seven decades (indeed, one might say the person with the most intimate perspective other than my parents themselves), I have often noticed that psychodrama is generally considered a less "intellectual," more simple-minded practice than psychoanalysis. In the words of a senior female psychoanalyst I encountered many years ago who was otherwise sympathetic to J.L., psychodrama is for "the simple people." (Said, I should add, with a wrinkled nose.)

Scott Giacomucci's book should permanently set that notion to rest. His careful investigation of the intricacies of psychodramatic interventions and their limitations is, at the very least, a breakthrough in the field and demands careful study.

A second immediate impression I took away from Giacomucci's text is the perspicacity of his focus on trauma as an entry way to understanding what psychodrama therapy is and can do. I have already referenced the familiar and somewhat cliched comparison with psychoanalysis, but candor requires noting that at least in its classical sense, psychoanalysis is a therapy only in the most liberal meaning of the word. Whether the intellectual explorations of psychoanalysis provide insight or not (a matter of contention since Freud's first forays into the "truth" about his patient Dora), few would reach for The Interpretation of Dreams as a guide to treating a person who has experienced trauma. Trauma, no matter how literary its ultimate expression, resists abstraction.

The third point that occurred to me by the time I was well into Giacomucci's investigation is that trauma and recovery demand a social perspective that neither talk therapy nor pharmacological treatment, whether separately or in combination, can provide. Particular attention should be paid to the way Giacomucci weaves sociometric assessments and implications into the guidance he provides in mapping psychodramatic interventions. Whatever else psychodrama is, it is a social therapy and requires confrontation with the immediate conditions of human life. This gives psychodrama both its power and its liability to be abused, or at least to be imposed on those unprepared for the raw emotional demands it sometimes engages. Giacomucci provides many moral and technical signposts that help avoid those tendencies.

This book appears at an important time. Although my evidence is anecdotal, from my well-traveled academic perspective in a different field, it does seem to me that psychodrama is undergoing a resurgence of interest. That cuts against the familiar worries about the 21st century's technologically driven social isolation, especially in developed countries. Practices like psychodrama, and especially psychodrama, could be pathways back toward the intensive social experiences that so many cultural critics advocate as a way back from a "loneliness epidemic." (On the other hand, my father wrote about loneliness in the 1930s as a social crisis his sociometric techniques could address; *plus ca change*.)

In the absence of breakthroughs in basic brain science that could be a decisive substitute, psychotherapy in one form or another is here to stay. Nor, so far at least, have virtual "communities" or visions of avatars powered by AI offered by tech enthusiasts and entrepreneurs provided anything like the immediacy of an actual encounter, or its potential for healing. The critique of "modern times" that emerged along with modernity itself more than a century ago is oddly alive again. For those engaged in psychotherapeutic work, Giacomucci's book places them at the center of history in a way that could not be more relevant.

Jonathan D. Moreno, PhD,
David and Lyn Silfen University Professor Emeritus,
University of Pennsylvania;
Author of Impromptu Man (2014) and Absolutely Essential (2025)

Acknowledgments

Acknowledgment sections are hard to write as there are too many people to thank, and I do not want to forget anyone! The motivation to write this book comes from my clients, students, trainees, and supervisees who are hungry to heal and learn. Without them, I would not have made the sacrifices necessary to undertake the production of this book. Thank you for pushing me to be a better psychodramatist, trainer, and educator. I would also like to acknowledge the pioneers in the development of recognizing complex trauma and complex post-traumatic stress disorder (CPTSD), which has been an uphill battle for decades. And to all the clients and survivors of complex trauma who knew what they experienced was real, even before we professionals had a name for it. This book builds off the experience and knowledge of those who came before me and paved the way for healing from and treating CPTSD.

Sending gratitude to my wife, Maria, and my dog, Azul, who spent countless hours by my side while I wrote this book, offering support and encouragement. Thank you to the countless teachers, role models, trainers, and supervisors who have demonstrated for me how to hold the role of psychodramatist and trauma therapist. I also want to thank my colleagues at the Phoenix Center for Experiential Trauma Therapy, Mirmont Treatment Center, and Bryn Mawr College Graduate School of Social Work and Social Research, who have helped me shape my treatment and teaching approaches related to complex trauma. I am also grateful to the team at Routledge for their interest and excitement in this book idea from the start, as well as their flexibility and guidance throughout the production process.

Finally, thank you to YOU, the reader. Thank you for your interest in this book and your interest in becoming a more effective trauma therapist. I appreciate and want to acknowledge you!

Chapter 1

Introduction to Trauma-Focused Psychodrama

> A psychodrama group is a place of action, love, truth, courage, and belonging.

Psychodrama is an effective modality in the treatment of trauma, PTSD, and CPTSD. The psychodramatic method offers potentialities for healing, restoration, posttraumatic growth, and empowerment that would be untouchable in traditional talk therapies. A psychodrama group is a place of action, love, truth, courage, and belonging. Almost anyone who has experienced a psychodrama session can attest to the power of the method and its capacity to draw people in while eliciting transformational emotional experiences.

My first experience with psychodrama was as a teenager. I do not remember much of the content of the sessions, but I remember the cathartic nature of the experience, even as an observer – as well as the meaningful bonds that were created between participants. Psychodrama played a big role in my adolescent and young adult years, contributing significantly to my personal growth and recovery journeys from addictions, mental health, trauma, and loss. I attended countless hours of psychodrama intensives, weekly groups, and other programs that used aspects of psychodrama.

After being introduced to other therapeutic approaches in my university studies, it became apparent to me that psychodrama was the path I was meant to take in terms of professional training and practice. After obtaining my Master's in Social Services, I devoted myself to learning all that I could about psychodrama and completed my 780 training hours for Certified Practitioner of Sociometry, Psychodrama, and Group Psychotherapy in just about three years. In the following four years, while pursuing my doctoral degree, I completed my Practitioner Applicant for Trainer process and was certified as a Trainer, Educator, and Practitioner of Sociometry, Psychodrama, and Group Psychotherapy.

DOI: 10.4324/9781003639497-1

Simultaneous to my psychodrama training, I was working in addiction treatment, volunteering in the Philadelphia prison system and my local county juvenile detention center, and was engaged in various social justice initiatives. At one point, I took a step back and realized that the commonality between these three areas of passion was trauma. Trauma seemed to play a role in every addiction client's story. Trauma seemed to be a precursor to each crime committed by the guys I worked with in juvenile detention or in prison. And trauma was underlying and/or resulting from every social justice issue. Every example of social injustice is essentially collective trauma. This realization propelled me to shift my focus beyond addiction, crime, and feelings of social injustice – the manifestations of past trauma – and to instead focus on the process of healing trauma itself. My professional journey of studying trauma included a blend of traditional trauma studies, trauma-focused psychodrama modalities, Eye Movement Desensitization and Reprocessing (EMDR) therapy, parts work, somatic psychotherapies, interpersonal neurobiology, collective trauma, and organizational trauma.

Having worked in inpatient, partial hospitalization program (PHP), outpatient, and multi-day intensive settings for addiction and mental health treatment, this book is a culmination of my experience treating trauma using psychodrama – learning from what worked and what did not work. This book is informed by my experience in various roles beyond being a psychodrama psychotherapist, but also a social worker, researcher, adjunct professor, trainer, supervisor, organizational leader, and an ongoing participant in psychodrama groups.

Any powerful method has the capacity to promote deep healing, but also for contributing to deep wounding or retraumatization. Psychodrama is no different. While psychodrama can be an effective and efficient approach in treating PTSD and CPTSD, it can also quickly lead to more harm to participants. The practice of psychodrama in the treatment of trauma must be done with an emphasis on trauma-informed principles, safety, and ethics. Psychodrama's reputation was tainted in the past due to unethical practice, untrained or unsupervised professionals using psychodrama, and an overemphasis on catharsis without considering the window of tolerance of the client and the group. As psychodrama regains its popularity in the United States and continues to spread internationally, it is imperative that we carefully consider the current standards for trauma-focused and trauma-informed treatment and develop our own best practices for trauma-focused psychodrama. This book is my attempt at summarizing these best practices based on my personal and professional experience.

As psychodrama continues to gain popularity as a trauma treatment, I continue to hear disturbing stories from clients, students, supervisees, and other trainers about ways that psychodrama is being practiced or taught that is resulting in harm. This book is my response – my attempt to organize and articulate both the basics and the complexities of utilizing psychodrama as a trauma therapy.

Psychodrama as a Treatment for Trauma

Psychodrama is uniquely situated as a treatment for trauma, PTSD, and CPTSD for a multitude of reasons. As humans, we regulate our emotions through relationships. If we are wounded in a relationship, it makes sense that the healing would also need to take place within relationships. Psychodrama is inherently a group therapy approach – developed within Moreno's triadic system of sociometry, psychodrama, and group psychotherapy (though also practiced effectively in individual therapy). The matrix of relationships and sociodynamics within the sociometry of the group can provide a holding environment and safe container for restoration. There could even be an argument made for sociometry as an effective treatment for trauma by itself, as it has the power to provide validation, belonging, and peer support in an efficient way.

> The psychodramatic method brings therapy to life and allows us to go beyond thinking and talking.

The psychodramatic method brings therapy to life and allows us to go beyond thinking and talking. Much of the new neuroscience of trauma shows how trauma impacts parts of the brain below thinking or talking (van der Kolk, 2014). It only makes sense then that our interventions must go beyond talk therapy and involve the body in the process of healing. A large portion of the symptoms of PTSD and CPTSD are related to the nervous system and the body. Psychodrama was one of the first body-oriented therapies and involves various interventions that facilitate enhanced sensory awareness and somatic processing. The experiential nature of psychodrama allows us to put healing into action. On the psychodrama stage, defenses can be honored and managed while cultivating the strengths and supports needed to safely face the trauma. Through the surplus reality of a psychodrama enactment, we can revisit moments from the past and change them, we can provide clients with the opportunity to complete a survival response related to the trauma, and we can change how trauma lives within us today.

> Perhaps one of the most powerful aspects of psychodrama is the reality that anything can happen in psychodrama, even the impossible.

It may seem like psychodrama is simply a role play and therefore unlikely to have any emotional impact. I tell my clients that it is not quite role-playing like we normally think of role play, but, instead, we are acting as if and bringing ourselves fully into the role and the scene. Moreno even gave an interesting commentary about "role-playing" as a poor choice of words, as it suggests that it is fake – instead, he emphasized the realness of it. However, I think philosopher Jacques Derrida's quote sums it up best – "to pretend, I actually do the thing:

I have therefore only pretended to pretend." We could think of the psychodrama experience as pretending to pretend. If a group is properly warmed up to the psychodrama process, it feels like a real experience and produces meaningful emotions and insights.

Perhaps one of the most powerful aspects of psychodrama is the reality that anything can happen in psychodrama, even the impossible. Experiences that a trauma survivor might crave for can be represented in surplus reality. This creates unlimited potentials for corrective emotional experiences, closure, and internal transformation. In any trauma-focused approach, there must be an equal focus on trauma recovery, as there is on the trauma itself. Psychodrama is a humanistic and strengths-based approach and lends itself effectively to the expression of recovery. Posttraumatic growth can be envisioned, explored, cultivated, and embodied using role-playing. The five domains of posttraumatic growth can be concretized and actualized in psychodrama rather than theoretical goals. Psychodrama can be employed to facilitate role training for trauma recovery.

In any trauma-focused approach, there must be an equal focus on trauma recovery as there is on the trauma itself.

Here is a simple example of Jada's psychodrama, which is focused on developing hope for a future beyond the depression and oppression that she feels has been holding her back.

> Jada is chosen by the group as the protagonist and shares her difficulty envisioning a future for herself in recovery. She shares about the societal pressure and oppression she feels due to being a queer, black woman. She says that the oppression she experiences has fueled her depression and made it hard to have hope for a future. We start by enrolling some support in the scene for Jada including the role of her best friend and the role of hope. Jada interacts with her best friend and reverses roles. As the director, I instruct her, as her best friend, to offer herself support and hope. "Jada, come on girl, we have plans for the future which means we have hope for the future. We won't let the world scare us from living our life." Jada reverses roles back to herself and the messages are repeated to her from the role player. Next Jada reverses roles with hope and is invited to speak to herself – "hope can you tell Jada how she can find you?." As hope, Jada says "you find me in music and dance and activism and community. You find me when you sing or when you help someone else." I continue directing – "hope, but what about all of the injustice in the world? How can Jada feel hope considering the state of the world?." In the role of hope, Jada pauses then says "holding onto hope is an act of defiance against the oppression and against society that wants to keep you down.

As long as there is breath, there is hope." Jada reverse roles back to self and a group member takes on the role of hope repeating the messages to her.

Next, I suggested we enroll the depression and the oppression to interact with them briefly. Jada invites two group members to take on these roles and I invite her to speak to oppression first. What do you want to say to all of this oppression that has been holding you back? Jada's best friend and hope step in closer and offer gentle support to her as she faces her oppression. She says, "you have been suffocating me my entire life and I am sick of it. It isn't fair that you impact me so much more than others. I deserve to have all the same opportunities as anyone else. It's your fault that I am depressed all of the time. Because of you, I feel like I can't plan for the future and am just trying to survive each day." As the director, I offer Jada a doubling statement and invite her to repeat it or change it to make it fit for her – "you fuel my depression." She smiles and repeats it. We enroll her depression into the scene with another role player for her to speak to – "and you depression, you make me feel like shit. I can't seem to get away from you. You tell me horrible things about myself and make me feel like I'm a failure." I motion for the supportive roles to step closer and help Jada speak to depression. "I'm done letting you control my life. I'm realizing that you are mostly just a result of the oppression that I experience, and that there isn't really anything wrong with me." I instruct Jada to tell her depression what she is going to do next time she feels it or it speaks to her. "Next time I feel you, I'm going to remember that you are just a side effect of injustice and oppression. But I have hope, and friends, and a community to resist you and prevent you from controlling my life!" I tell the group members who are playing the roles of depression and oppression to step away from Jada once they feel convinced in her conviction. As she continues talking to them and feels more empowered, they both begin to step away. The group celebrates Jada and the work she is doing.

I suggest that we have one more role to talk to for now – her future self. She agrees and chooses another group member to play this role. I ask Jada to describe the future self that she sees as a possible now that she has hope, support, and some space from depression and oppression. She begins to describe a version of herself in the future no longer held back by depression or yielding to oppression. She describes herself with hope, love, self-compassion, worth, confidence, and connection to her queer community. I ask her to reverse roles with this future self and speak to herself today. As future self, Jada says to herself today – "Jada I'm proud of you. You are a powerful and courageous woman. Just wait to see how many other women you are going to help and inspire through the change you create in the community." When Jada pauses, I step in – "future Jada, can you tell Jada today about how your relationship to hope, depression, and oppression now?" Future Jada looks to Jada today and says, "I'm not depressed anymore. I have hope and I won't let anyone take this hope from me. Sometimes I have a bad day, but I bounce back and don't let it get to me like I used to. All of this oppression and injustice is messed up, but you don't have control over what other people choose to do. I know now that I can control how I respond, and I don't have to allow people to treat me unfairly. Today, I have a community who loves me, supports me, and needs me. I feel like I belong." Jada reverses roles back to herself today and the role player repeats the messages to her. I invite her to really take it in and see herself in the future. As she listens to these messages, her smile grows, and her body relaxes. The psychodrama ends, role players de-role, and the group moves into sharing about how they were impacted by Jada's psychodrama.

This psychodrama depicts the power of the method as a treatment for mental health and trauma. Psychodrama looks different in every group and each session as it is adapted for the population, setting, issues, topics, and goals (this book will include more than 30 diverse examples of psychodrama scenes through future chapters). Jada's psychodrama demonstrates the versatility of the model in that we can address issues related to intrapsychic experience (such as depression) while also addressing larger social issues (such as oppression) at the same time. Some psychodramas are entirely interpersonal (composed of other people in the protagonist's life), some are entirely interpsychic (composed of parts of self or internal roles), and other psychodramas are purely transpersonal (made up of spiritual or collective roles). Psychodrama allows us to externalize inner experiences, change our relationship to internalized pain, trauma, oppression, or people, and then reintegrate the new configuration of relationships between roles in a new way.

Psychodrama has sometimes been described as a type of psychological surgery in that we are opening ourselves up, changing psychodynamics, and integrating our internal psychological parts in a new way. Psychodrama can also be emotionally draining and requires some recovery time, similar to a medical surgery. Others have described psychodrama as a sort of social and communal ritual or ceremony, emphasizing the relational and group components of the healing process. That, because we are wounded in groups and relationships, the healing must also take place within group and relational contexts. Furthermore, others have conceptualized psychodrama as similar to various indigenous, shamanic, religious, or spiritual practices from around the world (Moreno et al., 2000). Psychodrama is unique in that it encompasses psychological, relational, societal, spiritual, and somatic aspects in one approach (Giacomucci, 2021).

Psychodrama is unique in that it encompasses psychological, relational, societal, spiritual, and somatic aspects in one approach.

Trauma, Traumatic Stress, and Posttraumatic Growth

In our exploration of trauma-focused psychodrama, it is important that we are on the same page related to the term *trauma*. Some have been criticized for using a too narrowly defined conceptualization of trauma in the past (usually focused exclusively on war veterans). More recently, there has been discussion about the term trauma being used too liberally to label any uncomfortable experience. My favorite definition of trauma is that it is simply the wound that results from any experience that overwhelms our ability to cope. By its nature, trauma is a very subjective experience. Multiple people could experience the same adversity, but not all experience it as a trauma. Our identity, race, gender, age, belief systems, social support, internal strengths, past experience, and current state are all going to collectively impact the way we metabolize experience and make sense of the world.

In their seminal publication on trauma-informed care, the Substance Abuse and Mental Health Service Administration (SAMHSA, 2014) articulates three Es related to understanding trauma: (1) Event, (2) Experience, and (3) Effect.

> Individual trauma results from an *event*, series of events, or set of circumstances that is *experienced* by an individual as physically or emotionally harmful or life threatening and that has lasting adverse *effects* on the individual's functioning and mental, physical, social, emotional, or spiritual well-being.
> (2014, p. 7)

This definition seems to capture the complexities of trauma while underscoring the elements of traumatic experience. There are many different types of trauma including violence, abuse, sexual trauma, relational trauma, shock trauma, complex trauma, collective trauma, racial trauma, financial trauma, ancestral trauma, organizational trauma, and more. Throughout this book, I intend to depict how psychodrama can be used thoughtfully to promote healing from each of these types of trauma.

When someone experiences harm from adversity, the wound that emerges over time tends to manifest in the form of traumatic stress. Posttraumatic stress symptoms are organized into four categories (see Figure 1.1):

- **Re-Experiencing and Intrusions** – flashbacks, nightmares, emotional or somatic reliving of the trauma, disturbing memories, cues that trigger trauma-related memories, and the tendency to re-enact traumatic relationships
- **Arousal and Reactivity** – hypervigilance, irritability, difficulty concentrating or sleeping, exaggerated startle response, rage, and recklessness
- **Avoidance and Numbing** – dissociation, avoiding reminders of trauma, avoiding memories, thoughts, or feelings related to trauma

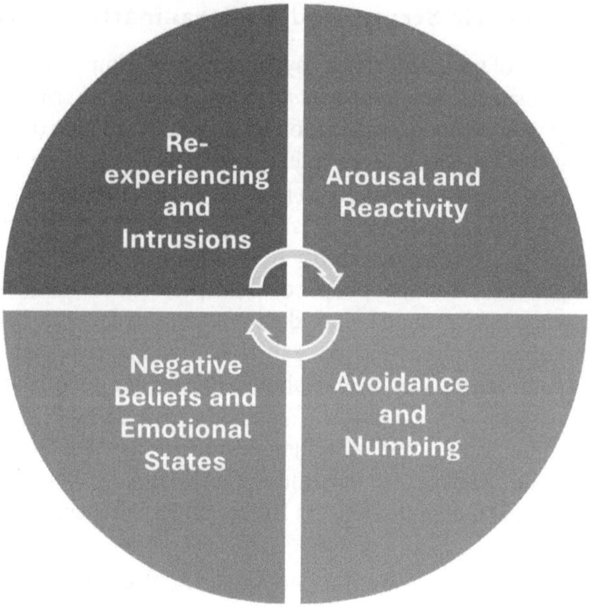

Figure 1.1 Symptom clusters of PTSD

- **Negative Beliefs and Emotional States** – distorted beliefs (about self, others, or the world), self-blame, strong negative emotional feelings, inability to feel positive emotions, loss of interest in activities or hobbies, feeling distant from others, and difficulty remembering parts of the trauma

These four symptom clusters make up the diagnostic symptoms for PTSD, as outlined in the Diagnostic and statistical manual of mental disorders, 5th Edition (DSM-5). There are also two additional dissociative subtypes of PTSD:

- **Depersonalization** – persistent feeling disconnected from one's self or body as if you were an observer (similar to a dream-like state, a sense of unreality, and/or that of time moving slowly)
- **Derealization** – persistent experience of one's surroundings being unreal (such as feeling like the world is not real, distant, or distorted)

Beyond the DSM-5, there has been a movement to recognize CPTSD as an additional diagnosis. Advocates for a CPTSD diagnosis highlight that classical PTSD was developed with a focus on adults (particularly war veterans and railway workers) who experienced a single incident trauma or a short period of adversity. Complex trauma, which is characterized by repeated exposure to trauma – usually relational trauma in childhood – seems to result in a different flavor of traumatic stress. The DSM-5 rejected this proposal, but the World Health Organization acknowledged CPTSD as an add-on diagnosis and created a code for it in the International Classification of Diseases (ICD-11). The CPTSD diagnosis not only includes the first three symptom clusters of PTSD, which are outlined earlier (re-experiencing and intrusions, avoidance and numbing, and arousal and reactivity), but also includes three new groups of symptoms:

- **Problems in Regulating Emotions** – disconnection from emotions or lack of containment when emotions are activated and difficulty regulating feelings
- **Negative Beliefs About Self** – feeling like a failure or worthless, guilt/shame related to the traumatic event
- **Difficulty With Relationships** – feel distant from other people or struggle to be close to others

These three new symptom clusters (see Figure 1.2) are often referred to as disturbances in self-organization (DSO). In my clinical practice, when I started to assess for CPTSD and provide psychoeducation to clients about CPTSD, I quickly found that it was a much more accurate diagnosis for the majority of my clients than classical PTSD.

I like to think of traumatic stress as essentially just the past showing up in the present. The content of the memory, the feelings, physical sensations or sensory

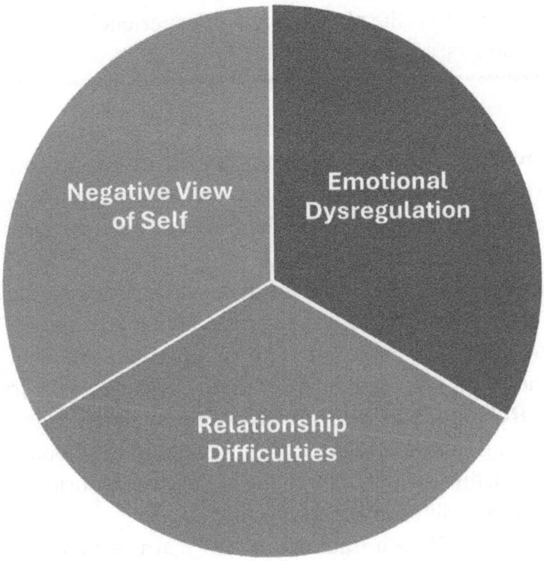

Figure 1.2 CPTSD add-on symptoms of disturbances in self-organization

input, and negative beliefs associated with trauma are simply being activated and re-experienced in the present moment. There was even a recent neuroscience study that confirmed that traumatic memory is relived, not remembered (Perl et al., 2023). In examining the symptoms of CPTSD, I also note that most of them seem to also be defenses or the brain/body's attempt to prevent additional harm or make sense of the past harm. Many trauma experts have gone as far as suggesting that PTSD is the least pathologizing diagnosis because it is less focused on something being wrong with you and more focused on the fact that something happened to you, and you are having a relatively common response to the adversity.

In any discussion of traumatic stress, it is also important that we recognize the possibility and likelihood of posttraumatic growth. Posttraumatic growth is the phenomenon of experiencing positive growth as a result of trauma or adversity. Posttraumatic growth is far more common than most people realize. Many studies even suggest that growth is statistically more likely after trauma than PTSD! While the prevalence of PTSD after trauma is around 25% for adults and 50% for children, the likelihood of posttraumatic growth is between 50% and 90% (Calhoun & Tedeschi, 2012; Wu et al., 2019). Sometimes, posttraumatic growth emerges organically after adversity, but sometimes, we have to actively cultivate it after trauma. I have come to look at posttraumatic growth as one of the primary goals of trauma therapy and the five domains of posttraumatic growth as a template for trauma recovery:

> Posttraumatic growth is the phenomenon of experiencing positive growth as a result of trauma or adversity.

1. **New Possibilities in Life** – trauma flips our lives upside down and forces us to develop new ways of looking at the world. Many times, survivors of trauma discover new opportunities in life that had not been considered prior to the traumatic experience.
2. **Increase in Personal Strengths** – trauma survivors are often astonished by the strength they are able to access while facing adversity. They frequently realize that they have more strength or different strengths than they had believed and/or develop new inner strengths because of the trauma.
3. **Enhanced Relationships** – the impact of trauma challenges us to seek support, which can enhance relationships. Trauma also frequently takes place within relationships, which can challenge us to reprioritize the healthy and supportive relationships in our lives.
4. **Appreciation of Life** – a traumatic event that threatens our life or the life of someone close to us reminds us how short and fragile life can be. This

existential realization has the power to promote new gratitude and appreciation for being alive or for aspects of life.

5. **Spiritual or Religious Growth** – many trauma survivors turn to religion or spirituality to help them navigate trauma and its aftermath. So, much of trauma happens because of other human beings, which can cause trauma survivors to seek support beyond humans.

Throughout this book, I will frequently reference these domains of posttraumatic growth as an inherent goal in trauma therapy and in trauma-focused psychodrama (especially in Chapter 14). Furthermore, Chapter 16 will highlight the very real potential of us as professionals experiencing these areas of posttraumatic growth vicariously through our clients. My experience has been that vicarious posttraumatic growth (VPTG) has been even more prominent in my work as a psychodramatist than in my other work as a trauma therapist.

Trauma-Informed versus Trauma-Focused

We must not confuse the terms "trauma-informed" and "trauma-focused" (see Figure 1.3). They are frequently used interchangeably, but are distinctly different. This book will focus primarily on trauma-focused psychodrama, which is simply the utilization of psychodrama in the treatment of trauma-related issues. In my presentation of trauma-focused psychodrama, I will also include considerable content on trauma-informed principles and the importance of trauma-informed psychodrama practice for all psychodramatists, regardless of if the sessions are focused on trauma. Trauma-informed practice is a broader framework and philosophy of providing services in a way that resists the potential of retraumatization while attempting to cultivate optimal environments for trauma survivors. It

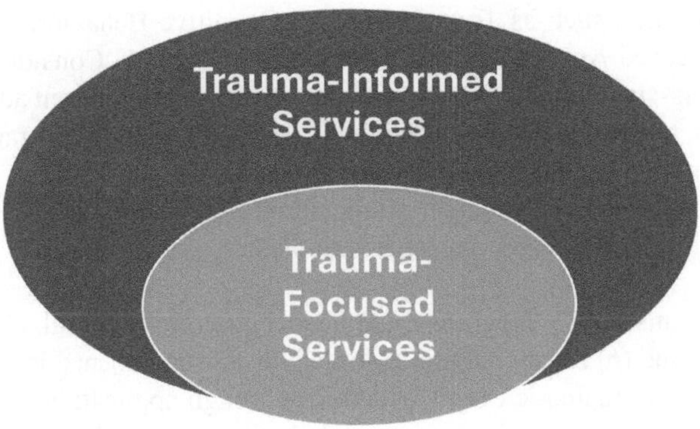

Figure 1.3 Trauma-informed and trauma-focused services

is dangerous to try to provide trauma-focused sessions without first implementing trauma-informed principles into the framework of service delivery. Practicing psychodrama with trauma survivors without regard to trauma-informed principles is liable to result in retraumatization (Giacomucci, 2023).

It is dangerous to try to provide trauma-focused sessions without first implementing trauma-informed principles.

Trauma-informed care roots can be traced back to the 1970s, but the term was first used in 2001 by Harris and Fallot. While some were writing and teaching about trauma-informed care in the early 2000s, it was not until 2014 that SAMHSA published their guidance for trauma-informed care, which further standardized and validated it as a framework. SAMHSA's motivation for bringing together a group of experts on the topic and publishing a trauma-informed care philosophy was largely fueled by the realization and concern that many treatment programs and practitioners were unknowingly retraumatizing the clients they were trying to help. After hearing from a number of clients and psychodrama trainees that they experienced retraumatization or harm in psychodrama therapy or training, I found it essential to write my last book emphasizing trauma-informed principles in psychodrama. Trauma-informed psychodrama is suitable for all psychodrama practice settings, while trauma-focused psychodrama is more specifically oriented to treating trauma, PTSD, and CPTSD.

The Clinical Practice Guidelines for PTSD, released by the Department of Veterans Affairs and Department of Defense, defines trauma-focused psychotherapy as "therapy that uses cognitive, emotional, or behavioral techniques to facilitate processing a traumatic event and in which the trauma focus is a central component of the therapeutic process" (2023, p. 48). Other established psychotherapy approaches have developed differentiated "trauma-focused" approaches for their models, such as Trauma-Focused Cognitive Behavioral Therapy and Trauma-Focused Acceptance and Commitment Therapy. Considering psychodrama's long-standing practice as a psychotherapy, and important adaptations for its use with trauma, it feels worthwhile to clarify the practice of trauma-focused psychodrama – which is what this book strives to do.

The American Psychological Association (APA) treatment guidelines for CPTSD outline seven essential areas with the acronym "HISTORY":

> (1) Humanistic, (2) Integrative, (3) Sequential, (4) Temporal, (5) Outcomes-focused, and (6) Relational principles, while assisting clients' in understanding (7) Why the traumatic events occurred. Through application of these guidelines, psychologists aspire to support their clients in seeking resilience, recovery and growth following their experience of complex trauma.
>
> (APA, 2024, p. 17)

These guidelines seem to be largely congruent with trauma-focused psychodrama practices. Psychodrama is a humanistic, integrative, and relational approach driven by an outcomes-oriented contract (or goal) between the protagonist and the director. Psychodrama is also a sequential method that has its own three phases for each session – warm-up, action, and sharing. Psychodrama is a method that allows us to move through time and interact with versions of self in the past and future, which experientially engages the temporal guideline. Trauma-focused psychodrama frequently involves helping the client to make sense of their experience on an existential or spiritual level related to questions of "why the trauma happened." These new action insights, or integrative catharses, frequently emerge in the interplay between the relationship between the protagonist and the other roles in the scene. While there is always more room to grow and further embody these guidelines, it seems clear that trauma-focused psychodrama is a method that is already inherently aligned with APA's treatment guidelines for complex trauma.

Limitations and Scope of This Book

The first limitation of this book is me. I write this book as the sole author through the lens of my own experience, identity, and bias. I am a white, male, cisgender, heterosexual, United States Citizen who grew up in the middle-class suburbs of Philadelphia. Although I have gained a diversity of experience through my life, work, and international travels, my identity and social location certainly influence my worldview and thus the development of the ideas in this book. I encourage you, as the reader, to consider your own identity and how it may influence your thinking and experience of this book and the ideas within. Do not take my suggestions and implement them exactly as I have; instead, critically reflect on the populations you serve and adapt these ideas to the cultural needs of the communities you work with.

The next limitation that I want to highlight is that this is a book, not a training program. This book may help you learn about trauma-focused psychodrama, but it will not prepare you to competently facilitate trauma-focused psychodrama without additional live training and supervision. As previously noted, many have attempted to use psychodrama in the past outside the scope of their competence, which has resulted in causing harm to clients and psychodrama's reputation. I encourage you to seek formal training in psychodrama; you can find a list of certified trainers on the website of the American Board of Examiners of Sociometry, Psychodrama, and Group Psychotherapy – www.PsychodramaCertification.org. The board recommends that trainees gain 80 hours of training before beginning to facilitate full psychodramas; however, there are various experiential techniques and interventions that can be safely implemented before then.

Additional limitations of the book include its narrow scope on trauma-focused psychodrama in clinical, in-person, group settings. Psychodrama is not only a trauma-focused modality, but it can also be employed with a focus on nearly any other mental health or social issue. Psychodrama was developed primarily as a group therapy, but can also be utilized effectively within individual therapy. This book will give limited attention to psychodrama in individual, couples, or family therapy settings. Other authors have focused their books or articles in these directions, which are outside the bounds of this book.

Psychodrama is primarily thought of as a psychotherapy; however, it is much more than a therapy. Psychodrama is used in various non-clinical settings in addition to treatment settings. It is seen as a therapy, an experiential teaching approach, a community organizing tool, social activism and social healing, a mystical tradition, a research methodology, and a theater approach. This book will orient specifically on psychodrama as a treatment for trauma and will not address its use in other non-clinical areas.

Psychodrama is primarily practiced in person, but the last five years have seen a rise of online psychodrama practice, especially since the onset of the COVID-19 pandemic. Though many were practicing psychodrama online before the pandemic, the large-scale shift to online work forced us to further develop online psychodrama methodologies. Perhaps more so than any others, Tele'Drama International has been at the forefront of this revolution, creating standards, training programs, and certifications for the practice of psychodrama online. I encourage you to explore this realm as psychodrama can be effectively implemented in online settings – however, this will be beyond the content of this book.

Chapters of this book were ordered in a way to build off of each other, starting with theory, philosophy, and sociometry in Chapters 2–5, before getting more fully into psychodrama practice. Foundational and advanced psychodrama interventions are presented in Chapters 6, 7, and 15, followed by trauma-related psychodrama practice areas in Chapters 8–14. These chapters are arranged based on the three-stage clinical map for safe and effective trauma work. Starting with strengths-based work to resource groups and protagonists, then honoring defenses and exploring parts of self. After phase 1 tasks of safety and stabilization have been established, we move into processing trauma and grief, while engaging in inner child and perpetrator work. The final phase of the clinical map shifts our attention to the future – trauma recovery, posttraumatic growth, integration, and meaning making. The final chapter of the book is dedicated to the psychodramatist and an exploration of vicarious trauma, countertransference, and vicarious growth for the professional.

Conclusion

Psychodrama is an effective treatment for trauma, PTSD, and CPTSD. The experiential, relational, and creative aspects of the approach situate it as a viable trauma therapy. Trauma-informed care principles must be integrated into safe and ethical trauma-focused psychodrama practice. Through the implementation of trauma-informed and trauma-focused approaches in psychodrama, we can offer healing from trauma while mitigating the risks of retraumatization.

Psychodrama is an effective treatment for trauma, PTSD, and CPTSD.

References

American Psychological Association. (2024). *Guidelines for working with adults with complex trauma histories*. Retrieved from https://www.apa.org/practice/guidelines/adults-complex-trauma-histories.pdf

Calhoun, L. G., & Tedeschi, R. G. (2012). *Posttraumatic growth in clinical practice*. New York: Routledge.

Department of Veterans Affairs and Department of Defense. (2023). *VA/DOD clinical practice guideline for the management of posttraumatic stress disorder and acute stress disorder*. Washington, DC: U.S. Government Printing Office. Retrieved from https://www.healthquality.va.gov/guidelines/MH/ptsd/

Giacomucci, S. (2021). *Social work, sociometry, and psychodrama: Experiential approaches for group therapists, community leaders, and social workers*. Springer Nature.

Giacomucci, S. (2023). *Trauma-informed principles in group therapy, psychodrama, and organizations: Action methods for leadership*. Routledge.

Harris, M., & Fallot, R. (2001). Using trauma theory to design service systems. In *New directions for mental health services* (p. 89). Jossey Bass.

Moreno, Z. T., Blomkvist, L. D., & Rutzel, T. (2000). *Psychodrama, surplus reality and the art of healing*. Routledge.

Perl, O., Duek, O., Kulkarni, K. R., Gordon, C., Krystal, J. H., Levy, I.,. . .& Schiller, D. (2023). Neural patterns differentiate traumatic from sad autobiographical memories in PTSD. *Nature Neuroscience, 26*(12), 2226–2236.

Substance Abuse and Mental Health Services Administration. (2014). *SAMHSA's concept of trauma and guidance for a trauma-informed approach*. HHS Publication No. (SMA) 14–4884. Rockville, MD: Substance Abuse and Mental Health Services Administration.

van der Kolk, B. A. (2014). *The body keeps the score: Brain, mind, and body in the healing of trauma*. New York: Viking Press.

Wu, X., Kaminga, A. C., Dai, W., Deng, J., Wang, Z., Pan, X., & Liu, A. (2019). The prevalence of moderate-to-high posttraumatic growth: A systematic review and meta-analysis. *Journal of Affective Disorders, 243*, 408–415.

Chapter 2

Trauma-Informed Principles, Safety, and Harm in Psychodrama

The effectiveness of the psychodramatic approach is inevitably linked to the implementation of trauma-informed principles, the cultivation of safety, and the prevention of harm throughout sessions. Until recently, very little had been written about explicitly integrating SAMHSA's six trauma-informed principles into psychodrama practice (Chesner, 2020; Giacomucci, 2021, 2023; Giacomucci & Briggs, 2025), though many had used the term "trauma-informed" in their psychodrama writing. SAMHSA's guidance for trauma-informed care has been integrated into countless organizations, treatment programs, therapeutic modalities, professional fields, and even in non-clinical settings. Many government organizations and third-party funders are routinely requiring that SAMHSA's trauma-informed care guidance be employed within treatment programs. The utilization of trauma-informed principles in psychodrama practice offers an avenue for establishing safety, promoting peer support, empowering the group, honoring identity, and preventing harm or retraumatization. Experiences of harm and retraumatization have been discussed occasionally in psychodrama literature, but no empirical research has been conducted in this area (at the time of this book submission, I have just begun recruitment for a qualitative study to examine factors related to harm and retraumatization in psychodrama therapy and training).

SAMHSA's Trauma-Informed Principles in Psychodrama

There are six trauma-informed principles outlined by SAMHSA (2014) (see Figure 2.1).

These principles offer an overarching framework for structuring psychodrama therapy sessions, psychodrama training, and psychodrama programs/organizations. Reference to these principles in psychodrama practice will be incorporated throughout this book; for a more complete discussion of trauma-informed psychodrama, see my previous book: *Trauma-Informed Principles in Group Therapy, Psychodrama, & Organizations: Action Methods for Leadership* (Giacomucci, 2023).

DOI: 10.4324/9781003639497-2

Figure 2.1 SAMHSA's trauma-informed principles
Reprinted with permission from Giacomucci (2021))

These six trauma-informed principles are already implicitly embedded within Morenian philosophy, psychodrama theory, and many psychodrama interventions (Giacomucci, 2023). Moreno's philosophy is humanistic and growth-oriented, rather than focused solely on pathology. Psychosocial problems are understood through the lenses of spontaneity, role, and sociometry theories rather than deficiencies of the individual. Moreno attempted to elevate every patient to the same level as the psychiatrist by referring to his patients as "doctors," emphasizing the therapeutic value that each group member possesses, and articulating that the healing in psychodrama comes from the group and the roles – not from the facilitator. The Morenos' conceptualization of healing revolved around the idea of the Autonomous Healing Center, which suggests that the client is healing themselves and the therapist is simply helping them to remove barriers to their own self-healing (Moreno, 2012).

Sociometry practices and attention to the warming-up process in psychodrama are inherently trauma-informed in that they create safety, peer support, collaboration, empowerment, voice, choice, and belonging. Sociometry practices help group members explore identity, power, privilege, oppression, in- and out-groups, and community. Psychodrama practice is fundamentally collaborative and empowering, with an explicit focus on co-creation between the director and group members. Many classical psychodrama interventions seem to embody trauma-informed care principles, such as doubling, enrolling a double as a role, utilizing the mirror position, and the pacing of a session from warm-up to action and group sharing.

Sociometry practices help group members explore identity, power, privilege, oppression, in- and out-groups, and community.

There are many ways to further integrate trauma-informed principles into psychodrama practice. Through my development of psychodrama training materials on trauma-informed care, I created a handout that I use in my 5-day Trauma-Informed Psychodrama Directing Intensives. The following are practical suggestions outlined in my handout, organized by the six principles. It is important to note that the implementation of each of these principles may need to look different depending on your practice context, level of care, profession, session goals, and the communities you work with.

Safety

- Facilitate an adequate warm-up for the group at hand.
- Establish a very clear and achievable contract.
- Employ strength-based roles in the psychodrama scene.
- Use a double role to stay with the protagonist throughout the enactment.
- Utilize the mirror position to provide titration for difficult emotions.
- Do not push the protagonist or group outside of their window of tolerance.
- Pay attention to the possibility of retraumatization for the protagonist, role players, and audience members.
- Consider safety through the lens of each participant's experience and identity.

Trustworthiness and Transparency

- Clearly outline the process and plan for the session.
- Stick to the contract/agreement with the group and protagonist.
- Build a therapeutic relationship with the group and protagonist.
- If known, let the protagonist know what the plan or some possibilities are for the psychodrama climax and psychodrama roles.
- Intervene to keep the process safe when needed by providing guidance, containment, or redirection
- Clearly outline and enforce group boundaries.
- Practice in a manner that demonstrates consistency, integrity, and ethics.

Peer Support

- Provide adequate time for warm-up and sharing.
- Invite group members to offer doubling statements when the protagonist is open to it.

- Use sociometry during the psychodrama to cultivate mutual aid.
- Encourage auxiliaries to offer support in their roles.
- Employ supportive roles in the psychodrama or simply ask group members to play the role of themselves as peer support in the scene.

Collaboration and Mutuality

- Provide adequate time for warm-up and sharing.
- Co-create the psychodrama with the protagonist and the group.
- Encourage group members to be involved throughout the process.
- Trust the protagonist and the group as experts in their experience.
- Initiate collaboration between the roles in the psychodrama.
- Find ways to integrate unchosen protagonist topics into the psychodrama scene.
- Believe in the protagonist/group's ability to heal.

Empowerment, Voice, and Choice

- Leverage sociometry for group and individual choices.
- Attend to social isolates in the warming-up process.
- Practice humility as a director and encourage the group/protagonist to make choices.
- Give the protagonist choices throughout the psychodrama.
- End the psychodrama with an integrative or growth-oriented scene, role, or action.
- Include opportunities for auxiliaries and audience members to step into the scene in moments of empowerment, integration, or growth.

Cultural, Gender, and Historic Issues

- Include content on identity in group norms and warm-up.
- Be aware of identity in the warming-up process.
- Set the tone/norms for the group by talking about identity and culture.
- Consider how the facilitator's identity may be experienced by the protagonist and the group.
- Consider the relationships between the identity of the auxiliaries and the identity of the roles they are playing.
- Position other community members as support for the protagonist when addressing a specific identity or cultural issues.
- Lead with a sense of cultural humility.

The adoption of these six trauma-informed principles and these suggestions into psychodrama practice would surely increase overall outcomes and effectiveness while reducing the risk of harm. In my experience, the risks and likelihood of harm and retraumatization increase when working with complex trauma and CPTSD.

Triggers, Harm, and Retraumatization in Psychodrama

Retraumatization describes the process of experiencing a new harm that also triggers and activates an old trauma at the same time. The layered experience of retraumatization increases the impact of the wound as it reinforces the original wounding. Retraumatization and being triggered are not the same thing, however. A trigger is when an action, inaction, feeling, or other sensory input activates past trauma and exacerbates traumatic stress symptoms. Triggers are going to be different and unique from person to person and can take the form of any object, action, or stimulus. Avoiding triggers is not entirely possible (nor healthy) for facilitators or trauma survivors. Triggers point to unprocessed traumatic content that needs to be addressed internally, not perpetually avoided externally. As facilitators, we need to be sensitive to our clients' triggers and offer them the support that they need to eventually face those triggers to change their relationship to those stimuli while also working to reprocess the trauma fueling the trigger.

Retraumatization describes the process of experiencing a new harm that also triggers and activates an old trauma at the same time.

Beyond triggers, harm, and retraumatization, it is also important to differentiate triggers from discomfort. The term trigger seems to be overused at times to label anything uncomfortable. If we avoid all discomfort in trauma recovery or trauma therapy, we are simply not going to grow or heal. Discomfort to some degree is part of the healing journey and part of the psychodrama process. Nevertheless, harm and retraumatization do not need to be part of the process. A future chapter will emphasize the importance of strength-based roles and supportive roles to help clients navigate discomfort and reduce the risks of being triggered, harmed, or retraumatized.

In my experience as a participant, facilitator, supervisor, and trainer of psychodrama, I have experienced, witnessed, and heard of various different incidents of harm and retraumatization in psychodrama. In reflecting on these various experiences, it seems that the majority of them are related to (1) an over emphasis on emotional catharsis (especially anger releases) without resourcing, (2) microaggressions or reenactments of identity-based trauma or oppression, (3) lack of sensitivity to (or disregard) of physical touch boundaries, (4) code of ethics violations, or (5) lack of attention to assessment, group structure, level of care, and pacing of the psychodrama process. Each of these areas will be further explored in the next subsections of this chapter. In one of my recent trainings, the topic of retraumatization emerged, and a participant made an important distinction that it is not psychodrama as a method that causes harm or retraumatization; it is the practitioner who uses it inappropriately.

Anger Catharsis in Psychodrama

One specific area linked to harm and retraumatization in psychodrama practice and training is the utilization of anger expression techniques, such as encouraging the protagonist to scream and yell at an antagonist or perpetrator role, physical fighting with the antagonist, hitting a punching bag or tackle dummy while imagining it is another person, or the use of a bat to hit pillows while expressing anger toward another. Traditionally, when anger emerges in psychodrama, the director encourages and even provokes an anger catharsis. Anger releases can be very empowering, helpful, and clinically appropriate, but also carry more risk than other interventions. Anger work must be handled sensitively with complex trauma survivors. There are three primary areas of concern and exploration related to this for me – (1) is it effective for the protagonist?, (2) how does it impact the rest of the group?, and (3) how much does the director's influence contribute to the movement toward (or away from) the anger catharsis?

Anger releases can be very empowering, helpful, and clinically appropriate, but also carry more risk than other interventions.

The first question is related to effectiveness for the protagonist. Many protagonists, including myself, have self-reported that anger catharsis in psychodrama has been helpful and empowering. However, after digging through the research on anger catharsis, there is very little or no evidence to support the idea that expression of anger is an effective way to reduce it. Most of the research concludes the opposite – that anger expression is not effective in reducing anger, hostility, or aggression (Kjærvik & Bushman, 2024), that ruminating on anger while hitting a punching bag imagining another person results in an increased level of anger and aggression (Bushman, 2002), and that arousal-decreasing activities such as mindfulness, breathing, and muscle relaxation are consistently effective at reducing anger, aggression, and hostility (Kjærvik & Bushman, 2024). Another study by Bushman et al. (1999) found that participants who received messaging that expressing aggression by hitting a punching bag had a higher desire to hit the bag, but that when doing so, it resulted in higher levels of anger and aggression compared to a control group that received messaging that anger catharsis was not helpful. Zerka Moreno's (1986) publication on ethical anger echoes some of the aforementioned concerns:

> The wave of humanistic psychology, particularly certain forms of gestalt therapy, have invested much energy in getting clients to express anger. This became an end in itself and was supposed to be the aim of therapy. What often resulted was that patients could not get beyond the anger. They were not getting purged, which was assumed to be the positive outcome; they were merely learning to be angry. There are no rewards for this type of learning.
>
> (p. 145)

This seems to contradict many people's experiences, including my own experience as a protagonist, that doing anger work as a protagonist can be quite empowering and helpful if done safely. Many trainers key in on specific aspects of anger work, such as avoiding role training violence, the target of the anger expression (at a person, not at a person, at the situation, etc.), or by suggesting that verbalization during anger releases keeps executive functioning online. We definitely do not want to encourage the suppression of anger. However, at the same time, I have also seen many people do the same types of anger/rage-related psychodramas without any lasting change in their life. I have begun to worry that the relief one feels after an anger catharsis in psychodrama is less about relief from the past trauma and more about relief from the stress of the session being over, exhaustion from the physical exertion, and a resulting flood of neurochemicals (including endogenous morphine) with pleasurable and painkilling characteristics designed to help us survive violence or threat. One study on crying and catharsis focused on a more nuanced question of when catharsis is healing; their conclusion was that crying is helpful when certain environmental factors are present, including social support, resolution to the event that provoked the emotions, and integrating a new understanding of the source of the emotions (Bylsma et al., 2008). These findings would point us as psychodrama directors to emphasizing group support, corrective emotional experiences, and integration when working with powerful catharses.

The second question revolves around the impact of anger catharsis on the other group members in a psychodrama. This has been one of the primary problems that I have seen with anger expressions in psychodrama, in that the director often is attuned to the protagonist who is ready to express the anger, but loses attunement to the rest of the group who may not be able to tolerate a big anger release. I have seen or heard of many clients and trainees being triggered or retraumatized through uncontained anger expressions in psychodrama groups. It is quite common for other participants to leave the room, dissociate, or become emotionally overwhelmed when witnessing a protagonist engage in an anger release. There are, of course, strategies that can be put into place to mitigate some of this and ensure the rest of the group is resourced enough for the anger work, but I have not heard much discussion about such strategies in psychodrama circles. I notice in my inpatient psychodrama group that, even after psychodramas with mild to moderate anger catharses, the number of clients who drop out of the group the following week seems to increase. I do believe that with some thoughtful preparation, social support, consent, grounding, and later debriefing that other group members can actually work through their triggers related to anger in these situations.

The third question has to do with the influence of the psychodrama director. When the topic of anger emerges in psychodrama, the response of the director certainly influences where the psychodrama goes next. Early in my directing experience, I was guilty of frequently pushing psychodramas toward anger catharses based on what I had seen, experienced, and learned through participation in psychodrama groups and training. For the past few years in my directing, I have been less convinced that anger expression is effective and prone to steer away from it – unless the protagonist explicitly states it as part of their contract for the session. More recently, I have been experimenting with different ways of directing anger catharsis in psychodrama, mostly focusing on boundary setting and empowerment (which will be further discussed in Chapter 13). Regardless, it seems clear to me that the beliefs, bias, and countertransference of the director significantly impact the direction of the psychodrama toward or away from anger. I have seen many psychodramas where the protagonist did not contract to focus on anger, but the topic emerged mid-session, and the director shifted the entire psychodrama climax to focus on anger release rather than the originally agreed-on contract for the session. This seems to be a problematic example of the director's countertransference impacting their practice. At the same time, I have occasionally worried that my more recent avoidance of anger could be from countertransference rather than from an unbiased review of the research and my experiences as protagonist and director. This is a complex issue that needs to be further explored with empirical research specific to psychodrama practice and trauma. It is clear that most of us were implicitly taught to believe in Freud's "hydraulic theory of emotion" – that releasing pent-up emotions was the key to healing. But more and more evidence is suggesting that this is a misleading metaphor and faulty theory for thinking about emotion.

Identity and Anti-Oppression

One of the most common causes of retraumatization and harm in psychodrama practice and training seems to be related to aspects of identity such as culture, gender, sexuality, race, religion, and age. I would argue that identity-based trauma is another form of complex trauma and is likely to result in CPTSD. These issues are also articulated in the sixth trauma-informed principle related to culture, history, and gender issues. Many people experience trauma as a direct result of their identity or social group memberships. The group is a microcosm of society (Yalom & Leszcz, 2020), which means that issues of oppression and discrimination are inevitably going to emerge within any group setting at some point. The unconscious and sometimes invisible nature of privilege, projection, and transference related to identity make it particularly complicated to address these issues in real time, however. The politicization of issues of identity has further complicated the process of addressing them for fear of ostracizing or offending group members of different political perspectives and, as a result, limiting our ability to help those group members. These issues, as tough as they are, must be addressed rather than brushed under the rug in psychodrama groups.

As psychodramatists, we must be aware of our own identities, social group memberships, biases, and projections. The action-based nature of our method is likely to enhance the presence of these issues rather than reduce them. This is where practicing with cultural humility and obtaining ongoing supervision and consultation becomes important. In my own work, I find it important to name some of these issues at the start of my groups through my group norms related to respect and identity. Before jumping into a psychodrama enactment, I challenge myself to take a moment with the protagonist to affirm their autonomy and choice throughout the psychodrama while also naming any differences in identity that seem related to the psychodrama contract. As a white, cis-gender, heterosexual, male trauma therapist, I often will name these identities when directing a psychodrama related to racial trauma, gender violence, or discrimination based on sexuality. In naming my difference in identity with the protagonist, I acknowledge that I may not fully understand the nuances of the issue and invite them to correct anything in the scene that is inaccurate. Helpful frameworks for exploring this further are Pamela Hay's ADDRESSING model (2008) and the work of Leticia Nieto and colleagues (Badis et al., 2025; Nieto, 2010; Nieto et al., 2010).

Identity-based trauma is another form of complex trauma and likely to result in complex PTSD.

Psychodrama practice without consideration of culture, identity, social group memberships, and oppression is unlikely to measure up to trauma-informed care standards. Awareness and action around these themes are especially important when working with groups composed of various identities and/or when the director comes from a different culture or social location from the participants of the group. All psychodramatists are encouraged and expected to consider their own identity as it relates to those that they are working with as a core component of the sociometry as well as the psychodramatic healing process.

Psychodrama practice without consideration of culture, identity, social group memberships, and oppression is unlikely to measure up to trauma-informed care standards.

Ethics and Physical Touch

Another common source of harm and retraumatization in psychodrama is the violation of ethical codes and the use of physical touch in psychodrama. Trauma survivors often experience harm in the world through the violation or abandonment of ethical conduct by people in power. Ethics and integrity are of utmost importance in trauma-focused and trauma-informed work. Without a solid ethical foundation and personal/professional integrity, the work is not trauma-informed. Trauma-informed psychodrama is ethical in nature. In the past, there have been various psychodramatists who have violated codes of ethics and caused harm to clients or trainees. Some of psychodrama's tarnished reputation can be attributed to the unethical practices of these psychodramatists. If we want our method to evolve with a good standing in the professional community, practicing with ethics and holding unethical psychodramatists accountable is vital.

Many trauma survivors experience trauma, which involves violent touch, unwanted sexual touch, or neglect involving an absence of physical touch. For these reasons, it is essential that psychodramatists consider ethics and sensitivity around physical touch as foundational to our work. Physical touch is a fundamental human need, something many people crave after a crisis, and something that can be quite healing and restorative. Professional codes of ethics limit the nature of physical touch that a professional can engage in with a client – which should always be done with multiple layers of consent and permission. One helpful framework to consider is seeking not only verbal consent but also somatic consent – tracking the client's physiological response(s) when moving toward and engaging in physical touch (after verbal consent has been provided). Another beneficial practice is to incorporate norms related to physical touch into the group rules and to explore aspects of physical touch in the warming-up process and sociometry. It can be helpful to assess the level of comfort for physical touch in sociometry, but also essential to assess group members' capacity for setting boundaries around physical touch, which might be more important to know as a facilitator. Furthermore, we must consider that comfort with touch and the ability to set boundaries related to touch are also going to be influenced by their present emotional state. A client who indicates in sociometric explorations that they are comfortable with touch and able to say no could find themselves emotionally activated mid-psychodrama in a manner that leaves them uncomfortable with touch and unable to state their boundaries. Similarly, a client who initially stated that they were not comfortable with physical touch may be experiencing difficult emotions mid-psychodrama and crave for supportive physical touch, such as a hand on the shoulder or a hug.

To further complicate the navigation of physical touch, we must also consider that there are varying degrees of normality, comfort, and permissiveness related to physical touch and its relationship to culture, gender, and religion. In some religious communities, it is not permitted for men and women to engage in physical touch of any kind with each other. On the other hand, in many cultures, physical touch is quite normal and expected. Recently, I attended the Brazilian Psychodrama Conference in Belo Horizonte. The very first difference that I noticed between psychodrama practice in the United States and in Brazil was the norms related to physical touch. Brazilian participants were very quick to engage in supportive physical touch with each other in psychodrama sessions, even when participants had never met before. Touch will be experienced differently based on culture, gender, age, religion, emotion, and context. For these reasons and more, it is important that we carefully consider the use of physical touch in psychodrama sessions between the director and participants, as well as between participants themselves.

Three-Phased Clinical Map

The safety and effectiveness of psychodrama practice can be further reinforced through the implementation of a three-phased clinical map for trauma work. The updated American Psychological Association guidelines for treating complex trauma endorse the use of a phase-based treatment model (APA, 2024). The use of three phases for trauma work can be traced back to Janet (1889), though popularized in modern trauma therapy by Herman (1992) and Courtios and Ford (2016) and integrated into psychodrama practice by Hudgins and Toscani (2013). While the terminology proposed in each of the three phases varies slightly, the main idea is consistent across all models and authors. Here are the three phases for sequenced trauma therapy (see Figure 2.2):

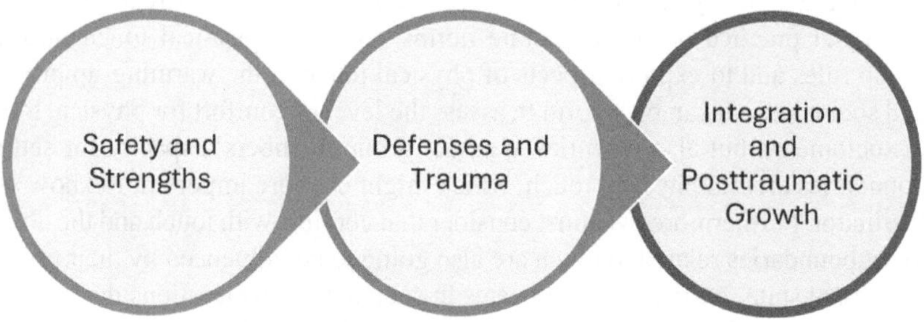

Figure 2.2 Three-phased clinical map for trauma work

1. **Safety and Strengths-Based Work** – development of coping skills, providing psychoeducation, practicing containment and grounding, building group cohesion and therapeutic relationship, working toward stabilization in the here-and-now
2. **Trauma Processing** – exploring trauma-related emotions (anger, grief, shame, guilt, fear, etc.), reprocessing traumatic memories, and working through defenses

3. **Integration and Growth** – promoting trauma recovery, cultivating posttraumatic growth, envisioning a future, and making meaning of the trauma

This simple clinical map starts with positive content, moves into negative content, and comes back to end in positive content. It offers a structure for cushioning the more difficult work between more tolerable work and titrating or pendulating in and out of the trauma safely. These three phases can be used throughout every aspect of psychodrama practice, including choice and pacing of sociometric prompts, pacing of group session focuses, sequence of roles enrolled in psychodrama scenes, and the ordering of psychodrama scenes in a longer multi-scene enactment. Many trauma practitioners skip over phase 1 in the map, which is prone to retraumatization. Many other trauma practitioners seem to address phase 1 before moving to phase 2, but stop there without addressing therapeutic content related to growth or recovery. There is also a risk of skipping from phase 1 directly to phase three while avoiding the feelings, sensations, beliefs, and memories related to the trauma, which is unlikely to be effective either. Together, these three phases offer psychodramatists an established architecture for effectively and safely pacing trauma-focused psychodrama.

Assessment, Group Structure, Level of Care, and Pacing

The safe and effective practice of trauma-focused psychodrama must also take into account the importance of assessment, group structure, level of care, and pacing – all of which we must be responsive to when facilitating groups. My experience has been that assessment and pre-group selection are one of the most underrated and key elements to setting up a therapy group for success. Yalom and Leszcz (2020) remind us that "good group therapy begins with good client selection. Clients improperly assigned to a therapy group are unlikely to benefit from their therapy experience" (p. 293). When group members are thoughtfully assessed for their appropriateness, we can craft together a group likely to be successful. Without proper assessment, we risk including clients who may need a higher level of care, may not be safe for the group, or may have goals unrelated to the group objectives.

Assessment for appropriateness for a group means that we must first have a vision and a concrete understanding of the nature of the group. We must consider the population the group is designed for in terms of age, gender, other aspects of identity, types of trauma, identified goals, and which phase of the clinical map the group is oriented toward. Will it be a group designed primarily to accomplish phase 1 tasks related to safety, cohesion, psychoeducation, strengths, support, and coping skills – or will it be a group focused on trauma processing – or a group oriented to growth after trauma? The phase of the clinical map that the group orients toward will have a major impact on how we assess appropriateness for the group. If we plan to offer a trauma processing group and do not exclude clients without any prior containment, resourcing, coping skills, or stability, then we risk moving fast for that individual to safely engage – or we risk being forced to slow the rest of the group down to avoid potentially overwhelming the other less resourced member.

The level of care that the group is held within will also impact the necessary pacing and structure of the group process.

The level of care that the group is held within will also impact the necessary pacing and structure of the group process. Psychodrama practice must be modified to meet clients where they are at. Psychodrama in a psychiatric hospital must be facilitated differently from psychodrama in an outpatient mental health clinic. Psychodrama in a residential addiction program and an Intensive Outpatient Program (IOP) will inevitably look different. A multi-day psychodrama workshop and a two-hour psychodrama open session allow for different-sized emotional containers. As a general rule of thumb, higher levels of care (inpatient, residential, and PHPs) provide more external support and containment due to the client lacking the internal supports and containment to function on their own. Lower levels of care (such as IOP and outpatient) provide less containment and external support because clients at those levels of care inherently are more resourced and stable. Having provided psychodrama groups at each level of care, I also notice that clients in higher levels of care seem to have an overall greater sense of urgency and willingness to dive deep quicker. Facilitating psychodrama groups in higher levels of care requires more resourcing but less closure and integrative work because participants have 24/7 support and ongoing opportunities for integration while in the hospital or residential program. Psychodrama groups in outpatient settings involve clients who are going back to their homes, work, and school after sessions, which requires that we provide more integration and closure before ending our outpatient sessions.

The pacing of a psychodrama group will also be impacted significantly by whether it is an open group or a closed group. Closed groups are often a better option for group cohesion as they do not permit new members to join after a certain point. This allows the group to establish connection and safety, which is essential for trauma processing. Sometimes, closed groups are not possible due to program structure, logistics, financial constraints, or level of care. For example, the trauma-focused psychodrama group I have facilitated at Mirmont Treatment Center for the past decade is within an inpatient addiction treatment center with an average length of stay of around three weeks. Clients join the group and are discharged from the group every week. This open group structure limits the potential of cohesion but creates more opportunities for mutual aid between the longer-term group members and the new clients joining the group. In open groups, when new clients join, we must attend to re-establishing group cohesion each time a new participant joins and orienting them to the group norms, rules, and process – which limits the depths that we can safely go to in a psychodrama session.

The pacing of a trauma-focused psychodrama group must also take into consideration the experience level of the participants with the psychodramatic method. In a group where everyone is new to psychodrama, we will need to slow the pace down and ease into fuller psychodramas – perhaps starting with sociodrama, psychodrama-like techniques, and psychodrama vignettes that are strength-based or shorter. In my inpatient group, I have found that if I move too quickly, the patients return to the group the following week, intimidated by the psychodrama session, and are less likely to volunteer as protagonists (or, I have more patients dropping out of the group). When facilitating a group with participants already experienced in psychodrama, we can move much quickly into more complex and emotionally intense psychodramas. The pacing of psychodrama sessions feels illusive for many new trainees due to the fact that psychodrama training demonstrations often move much faster, smoother, and deeper than psychodrama enactments with real patients.

Conclusion

Psychodrama is a powerful method with great potential for healing and harm. SAMHSA's trauma-informed care guidance offers concrete principles to guide psychodrama practice and training with an emphasis on resisting retraumatization and harm. Sensitivity and thoughtful navigation of anger catharsis, physical touch, ethics, identity, and anti-oppressive stances are essential for trauma-informed practice. Psychodrama must be modified to meet the group where they are at, which underscores the importance of considering the level of care, group structure, and group focus when facilitating trauma-focused psychodrama. In accordance with best practice guidelines for CPTSD treatment, psychodramatists are encouraged to adopt a three-staged, sequential treatment approach to trauma.

Psychodrama is a powerful method with great potentials for healing and harm.

References

American Psychological Association. (2024). *Guidelines for working with adults with complex trauma histories*. Retrieved from https://www.apa.org/practice/guidelines/adults-complex-trauma-histories.pdf

Badis, D., Hernandez, C. L., Nieto, L., Ruiz Esparza, M. P., & Tkachuck, C. (2025). A world with many worlds: Decolonizing education with action methods. In S.

Giacomucci, H. Fleury, & D. Altinay (Eds.), *Psychodrama in education: Creativity and experiential teaching around the world* (pp. 137–161). Springer Nature.
Bushman, B. J. (2002). Does venting anger feed or extinguish the flame? Catharsis, rumination, distraction, anger, and aggressive responding. *Personality and Social Psychology Bulletin, 28*(6), 724–731.
Bushman, B. J., Baumeister, R. F., & Stack, A. D. (1999). Catharsis, aggression, and persuasive influence: Self-fulfilling or self-defeating prophecies? *Journal of Personality and Social Psychology, 76*(3), 367.
Bylsma, L. M., Vingerhoets, A. J., & Rottenberg, J. (2008). When is crying cathartic? An international study. *Journal of Social and Clinical Psychology, 27*(10), 1165–1187.
Chesner, A. (2020). Psychodrama and healing the traumatic wound. In A. Chesner & S. Lykou (Eds.), *Trauma in the creative and embodied therapies: When words are not enough* (pp. 69–80). London: Routledge.
Courtois, C. A., & Ford, J. D. (2016). *Treatment of complex trauma: A sequenced, relationship-based approach.* New York: The Guildford Press.
Giacomucci, S. (2021). *Social work, sociometry, and psychodrama: Experiential approaches for group therapists, community leaders, and social workers.* Springer Nature. https://doi.org/10.1007/978-981-33-6342-7
Giacomucci, S. (2023). *Trauma-informed principles in group therapy, psychodrama, and organizations: Action methods for leadership.* Routledge.
Giacomucci, S., & Briggs, H. (2025). Trauma-focused psychodrama. In E. Senreich, S. L. A. Straussner, & J. Dann (Eds.), *Experiential therapies for treating trauma* (pp. 21–38). Routledge.
Hays, P. A. (2008). *Addressing cultural complexities in practice: Assessment, diagnosis, and therapy.* American Psychological Association.
Herman, J. L. (1992). *Trauma and recovery: The aftermath of violence – from domestic abuse to political terror.* New York: Basic Books.
Hudgins, M. K., & Toscani, F. (2013). *Healing world trauma with the therapeutic spiral model: Stories from the frontlines.* London: Jessica Kingsley Publishers.
Janet, P. (1889). *L'Automatisme psychologique* Félix Alcan: Paris.
Kjærvik, S. L., & Bushman, B. J. (2024). A meta-analytic review of anger management activities that increase or decrease arousal: What fuels or douses rage? *Clinical Psychology Review*, 102414.
Moreno, Z. T. (1986). JL Moreno's concept of ethical anger. *Journal of Group Psychotherapy, Psychodrama & Sociometry, 38*(4), 145–153.
Moreno, Z. T. (2012). *To dream again: A memoir.* Mental Health Resources.
Nieto, L. (2010). Look behind you: Using anti-oppression models to inform a protagonist's psychodrama. In E. Leveton (Ed.), *Healing collective trauma using sociodrama and drama therapy* (pp. 103–125). Springer Publishing Company.
Nieto, L., Boyer, M. F., Goodwin, L., Johnson, G. R., Smith, L. C., & Hopkins, J. P. (2010). *Beyond inclusion, beyond empowerment: A developmental strategy to liberate everyone.* Cuetzpalin Publishing.
Substance Abuse and Mental Health Services Administration. (2014). *SAMHSA's concept of trauma and guidance for a trauma-informed approach.* HHS Publication No. (SMA) 14-4884. Rockville, MD: Substance Abuse and Mental Health Services Administration.
Yalom, I. D., & Leszcz, M. (2020). *The theory and practice of group psychotherapy (6th edition).* Basic Books.

Chapter 3

Psychodrama Theory and Trauma Treatment

This chapter contains content from my previous books (Giacomucci, 2021a and 2023) with updated material throughout. Reprinted with permission.

Psychodrama is a complex system with its own theories, philosophy, and interventions. Similar to trauma-informed care, psychodrama is also a process-oriented approach that can be modified for any setting, any clinical issue, and any population, and is even used beyond therapy in education, religion, community organizing, theater, and other settings. Many of psychodrama's core theories are echoed through other modern trauma therapy theories and modalities. Moreno's mystical philosophy provides a conceptualization of the human essence at a level untouched by trauma. Psychodrama's spontaneity-creativity theory initiates as a view of the process of change through the simple steps of harnessing the available resources (cultural conserve), readying ourselves for action (warm-up), accessing spontaneity, and implementing a new and adequate way of responding. Moreno's contributions to our understanding of catharsis go beyond the simplicity of crying for release but also include the importance of integration, the nuances of audience versus actor catharses, and consideration of the influences of social contexts, spontaneity, and movement on the cathartic experience. Role theory provides a humanistic understanding of personality, similar to parts work, but more dynamic and expansive. Furthermore, psychodrama's developmental theory offers an understanding of child development stages through the lens of psychodrama's three core interventions – doubling, the mirror, and role reversal. Zerka's contributions to the developmental theory articulate how it applies to the entire lifespan – from life to death. Sociometric theory delivers extensive insight into the sociodynamics that impact all social spheres from relationships, groups, communities, and society. The very theories and philosophies that psychodrama emerged from inherently embody SAMHSA's trauma-informed principles of (1) safety, (2) trust and transparency, (3) peer support, (4) collaboration and mutuality, (5) empowerment, voice, and choice, and (6) issues related to gender, culture, and history.

DOI: 10.4324/9781003639497-3

> Moreno's mystical philosophy provides a conceptualization of the human essence at a level untouched by trauma.

Psychodrama theories were developed long before PTSD was recognized as a diagnosis, but they offer an effective approach in the treatment of trauma and complex trauma. In the context of complex trauma and CPTSD, the treatment can be modified to include a longer warming-up process and more focus on strengths-based content before activating past traumatic memories. The three add-on symptoms for CPTSD (disruptions in emotional regulation, relationships, and sense of self) seem to be three of the most common focuses in psychodrama therapy. The core interventions of psychodrama (which will be covered in Chapter 6) can all be used to help clients with emotional expression and emotional regulation. Psychodrama even allows us an avenue to concretize or enroll a particular emotion into a scene and have a conversation with it to explore our relationship to it (kind of like the movie "Inside Out"). Psychodrama is inherently a group therapy that puts a strong focus on the importance of relationships. This is evident especially in psychodrama's sociometric system, theory, and interventions. Many psychodrama enactments end up being about specific relationships, and psychodrama allows us to examine what is not working in relationships while practicing new ways of being in relationships. Psychodrama is also adept at addressing the negative view of self that can emerge from complex trauma. These negative views of self get dislodged during many sociometric warm-ups, where clients get to see how others experience them. Psychodrama scenes with strength-based roles help clients to see themselves in a new light, from the position of strength or from a supportive role. With psychodrama, we can even enroll a negative belief into a scene and interact with it directly to change our relationship to it.

The safe and effective practice of psychodrama, especially with trauma survivors, relies on a strong understanding of methodology, theories, and philosophy. This is true of any modality. Practicing without knowing the underlying theory is practicing blind. Wielding the powerful tools of psychodrama blindly is likely to result in someone getting hurt. Theory offers us a framework for understanding the client's (and group's) presentation, organizing the treatment, timing the interventions, and selecting from the assortment of interventions in each moment. Psychodrama practice developed from psychodrama theory, which originates from Moreno's philosophy. In order to understand psychodrama interventions and when to utilize them, we must first comprehend psychodrama's theories and underlying philosophy.

> The safe and effective practice of psychodrama, especially with trauma survivors, relies on a strong understanding of methodology, theories, and philosophy.

Morenean Philosophy as Trauma-Informed Philosophy

Jacob Moreno describes his philosophy as an existential and mystical philosophy emerging from his spiritual beliefs and commitment to Sociatry – healing for society (Giacomucci et al., 2021). He was disappointed at the end of his life as his methods had become largely integrated into other approaches and the culture but had become disconnected from the philosophy from which they came (J. D. Moreno, 2014). He likened this to ripping children from their parents (Z. T. Moreno, 1969). Moreno's philosophy was radical for its time and was rejected by many as it significantly challenged the generally accepted paradigms in the field. Though he developed his method and philosophy decades before PTSD was recognized as a diagnosis, careful examination of his philosophy reveals its congruence with modern trauma theory, trauma therapies, and trauma-informed principles. Most of the communities that Moreno directly worked with, and particularly the populations he worked with when developing his ideas, were highly traumatized and marginalized groups (Giacomucci, 2021b). His ideas of group psychotherapy emerged from his work with immigrants and sex workers, his sociometric system was generated from work with refugees, inmates, and a residential girls' reform school, and his psychodramatic approach developed from work with hospitalized psychiatric patients.

Morenian philosophy is expansive and therefore difficult to summarize concisely; nevertheless, I will do my best here. Moreno starts by proposing that humans are more than biological, psychological, or social beings, but are first of all cosmic beings (Z. T. Moreno, 2012). His conceptualization of human nature is fundamentally biopsychosocial-spiritual; thus, his methods are designed to address the biological, psychological, social, and spiritual/existential nuances of experience (Giacomucci, 2021a). In describing the Morenian approach, Zerka Moreno (2012) writes, "our instruments are basically spiritual and existential, pointing to and supporting the value of the human spirit" (p. 515).

In his 1912 encounter with Sigmund Freud, he articulates how his approach is different from psychoanalysis:

> Well, Dr. Freud, I start where you leave off. You meet people in the artificial setting of your office. I meet them on the street and in their homes, in their natural surroundings. You analyze their dreams. I give them the courage to dream again. You analyze and tear them apart. I let them act out their conflicting roles and help them to put the parts together again.
>
> (J. L. Moreno, 2019, p. 187)

He developed his ideas in opposition to Freud and psychoanalysis, which seems to have contributed to psychodrama's marginalization in the larger mental health system.

Moreno's approach is growth-oriented, compatible with modern strengths-based approaches and positive psychology (Giacomucci, 2021b). His humanistic perspective suggests that we should emphasize the genius and strengths of each person rather than pathology and shortcomings (J. L. Moreno, 2019). Moreno takes this as far as declaring all humans as potential geniuses, emphasizing each person's godlikeness, and even referring to his patients as "doctors" at times. In doing so, he emphasizes each person's dignity and worth while disrupting the inherent power dynamics within psychotherapy. He believed so much in each group member's therapeutic power that his code of ethics even suggests each group member taking the Hippocratic Oath to formalize their role as co-healers in the group therapy process (J. L. Moreno, 1957). This simple but revolutionary shift in the role expectations of therapist and group participants promotes nearly all of SAMHSA's trauma-informed principles (2014) – particularly safety, collaboration, mutuality, empowerment, voice, trustworthiness, and peer support.

Moreno's spiritual philosophy promotes the idea of a Godhead, the source of all spontaneity and creativity, while suggesting that each human being is also divine. He believed in the existence of a parallel universe where all things are sacred – a place containing a "primordial nature" that fuels the life force of each new generation. Morenean philosophy suggests that this is the First Universe from which we come at birth and return to after death. The Second Universe describes the world of form, space, and time where we primarily live in. He believed that one could tap into the First Universe through mystical experience and that psychodrama could provide a portal into this surplus reality where all things are possible. The intersection of these two universes is depicted through the encounter symbol in Figure 3.1.

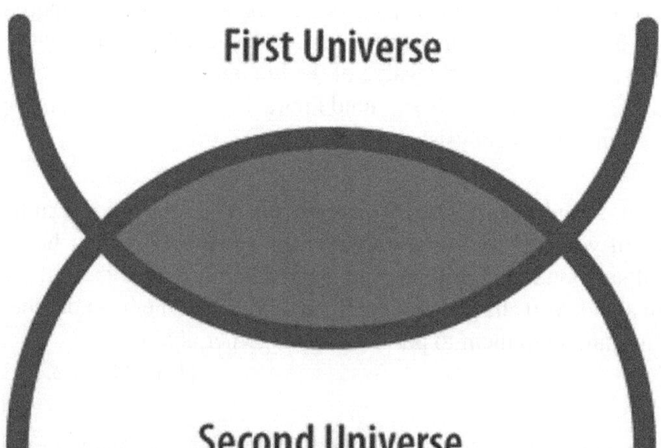

Figure 3.1 The encounter symbol

Republished with permission from Giacomucci (2021a)

Within Moreno's mysticism, spontaneity, psychodrama's curative agent, is conceptualized as a spiritual energy, originating with the Godhead, that promotes adequate responses to new situations and new responses to old, reoccurring situations. Spontaneity and creativity are conceptualized as twin principles, foundational to psychodrama's theory of change, and underpinning all human progress (Nolte, 2014).

The Morenos articulate that the primary goal of all forms of therapy is to help a client access the *Autonomous Healing Center* within. In describing her husband's philosophy, Zerka writes that healing is attributed to a quiet process deep within the body and the self, untouched by words but stimulated through action (Z. T. Moreno, 2012). The strong emphasis on the autonomous healing center demonstrates synchronicity with modern trauma theories (such as Interpersonal Neurobiology's focus on integration, the Adaptive Information Processing Model in EMDR, SELF in Internal Family Systems (IFS), and the body's ability to restore itself to goodness in Somatic Experiencing) which also underscore the self-healing nature of the human mind and nervous system (Levine, 2010; Schwartz, 2021; Shapiro, 2018; Siegel, 2020).

Moreno's philosophy emphasizes the here-and-now, even conceptualizing the past and future within the context of the present. The past is considered "memory-in-the-moment of past experiences," and the future is regarded as "here and now anticipation-in-the-moment of what might be eventually experienced" (Nolte, 2020, p. 131). This is particularly congruent with EMDR, somatic psychotherapy, and other theories of traumatic memory processing, which are more concerned with the here-and-now experience of remembering trauma than the actual details of a traumatic event. Morenean philosophy teaches that spontaneity and creativity are only accessible in the moment and that each moment is wide-open with possibility. This fundamentally supports a view of human beings as active actors with agency in their life and situation rather than helpless victims of predeterminism. Psychodrama enactments are co-created in the here-and-now, acting as if they were currently real. In this way, psychodrama provides participants with access to experiences in surplus reality that would be impossible otherwise. Furthermore, psychodrama insists on honoring the subjective reality of the protagonist based on their experience and perspective. This approach meets the client where they are through a postmodern and social constructivism lens, supporting participants' unique meaning-making process rather than imposing the therapist's judgment of reality or interpretation upon them (Blatner, 2000; Oudijk, 2007).

Morenean philosophy teaches that spontaneity and creativity are only accessible in the moment and that each moment is wide-open with possibility.

Psychodrama, the first body-oriented therapy, is perhaps most fundamentally different from other approaches with its focus on action rather than talking. Moreno believed that "what was learned in action, must be unlearned in action" (Dayton, 2005, p. xxvii). While a traditional group psychotherapy session only involves participants sitting in their seats in discussion, every psychodrama group session involves multiple action structures initiating movement for participants. Through movement and action, psychodrama brings the body and nervous system into the treatment process. The influx of trauma research continues to support the use of body-oriented interventions to address the somatic imprint of trauma, which exists within the brain and body at levels below thinking and talking (Cozolino, 2014; Levine, 2010; Malchiodi, 2020; Perry & Szalavitz, 2006; van de Kamp et al., 2019; van der Kolk, 2014). The interpersonal neurobiologists have declared the most significant finding of the century to be that the human brain is constantly changing and evolving based on experience (Cozolino, 2014; Siegel, 2020). Psychodrama's action approach provides participants with opportunities for healing trauma through corrective experiences that would be impossible through talk therapy (Giacomucci, 2018, 2019, 2020; Giacomucci & Ehrhart, 2021; Giacomucci & Stone, 2019). Psychodrama provides a safe space for doing, undoing, and redoing in the context of renegotiating traumatic experience (Schreiber & Giacomucci, 2024). Redfern (2014) beautifully articulates this same process in the context of trauma healing in dramatherapy – "a completed release (after some struggle) from a well-held pattern or structure and the embrace of a missing opposite that takes place in the arts/playspace and leaves the client significantly changed afterwards" (p. 384).

Psychodrama Theories as Trauma Theories

Leszcz (2018) reminds us that "Theory teaches us where to head therapeutically. Technique teaches us what to do once we arrive there" (p. 285). This is important wisdom for practitioners to consider. Many contemporary practitioners seem to juxtapose various techniques together while neglecting theoretical frameworks. This is particularly true when it comes to psychodrama practice and the ways in which psychodrama techniques have been adopted by non-psychodramatists and employed without regard for their underlying philosophy and theories.

Psychodrama offers multiple theories that support its interventions and operationalize its philosophy. The core theories of psychodrama range from action theory, spontaneity-creativity, role theory, developmental theory, sociometry, and catharses. Psychodrama theories are intrinsically connected to psychodrama techniques. These primary theories will be presented below while drawing connections between them and trauma theory. Psychodrama interventions and techniques will be outlined and described in Chapter 6.

Spontaneity-Creativity Theory

Moreno's theory of change is spontaneity-creativity theory, depicted through the Canon of Creativity (1953). This process shows how new cultural conserves are generated through a warming-up process that cultivates spontaneity and creativity, resulting in the creation of something new (see Figure 3.2).

Spontaneity is only accessed through a warming-up process, but once tapped into provides the readiness for new action and creation. The warming-up process helps overcome ambivalence and prepare for new action. In psychodrama theory, there is no such thing as "resistant clients"; instead, they are conceptualized as clients who are warmed up to something else.

The Spontaneity Assessment Inventory Revised (SAIR) was developed by David Kipper and colleagues while validating its psychomctric validity and reliability (it has also been translated into multiple languages). The SAIR has been used in multiple studies demonstrating spontaneity's inverse relationship to mental health symptoms and its positive relationship to other measures of well-being. Nearly a century ago, Moreno postulated that spontaneity and anxiety are inversely correlated – an idea later validated by research (Tarashoeva et al., 2017). Moreno suggested that the warming-up process helps to mitigate anxiety while propelling one toward spontaneous action. PTSD, formerly categorized as an anxiety disorder but now a stress disorder, appears to have a similarly inverse relationship to spontaneity (Giacomucci, 2021b; Giacomucci

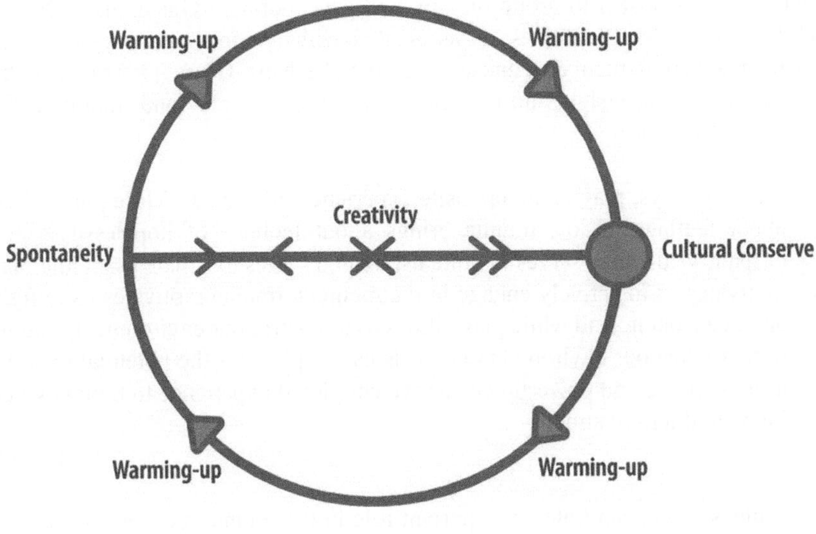

Figure 3.2 Moreno's Canon of Creativity

Republished with permission from Giacomucci (2021a)

et al., 2022, 2025). In our most recent study, we actually found that spontaneity and PTSD were more closely related than spontaneity and anxiety (Giacomucci et al., 2025). Through the lens of Moreno's spontaneity theory, we would conceptualize PTSD as a condition perpetuated through the disconnection from healthy spontaneity (Giacomucci, 2021b). PTSD, like other psychosocial problems, would be described by Moreno as being characterized by an absence of spontaneity (immobilization or reenactment) or the presence of pathological spontaneity (novel but inadequate action). The Canon of Creativity provides us with a simplified map for trauma recovery and reminds us of the importance of the warming-up process, which is likely to take longer for trauma survivors. The importance of warming-up is a core idea of this book, which will be revisited in later sections and chapters as it relates to playfulness, internalized trauma roles, sociometric warm-ups, and SAMHSA's core principles of trauma-informed care.

In order to access spontaneity, safety must first be established.

Traumatic stress is characterized by intrusive images or thoughts, negative moods and beliefs, arousal and reactivity, as well as avoidance and dissociation. These symptoms provide blocks from safety, well-being, joy, and happiness. In order to access spontaneity, safety must first be established. The role of playfulness in cultivating safety for adults is beginning to be discussed, particularly as it relates to group therapy and psychodrama (Giacomucci, 2021a; Goldstein, 2018). Playfulness is associated with relationships, joy, and even resilience (Trevarthen & Panksepp, 2016). Perhaps Gross (2018) provides the most striking insights on the relationship between play and trauma in the following passage:

> In many ways, play is the opposite experience of trauma. While play brings about feelings of joy, trauma brings about feelings of hopelessness and despair. While play serves to unite us, trauma serves to isolate us. While play motivates us to actively engage in the moment, trauma motivates us to fight and flee from it. And while play allows us to control our environment, trauma occurs when our environment controls us . . . play has the potential to serve as an antidote and powerful corrective emotional experience to trauma when integrated into treatment.
>
> (p. 369)

Playfulness then, can hold an important role in the trauma recovery process as it cultivates safety, connection, engagement, control, and joy. Play may be a core component in one's warming-up process on the Canon of Creativity as it appears to help many access their spontaneity and creativity. Role-playing is, of course, one form of play. The psychodramatic process inherently involves play as an undercurrent through its reliance on role-playing techniques. In a recent trauma-focused psychodrama study by this author, after completion of a psychodrama group, patients commented on their surprise that trauma therapy could be "fun" (Giacomucci & Marquit, 2020). A psychodrama enactment is a unique experience that often encompasses experiences of playfulness, catharsis, and the integration of new ideas.

Catharsis

Psychodrama has developed a reputation for its potential in facilitating powerful catharsis. Catharsis is usually part of the trauma therapy process and generally something experienced during a psychodramatic role play. Moreno was perhaps one of the most prolific writers on the theory of catharsis since Aristotle, Breuer, and Freud. He expanded the concept of catharsis, finding positive correlations between catharsis and spontaneity, action, and group experience (J. L. Moreno, 1940; Nolte, 2014). Moreno identified multiple distinctly different types of catharsis, most notably – audience catharsis, actor catharsis, catharsis of abreaction, and catharsis of integration. Developing on Aristotle's concept of spectator catharsis, Moreno noted how an audience's cathartic experience was enhanced when the action observed was novel (spontaneous), when the audience shared a common bond, and when the action related to the audience's own personal lives. Through his research with the *Theater of Spontaneity*, he also became acutely aware of the catharses his actors were experiencing through role-playing characters and situations that related to their personal lives. "The greater catharsis achieved through action is undeniable. The patient is able to express kinesthetically many feelings for which he has no words" (J. L. Moreno & Enneis, 1950, p. 13). Moreno differentiates between catharsis of abreaction and catharsis of integration, suggesting that both are necessary, but that abreaction alone is not healing – integration is the ultimate goal (Nolte, 2014). Catharsis of abreaction describes the discharging, releasing, and expressing of built-up feelings or resistances, while catharsis of integration labels the reconfiguration and inner transformation associated with meaning-making and growth (Kellermann, 1984). Group therapy research supports that catharsis is only effective in promoting change when it includes cognitive learning (Lieberman et al., 1973).

Zerka Moreno (2000) further adds that many of the most healing catharses occur through psychodrama scenes of experiences impossible in reality – for example, a client having a conversation for closure with a deceased family member, a childhood trauma survivor nurturing themselves as a child, or an assault survivor confronting their perpetrator and receiving an authentic amends from them. Kellerman articulately summarizes Moreno's contribution to the theory of catharsis:

> To include not only release and relief of emotions, but also integration and ordering; not only intense reliving of the past, but also intense living in the here-and-now; not only a passive, verbal reflection, but also an active, non-verbal enactment; not only a private ritual, but also a communal, shared rite of healing; not only an intrapsychic tension reduction, but also an interpersonal conflict resolution; not only a medical purification, but also a religious and aesthetic experience.
>
> (1984, pp. 10–11)

Role-playing often leads to catharses, action insights and the integration of new ideas that were not previously available to an individual from the role of self. Spontaneous role-playing, in many ways, is an action-based free association method. Taking on different roles in a psychodrama offers participants a chance to step into the shoes of others, give voice to parts of self, and develop new roles or skills previously unintegrated into their sense of self. Psychodrama enactments may include a variety of roles ranging from intrapsychic roles (strengths, parts of self, visions of self, internalized trauma roles, defenses, etc.), interpersonal roles (family members, friends, colleagues, etc.), or transpersonal roles (God, ancestors, archetypes, etc.).

Role Theory

Moreno's theory of personality is role theory – which suggests that the "self" is composed of all the roles one holds in their life and that a healthy (spontaneous) personality has a wide role repertoire (J. L. Moreno, 1953). The idea of the role is a non-pathologizing way of labeling clusters of behavior, cognition, affect, somatic experience, and social phenomenon. It bridges the gap between psychiatry and the social sciences (J. L. Moreno, 1961) while offering a simple-to-understand language for describing the behavior of clients. Psychodrama's role theory is comprehensive including a theory of role development (role taking, role-playing, and role creating), categories of roles (somatic, psychodramatic, and social), and various role dynamics and role phenomenon including role reciprocity, role lock, role fatigue, role-self congruence, role conflict, sub-roles, and others (Clayton, 1993, 1994; Giacomucci, 2021a).

One of the most important teachings from role theory is that of the three stages of role development (see Figure 3.3).

Moreno teaches that when we begin to adopt new roles in our life and our self, we are in a role-taking phase. The role is new and unfamiliar at this point, and there may be resistance to the role. Here, we look to role models for help in learning the new role. After a role is adequately learned, we move into a role-playing

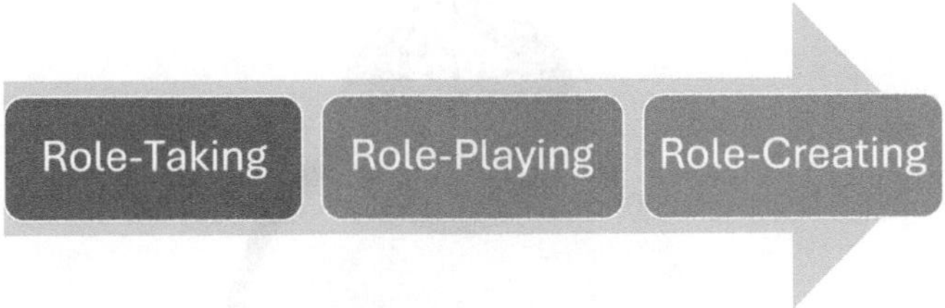

Figure 3.3 Moreno's stages of role development

phase of development, which is characterized by one's ability to hold the role and start to bring themself into it. The final phase of development, role creating, is when one brings enough spontaneity and creativity into the role to transform it into something completely new. The role development theory can be particularly useful when thinking about professional development or staff development within organizations, as well as when helping clients integrate new internal or interpersonal roles related to trauma recovery.

Role theory provides a simple language for describing parts of self that translates easily across cultures. Moreno outlines three categories of roles – somatic, psychodramatic, and social roles. Somatic roles are the first to develop in one's life at the preverbal stage and include the eater, the crawler, the sleeper, and so on. Though somatic roles are their own category or role, both psychodramatic and social roles also have somatic aspects to them. Psychodramatic roles are the roles we play out in our mind or psyche relating to the internal dimensions of life – the dreamer, the thinker, idealized or distorted parts of self, future or past projections of self, and so on. Social roles are ones we play in relation to others in our life and society, such as brother, mother, therapist, client, and so on (J. L. Moreno, 1953). Roles can be integrated parts of self, or here-and-now manifestations of behavior and experience. J. L. Moreno (1972) writes of a somatic self, psychodramatic self, and social self, composed of all the roles within each category which integrate into a singular sense of a biopsychosocial self (see Figure 3.4). Baer (2024) describes how CPTSD symptoms correlate strongly to physiological responses and a loss of safety in the body, which impacts somatic roles. These somatic roles, in turn, impact both our psychological experience (psychodramatic self) and the social roles that we hold in our life. Psychodramatic roles mediate inner conflict or harmony between somatic and social roles, which highlights the potential of psychodrama to help promote further harmony on a biopsychosocial level.

Moreno viewed human beings as role players and actors on the stage of life, and that an individual's personality emerges from their roles and relationships. Roles also emerge and are embodied in situations, often with reciprocity to others. This theory of personality highlights the impacts of relationships and social

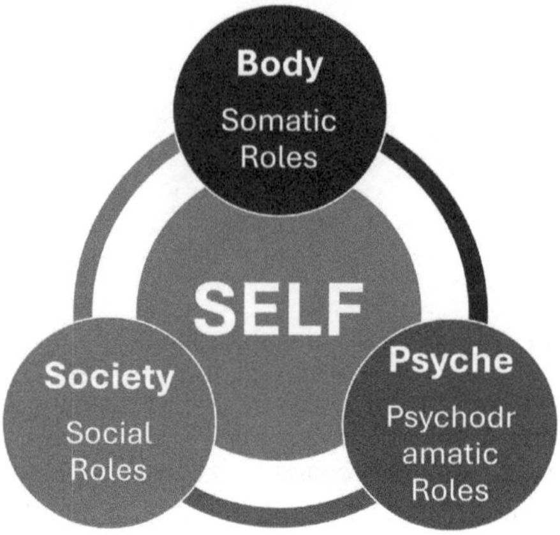

Figure 3.4 Roles and their relation to the biopsychosocial self

forces upon our lives and thus takes into account how relational and collective trauma may impact personality and a sense of self. Traumatic responses to adversity lead to the internalization of trauma-based roles (Giacomucci, 2018). The trauma recovery process involves transforming these trauma-based roles into roles of posttraumatic growth (Giacomucci, 2021b). Role theory provides a non-pathologizing approach to conceptualizing self that is similar to other popular trauma theories based on ego states or parts work.

Moreno's Developmental Theory

J.L. Moreno proposed a new developmental theory composed of three distinct stages, which also reflect three primary psychodrama interventions – the double, the mirror, and the role reversal. Moreno's three stages of development describe a child's movement from the first universe of formlessness into the second universe. After birth, a child lives in a state of undifferentiated identity having not yet formed a sense of self or ego strength. Moreno described this as the *matrix of identity* and theorized that during this time the child experiences themselves as one with their mother, caregivers, and all of their surroundings (J. L. Moreno, 1953).

The first development stage is *doubling*, which is when caregivers and others help to give voice to a pre-verbal infant's experience and needs. Accurate doubling requires an attuned caregiver and helps the child develop a sense of self and of their needs, feelings, and experiences (Dayton, 2005). Doubling is required for healthy attachment and helps a child feel understood and seen – neurobiologically developing the internal brain circuitry for self-regulation later in life (Cozolino, 2014). When a child grows up without accurate doubling from others, "the child may feel that he is incomprehensible to others and a sort of fissure may occur within the self due to feeling misunderstood or out of sync with his external representations of self" (Dayton, 2005, p. 161). This frequently occurs in the context of childhood trauma. The second developmental stage is that of *the mirror*. This is when a child begins to develop a sense of individuality and a sense of self, to the point of being able to recognize their reflection in the mirror (J. L. Moreno, 1952). At this stage, the child develops awareness of themself as separate from others and separate from the world (Dayton, 2005). Children whose developmental needs are not met in this stage may struggle with co-dependency, enmeshment, or a distorted sense of self. This is also quite common for childhood trauma survivors. The third developmental stage, role reversal, describes a stage when a child can empathize with others, see things from another's perspective, and understand that each person has their own subjective experience, feelings, and thoughts. Tian Dayton (2005) writes that "in role reversal the sense of self is intact enough so that we can temporarily leave it, stand in the shoes of another, and return safely home" (p. 439). A child experiencing complex trauma at this phase may not develop the capacity to consider other people's perspectives, emotions, and experiences. It may manifest as a rupture in empathy and consideration for others. These three stages of child development offer a simplified conceptualization of how traumatic disruptions at these three stages may impact an individual. The clinician's assessment in this framework then offers guidance on which of these psychodramatic interventions (doubling, mirroring, or role reversal) to emphasize (Giacomucci, 2021a).

Zerka Moreno later expanded upon Moreno's three stages, influenced by Erickson's eight psychosocial stages, outlined in *The Eight Stages of Cosmic Being in Terms of Capacity and Need to Double and Role Reverse* (2006). Zerka's expanded developmental theory goes a step further, describing one's development through adulthood. It depicts how the child-caregiver roles often reverse, wherein the adult child becomes the double and mirror for their aging parent, helping them as they transition from this world back to the first universe. Moreno's theories are deeply relational, highlighting the importance of relationships and social forces in each human's life. His 1914 poem, *An Invitation to an Encounter*, synthesizes the core of his interpersonal theory as well as the essence of role reversal:

> A meeting of two: eye to eye, face to face. And when you are near I will tear your eyes out and place them instead of mine and you will tear my eyes out and place them instead of yours then I will look at you with your eyes and you will look at me with mine.
>
> (J. L. Moreno, 1914)

Sociometric Theory

He later developed his interpersonal theory into a more comprehensive sociometric theory, which became the foundation of his group therapy and psychodrama approaches. His sociometry theory offers a bridge between psychology and sociology while emphasizing a view of the person within their environment

(Giacomucci, 2021a). One of the most important aspects of sociometry is the social atom, which is a visual depiction of an individual's closest relationships. Moreno's creation of the social atom appears to have also influenced the later development of the genogram and the ecomap (Dayton, 2005). The social atom is essentially a relational map showing the nature of an individual's connection to others in their life (see Figure 3.5).

The social atom is a useful assessment tool and future visioning tool for clinical work, as it helps to illuminate social relationships and dynamics within one's life. Having a client draw their social atom will often provide a clinician with more insight into their social life than simply interviewing them. In the aforementioned example, individuals in the client's life are down to scale and proximity based on closeness and the amount of social space the individual or entity occupies in their life. The line connecting the two individuals also provides

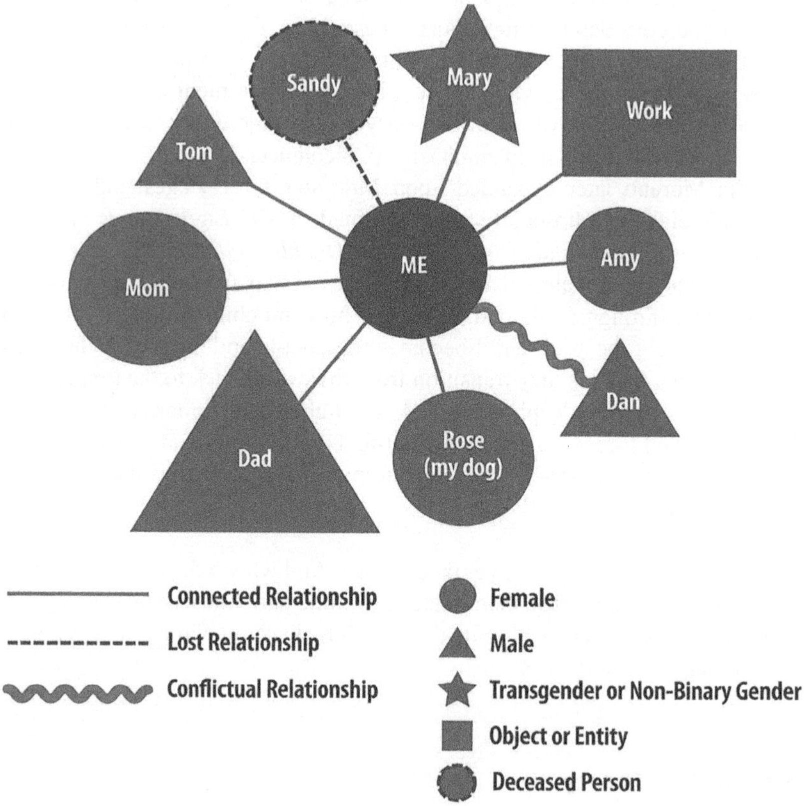

Figure 3.5 The social atom

Republished with permission from Giacomucci (2021a)

information related to the nature of the connection – a straight line representing a connected relationship, a dotted line to represent a lost relationship, and a squiggly line to indicate a conflictual relationship. Traditionally, circles were used for women, triangles for men, and squares for non-human roles. The social atom has been further developed in the past several years by modern psychodramatists to offer options for non-gender-conforming and transgender folks, such as the use of a star or simply giving participants the option of using any shape for any person on the social atom (as suggested by this writer's former graduate student Jordan Briem) (Giacomucci, 2021a). The social atom can be used in a variety of different ways, including as an assessment tool, as a treatment planning or evaluation tool, for self-examination, or as a warm-up for a psychodrama.

While the social atom is a person-centered view of one's relationships, Moreno also developed a tool called the sociogram, which is a group-centered exploration of relationships and sociodynamics. Moreno's sociograms, generated through a sociometric test, depict the distribution of choices, preferences, connections, and social wealth within a group of any size (see Figure 3.6).

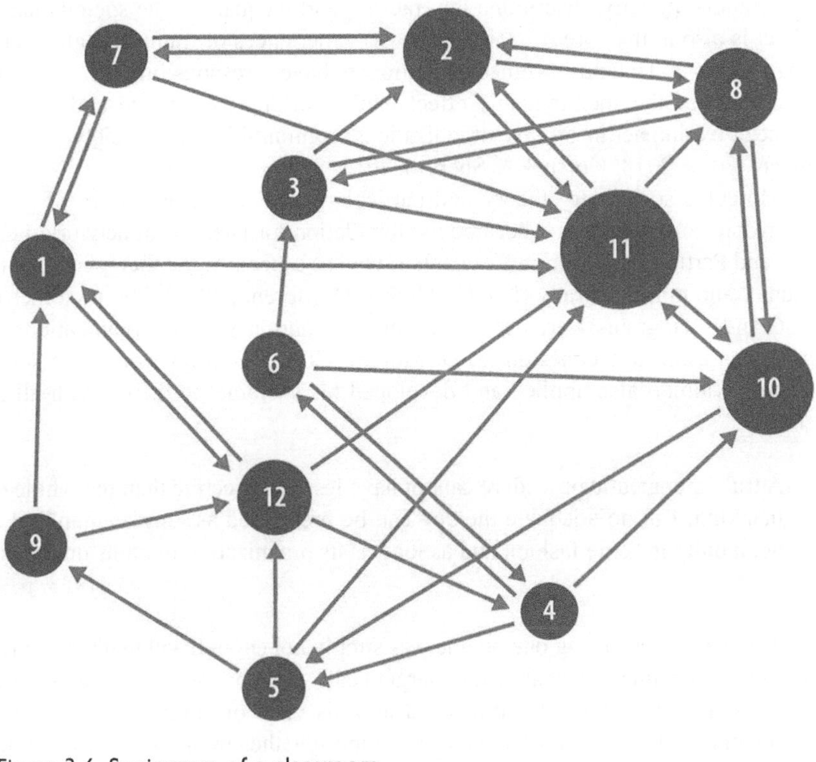

Figure 3.6 Sociogram of a classroom

Republished with permission from Giacomucci (2021a)

Sociograms can be drawn on paper, generated by computer programs (Raimundo & Raimundo, (2021)), or done experientially through "hands-on-shoulder sociometry," which will be described in Chapter 5. The sociogram was one of Moreno's earlier sociometric tools and illuminated the presence of two core sociometric phenomena – *tele* and the *sociodynamic effect*. Tele describes "the socio-gravitational factor, which operates between individuals, drawing them to form more positive or negative pair-relations . . . than on chance" (J.L. Moreno, 1947, p. 84). Moreno further explains tele as a type of two-way empathy, as the opposite of transference, as a knowing and insight into another person, and as the foundation for all wholesome relationships (1953, 1959). Tele appears to be related to non-verbal, right-brain to right-brain communication and intuition that promotes synchronicity and unexpected connection (Dayton, 2005, Giacomucci, 2021a, Yaniv, 2014). On the other hand, the sociodynamic effect is a term labeling an underlying social force in all groups that leads to the unequal distribution of connections, choices, preferences, and social wealth (J. L. Moreno, 1943). This effect leads to the presence of social stars and social isolates in every group while also underlying most social problems in the world, such as collective trauma, poverty, discrimination, racism, and inequality. The sociodynamic effect is also at the core of many (or most) experiences of trauma, neglect, and abandonment. Trauma-informed practitioners have a responsibility to maintain awareness of the sociodynamic effect while working to mitigate and reverse its negative impact in groups, organizations, communities, and society (Giacomucci, 2017, 2018; Korshak & Shapiro, 2013; Schreiber, 2018).

Moreno's sociometry theory and particularly his sociograms were of great interest to sociologists and became the foundation for later social network theories and Participatory Action Research as well as aspects of the therapeutic community and milieu therapy (Landy, 2008; J. D. Moreno, 2014). His sociometric tests and sociograms were used in the military and in various organizations to assess and improve cohesion (J. D. Moreno, 2014). Beyond work with small groups, Moreno also applied and developed his sociometric theory with all of society:

> A truly therapeutic procedure cannot have less an objective than the whole of mankind. But no adequate therapy can be prescribed as long as mankind is not a unity in some fashion and as long as its organization remains unknown. (1953, p. 3)

He believed that working one on one was simply not enough and that we needed to promote healing and change on a larger scale. His philosophy of viewing the group as its own entity also translated into his view of humankind as having an organic unity – that all humans are bound together by a core commonality that transcends all differences (J. L. Moreno, 1953). His sociometric system, he believed, was an essential prerequisite for assessing groups, communities, and society in order to offer adequate interventions for change. Moreno's sociometry on a macro level is designed to address, mitigate, and prevent social injustice while promoting equity and equality in all spheres of life.

Sociodrama

Beyond psychodrama, sociodrama is another method that can be employed. Sociodrama is similar to psychodrama but provides a greater sense of emotional and aesthetic distance for participants as the sociodramatic roles are more broadly defined without using anyone's story as a script. In sociodrama, we emphasize collective group themes rather than a single person's story. For example, in psychodrama, we might enact the relationship between John and his mother, but in sociodrama, we would enact the relationship between a client and a mother. The roles, themes, and issues are usually co-created by the group spontaneously, but can also be inserted by the director to keep the process on track or focused on a specific objective. Sociodrama often tends to be more playful and educational than psychodrama, but this is not always the case. I have done many sociodramas that were as emotionally powerful as most of the psychodrama sessions I have been a part of. Sociodrama is concerned with collective issues, which often means that it focuses on social justice or collective trauma issues.

Sociodrama is sometimes a better option than psychodrama when working with collective issues, as sociodrama orients on the group's collective experience rather than an individual's specific story (Giacomucci, 2017). This provides an enhanced sense of safety, distance, playfulness, and spontaneity that is often beneficial to groups when addressing uncomfortable and painful topics related to identity or social injustice.

> In the midst of the "MeToo Movement" in the United States, I was facilitating a workshop on sociodrama. The workshop participants, composed primarily of female therapists and graduate students, chose the topic of sexism, gender violence, rape culture, and sexual harassment for the sociodrama topic during the training. As a male facilitator, I determined it was necessary to acknowledge my position as a male in authority during the session while committing to facilitate the sociodrama with a sense of humility, following the lead of the group (follow-lead-follow). The group collectively co-created a scene of a mother prompting a difficult discussion with their teenage daughter about consent, sex, and sexual harassment. In the sociodrama, the daughter expressed her confusions with current events and national news related to prominent court cases during which men in positions of power seemed to be getting away with sexual harassment or even rape without punishment or accountability. Feeling disempowered, both expressed their shared frustrations, fears, and hopes for a more equitable future. Group members offered doubling statements from each role to deepen their understanding and expression of

> the issues at hand. As the group articulated the important feelings and perspectives from each role, a sense of catharsis and new insight was achieved. The sociodrama still felt quite heavy as we organically were moving towards closure, so I suggested we incorporate an archetypal feminine role model to guide the teenager and mother in navigating these issues. The group chose Wonder Woman (the 2017 movie had recently been released at that time) who was enrolled into the scene to offer an enhanced sense of empowerment, safety, and powerful feminine energy. The sociodrama came to closure with Wonder Woman offering her guidance to the mother, the teen, and the group.

In this example, we can see the power of sociodrama in exploring collective issues within groups and society. Though sociodrama is often much less emotionally intense and involved as psychodrama, this specific sociodrama is a testament to the fact that sociodrama scenes can be equally as intense and powerful as psychodrama scenes. This book will reference sociodrama at times, but is mostly focused on psychodrama. See chapter 7 for more on sociodramatic use of the empty chair.

Neuroscience of Trauma-Focused Psychodrama

In addition to the empirical research, the constantly evolving neuroscience research also supports psychodrama as an effective treatment for trauma, PTSD, and CPTSD. Moreno suggested nearly 100 years ago that the body remembers what the mind forgets. This wisdom is echoed throughout the core philosophies of many of the foremost trauma experts today, who regularly emphasize the somatic imprints of trauma and how the body keeps the score (van der Kolk, 2014; Levine, 2010):

> Prone to action, and deficient in words, these patients (trauma survivors) can often express their internal states more articulately in physical movements or in pictures than in words. Utilizing drawings and psychodrama may help them develop a language that is essential for effective communication and for the symbolic transformation that can occur in psychotherapy.
>
> (van der Kolk, 1996, p. 195)

Our understanding of the neuroscience of trauma is constantly evolving. The research points to how trauma impacts the brain at levels below thinking, cognition, and talking. Trauma leaves an imprint on the nervous system and within the body – even when the traumatic experience is not consciously remembered by the survivor. In the case of repressed traumatic memories, the body continues to keep the score and respond to stimuli or triggers related to the traumatic event. Research shows that when someone remembers a traumatic experience, the left hemisphere of the brain is largely inactive (including Broca's area, which is dedicated to speech and language), while the right hemisphere is overactive (Rauch et al., 1996; van der Kolk, 2014). This finding strongly challenges the use of talk therapies alone in the treatment of PTSD and trauma-related issues. Bessel van der Kolk, MD, describes how the limbic system is impacted, "the imprint of trauma doesn't sit in the verbal, understanding part of the brain . . . but in much deeper regions – amygdala, hippocampus, hypothalamus, brain stem – which are only marginally affected by thinking and cognition" (as cited in Wylie, 2004, pp. 30–41). These neuroscience findings provide further validation for trauma survivors who so often report that it is difficult to talk about their trauma or that they struggle to remember it and describe it in words (Malchiodi, 2020). The voicelessness that commonly results from trauma can now be understood partially as a neurobiological process. Psychodrama's emphasis on symbolic representation, body movement, action, relationship, and other right-brain processes positions it as an ideal trauma treatment in that it can access and renegotiate trauma in the places it is stored within the mind, body, and brain.

Psychodrama's emphasis on symbolic representation, body movement, action, relationship, and other right-brain processes positions it as an ideal trauma treatment in that it can access and renegotiate trauma in the places it is stored within the mind, body, and brain.

The limbic system of the brain is significantly involved in attachment and relationships. So much of complex trauma is experienced in the context of a relationship and results in later complications in one's social life. Cozolino articulates how "our brains are structured and restructured by interactions with our social and natural environments" (2014, pp. 77–78). After birth, human beings are entirely dependent on caregivers and attachment figures longer than any other species on the planet. Early childhood experiences and attachments provide the psychological and neurobiological architecture for a sense of self, template of relationships, core belief systems, and abilities for self-regulation later in life (Cozolino, 2014; Shapiro & Applegate, 2018; Wallin, 2007). Throughout the first several months of life, all communication is non-verbal and through action, such as facial expression, body language, posture, pointing, and gesturing. As a child develops, their communication evolves to include language and words while continuing to also be largely composed of action and non-verbal language. The emphasis on action, interaction, and non-verbal communication in psychodrama further validates its effectiveness in addressing childhood adversity and relational trauma. In addition to thought and cognition, the brain's primary languages are action and relationship. Louis Cozolino (2014) informs us that the field of "interpersonal neurobiology assumes that the brain is a social organ built via experience" (p. xvii).

Perhaps the most groundbreaking neuroscience finding of the century is that the brain changes through experience and maintains its neuroplasticity throughout the entire lifespan (Siegel, 2020). This highlights how adversity and traumatic experiences change the brain, but also points to the power of new positive experiences in promoting neurobiological change (Shapiro & Applegate, 2018). The surplus reality of the psychodrama stage provides an avenue for new experiences that are otherwise impossible in real life (Giacomucci & Stone, 2019). Though the psychodramatic role play is different from a real experience, when the group is fully warmed-up and acting as if in the here-and-now, it appears that the brain/body processes the psychodrama experience in the same way any other experience is processed. Psychodrama participants often comment on how real the role play felt for them, which further validates this idea. Psychodrama offers the potential of changing both psychological and somatic impacts of past adversity by activating one's traumatic neural network in the safety of the group; the traumatic memory is renegotiated through new corrective experiences on the psychodrama stage (Giacomucci, 2021a). Previously incomplete survival responses from the moment of the trauma can be resolved. A client immobilized or frozen in their trauma, stuck in a chronic freeze response (dorsal vagal), can be released through the safe activation of a fight or flight response (sympathetic nervous system), and a resulting return to social engagement (as described in Polyvagal theory). In this way, the nervous system can discharge pent-up somatic energy related to the trauma and be restored to a state of equilibrium (Levine, 2010; Porges, 2011). For example, a survivor of complex childhood abuse who perpetually is stuck in a freeze response long into adulthood, could engage in a series of psychodrama scenes that involve building up the strengths, support, and safety to face the trauma; nurturing and validating their younger self; address any abandoning authorities that failed in their responsibility to prevent or stop the abuse; have an embodied experience of successfully defending themselves and fighting off their perpetrator or successfully fleeing from their perpetrator; experience correction and the fulfillment of unmet developmental needs through scenes of repair with a perpetrator or idealized/archetypal parent figure; and engage in future projection scenes that involve role training aspects of posttraumatic growth.

Conclusion

Psychodrama theories and Morenean philosophy are a foundation for the safe and effective practice of psychodrama with complex trauma. Without a strong grasp on the theory and philosophy, the risks of harm and retraumatization increase. Psychodrama theories provide paradigms for understanding human nature, the change process, catharsis and integration, personality and roles, child development, and social phenomena in relationships, groups, communities, and society. Psychodrama theories from 100 years mirror many contemporary trauma theories from modern-day trauma therapy approaches and are progressively more supported by the ever-growing body of neuroscience research.

References

Baer, J. (2024). Applying the role-oriented integrated model to treat clients with complex trauma. *Journal of Psychodrama, Sociometry, and Group Psychotherapy, 70*(1), 16–30.

Blatner, A. (2000). *Foundations of psychodrama: History, theory, and practice (4th edition)*. New York City: Springer Publishing Company.

Clayton, M. (1993). *Living pictures of the self. Applications of role theory in professional practice and daily life*. ICA Press.

Clayton, M. (1994). Role theory and its application in clinical practice. In P. Holmes, M. Karp, & M. Watson (Eds.), *Psychodrama since Moreno: Innovations in theory and practice* (pp. 121–144). Routledge.

Cozolino, L. J. (2014). *The neuroscience of human relationships (2nd edition)*. New York: W.W. Norton & Company.

Dayton, T. (2005). *The living stage. A step-by-step guide to psychodrama, sociometry, and experiential group therapy*. Deerfield, FL: Health Communications Inc.

Giacomucci, S. (2017). The sociodrama of life or death: Young adults and addiction treatment. *Journal of Psychodrama, Sociometry, and Group Psychotherapy, 65*(1), 137–143.

Giacomucci, S. (2018). The trauma survivor's inner role atom: A clinical map for post-traumatic growth. *Journal of Psychodrama, Sociometry, and Group Psychotherapy, 66*(1), 115–129.

Giacomucci, S. (2019). *Social group work in action: A sociometry, psychodrama, and experiential trauma therapy curriculum*. Doctorate in Social Work (DSW) Dissertations. 124. https://repository.upenn.edu/cgi/viewcontent.cgi?article=1128&context=edissertations_sp2

Giacomucci, S. (2020). Addiction, traumatic loss, and guilt: A case study resolving grief through psychodrama and sociometric connections. *The Arts in Psychotherapy, 67*, 101627.

Giacomucci, S. (2021a). *Social work, sociometry, and psychodrama: Experiential approaches for group therapists, community leaders, and social workers*. Singapore: Springer Nature.

Giacomucci, S. (2021b). Traumatic stress and spontaneity: Trauma-focused and strengths-based psychodrama. In J. Maya & J. Maraver (Eds.), *Psychodrama advances in psychotherapy and psychoeducational interventions*. Nova Science Publishers.

Giacomucci, S. (2023). *Trauma-informed principles in group therapy, psychodrama, and organizations: Action methods for leadership*. Routledge.

Giacomucci, S., & Ehrhart, L. (2021). Introduction to psychodrama psychotherapy: A trauma and addiction group vignette. *Group, 45*(1), 69–86.

Giacomucci, S., Karner, D., Nieto, L., & Schreiber, E. (2021). Sociatry, psychodrama, and social work: Moreno's mysticism and social justice tradition. *Social Work with Groups, 44*(3), 288–303.

Giacomucci, S., & Marquit, J. (2020). The effectiveness of trauma-focused psychodrama in the treatment of PTSD in inpatient substance abuse treatment. *Frontiers in Psychology, 11*, 896.

Giacomucci, S., Marquit, J., Briggs, H., & Gupta, R. (2025). Psychodrama's effects on PTSD, depression, anxiety, traumatic grief, prolonged grief disorder, and spontaneity: A mixed methods study in inpatient addiction treatment. *The Arts in Psychotherapy, 93*, 102293.

Giacomucci, S., Marquit, J., & Miller Walsh, K. (2022). A controlled pilot study on the effects of a therapeutic spiral model trauma-focused psychodrama workshop on post-traumatic stress, spontaneity and post-traumatic growth. *Zeitschrift für Psychodrama und Soziometrie, 21*(1), 171–188.

Giacomucci, S., & Stone, A. M. (2019). Being in two places at once: Renegotiating traumatic experience through the surplus reality of psychodrama. *Social Work with Groups*, *42*(3), 184–196.
Goldstein, B. (2018). Cultivating curiosity, creativity, confidence, and self-awareness through mindful group therapy for children and adolescents. In T. Marks-Tarlow, M. Solomon, & D. J. Siegel (Eds.), *Play & creativity in psychotherapy* (pp. 338–358). New York: W.W. Norton & Company.
Gross, S. (2018). The power of optimism. In T. Marks-Tarlow, M. Solomon, & D. J. Siegel (Eds.), *Play & creativity in psychotherapy* (pp. 359–375). New York: W.W. Norton & Company.
Kellermann, P. F. (1984). The place of catharsis in psychodrama. *Journal of Group Psychotherapy, Psychodrama, and Sociometry*, *37*(1), 1–13.
Korshak, S. J., & Shapiro, M. (2013). Choosing the unchosen: Counteracting the sociodynamic effect using complementary sharing. *Journal of Psychodrama, Sociometry, and Group Psychotherapy*, *61*(1), 7–15.
Landy, R. J. (2008). *The couch and the stage: Integrating words and action in psychotherapy*. Lanham, MD, US: Jason Aronson.
Leszcz, M. (2018). The evidence-based group psychotherapist. *Psychoanalytic Inquiry*, *38*(4), 285–298.
Levine, P. A. (2010). *In an unspoken voice: How the body releases trauma and restores goodness*. Berkeley, CA. North Atlantic Books.
Lieberman, M. A., Yalom, I. D., & Miles, M. (1973). *Encounter groups: First facts*. New York: Basic Books.
Malchiodi, C. A. (2020). *Trauma and expressive arts therapy: Brain, body, and imagination in the healing process*. Guilford Publications.
Moreno, J. D. (2014). *Impromptu man: J.L. Moreno and the origins of psychodrama, encounter culture, and the social network*. New York: Bellevue Literary Press.
Moreno, J. L. (1914). *Einladung zu einer Begegnung*. Vienna: Anzengruber Verlag.
Moreno, J. L. (1940). Mental catharsis and the psychodrama. *Sociometry*, *3*, 209–244.
Moreno, J. L. (1943). Sociometry and the cultural order. *Sociometry*, *6*(3), 299–344.
Moreno, J. L. (1947). Progress and pitfalls in sociometric theory. *Sociometry*, *10*, 268–272.
Moreno, J. L. (1952). Psychodramatic production techniques. *Group Psychotherapy, Psychodrama, & Sociometry*, *4*, 273–303.
Moreno, J. L. (1953). *Who shall survive? Foundations of sociometry, group psychotherapy and sociodrama (2nd edition)*. Beacon, NY: Beacon House.
Moreno, J. L. (1957). Code of ethics of group psychotherapists. *Group Psychotherapy*, *10*, 143–144.
Moreno, J. L. (in collaboration with Z. T. Moreno) (1959). *Psychodrama second volume, foundations of psychotherapy*. Beacon, NY: Beacon House.
Moreno, J. L. (1961). The role concept, a bridge between psychiatry and sociology. *American Journal of Psychiatry*, *118*(6), 518–523.
Moreno, J. L. (1972). *Psychodrama and group psychotherapy: First volume (4th edition)*. Beacon House.
Moreno, J. L. (2019). *The autobiography of a genius* (E. Schreiber, S. Kelley, & S. Giacomucci, Eds.). United Kingdom: North West Psychodrama Association.
Moreno, J. L., & Enneis, J. M. (1950). *Hypnodrama and psychodrama*. Beacon House.
Moreno, Z. T. (1969). Moreneans: The heretics of yesterday are the orthodoxy of today. *Group Psychotherapy*, *22*, 1–6.
Moreno, Z. T. (2000). The function of 'Tele' in human relations. In J. Zeig (Ed.), *The evolution of psychotherapy: A meeting of the minds*. Erickson Foundation Press.
Moreno, Z. T. (2012). *To dream again: A memoir*. Mental Health Resources.

Nolte, J. (2014). *The philosophy, theory, and methods of J.L. Moreno: The man who tried to become god.* Routledge.

Nolte, J. (2020). *J.L. Moreno and the psychodramatic method: On the practice of psychodrama.* Routledge.

Oudijk, R. (2007). A postmodern approach to psychodrama theory. In C. Baim, J. Burmeister, & M. Maciel (Eds.), *Psychodrama: Advances in theory and practice* (pp. 139–150). London: Routledge.

Perry, B. D., & Szalavitz, M. (2006). *The boy who was raised as a dog and other stories from a child psychiatrist's notebook: What traumatized children can teach us about loss, love, and healing.* Basic Books.

Porges, S. W. (2011). *The polyvagal theory: Neurophysiological foundations of emotions, attachment, communication, and self-regulation.* W. W. Norton & Company.

Raimundo, C. A., & Raimundo, M. (2021). RCompass, a digital sociometry. what would Moreno think about it? Celebrating 100 years of Moreno's psychodrama and 60 years of Rojas-Bermúdez Psychodrama. *Journal of the Psychodrama, Sociometry, and Group Psychotherapy, 68*(1), 39–62.

Rauch, S. L., van der Kolk, B. A., Fisler, R. E., Alpert, N. M., Orr, S. P., Savage, C. R.,. . .& Pitman, R. K. (1996). A symptom provocation study of posttraumatic stress disorder using positron emission tomography and script-driven imagery. *Archives of General Psychiatry, 53*(5), 380–387.

Redfern, M. (2014). Safe spaces and scary encounters: Core therapeutic elements of trauma-informed dramatherapy. In N. Sajnani & D. R. Johnson (Eds.), *Trauma informed drama therapy: Transforming clinics, classrooms, and communities* (pp. 365–388). Charles C Thomas Publisher.

Schreiber, E. (2018, Winter). Sociatry part 2: Moreno's mysticism. In *Psychodrama network news* (pp. 24–25). American Society of Group Psychotherapy and Psychodrama.

Schreiber, E. W., & Giacomucci, S. (2024). Psychodrama, sociodrama, sociometry, & sociatry. In B. J. Sadock, V. A. Sadock, & P. Ruiz (Eds.), *Kaplan & Sadock's comprehensive textbook of psychiatry (11th edition).* Lippincott Williams & Wilkins publishers.

Schwartz, R. C. (2021). *No bad parts: Healing trauma and restoring wholeness with the internal family systems model.* Sounds True.

Shapiro, F. (2018). *Eye-movement desensitization and reprocessing (EMDR) therapy (3rd edition).* Guilford Press.

Shapiro, J. R., & Applegate, J. S. (2018). *Neurobiology for clinical social work: Theory and practice (2nd edition).* W.W. Norton & Company.

Siegel, D. J. (2020). *Developing mind: How relationships and the brain interact to shape who we are (3rd edition).* Guilford Press.

Substance Abuse and Mental Health Services Administration. (2014). *SAMHSA's concept of trauma and guidance for a trauma-informed approach.* HHS Publication No. (SMA) 14–4884. Rockville, MD: Substance Abuse and Mental Health Services Administration.

Tarashoeva, G., Marinova-Djambazova, P., & Kojuharov, H. (2017). Effectiveness of psychodrama therapy in patients with panic disorders: Final results. *International Journal of Psychotherapy, 21*(2), 55–66.

Trevarthen, C., & Panksepp, J. (2016). In tune with feeling. *Inclusion, Play and Empathy: Neuroaffective Development in Children's Groups*, 29.

van de Kamp, M. M., Scheffers, M., Hatzmann, J., Emck, C., Cuijpers, P., & Beek, P. J. (2019). Body-and movement-oriented interventions for posttraumatic stress disorder: A systematic review and meta-analysis. *Journal of Traumatic Stress, 32*(6), 967–976.

van der Kolk, B. A. (2014). *The body keeps the score: Brain, mind, and body in the healing of trauma.* Viking Press.

van der Kolk, B. A., & McFarlane, A. C. (Eds.). (1996). *Traumatic stress: The effects of overwhelming experience on mind, body, and society*. Guilford Press.
Wallin, D. J. (2007). *Attachment in psychotherapy*. Guilford Press.
Wylie, M. S. (2004). The limits of talk: Bessel van der Kolk wants to transform the treatment of trauma. *Psychotherapy Networker*, *28*, 30–41.
Yaniv, D. Z. (2014). Tele and the social atom: The oeuvre of J. L. Moreno from the perspective of neuropsychology. *Zeitschrift für Psychodrama und Soziometrie*, *13*(1), 107–120.

Chapter 4

Healing Complex Trauma With Psychodrama

Psychodrama is an effective approach in the healing of trauma, PTSD, and CPTSD. The research to support this claim continues to grow, demonstrating psychodrama's positive impacts for various subgroups of trauma survivors. Beyond the question of effectiveness, we must also explore the question of how and why it is effective for trauma. This chapter explores the how and why of psychodrama's capacity to reduce traumatic stress and promote trauma recovery. The power of community witnessing and validation provides psychodrama protagonists with a remedy for shame and isolation that comes with trauma. Trauma-focused psychodrama enactments involve a process of gradual exposure to aspects of the traumatic memory with desensitization and a renegotiating of one's relationship to the memory. By externalizing, reorganizing, and internalizing aspects of the trauma, we can change how it lives within us. The process of resourcing, undoing, and redoing memories of trauma offers a structure for safe and effective psychodramatic healing. Within the surplus reality of psychodrama, we also find unlimited potentials for corrective emotional experiences and embodiments of trauma recovery.

The power of community witnessing and validation provides psychodrama protagonists with a remedy for shame and isolation that comes with trauma.

Psychodrama as an Effective Treatment for Trauma and CPTSD

The empirical evidence supporting psychodrama as an effective treatment for PTSD continues to grow and evolve. Current research positions psychodrama as a promising modality, but more research is needed, particularly research trials with rigorous study designs (Orkibi & Feniger-Schaal, 2019). Multiple studies have already been published that demonstrate psychodrama's effectiveness

DOI: 10.4324/9781003639497-4

in significantly reducing PTSD symptoms or trauma-related issues in various populations including military veterans (Cowden et al., 2021; Perry et al., 2016), patients in addiction treatment (Giacomucci & Marquit, 2020; Giacomucci et al., 2023, 2025), mass shooting survivors (Cowden et al., 2022), child survivors of natural disasters (Hamidi & Sobhani Tabar, 2021; Tabar et al., 2020), women victims of intimate partner violence (Damra, 2022; Ron & Yanai, 2021; Mondolfi Miguel & Pino-Juste, 2021), abused women (Avinger & Jones, 2007; Bucuţă et al., 2018), and men with varied trauma histories (Giacomucci et al., 2022) and other forms of interpersonal trauma (Seppälä, 2020). Furthermore, psychodrama has been included in the literature bases of other larger categories of modalities that have significant evidence of effectively treating PTSD and trauma such as the experiential psychotherapies (Benish et al., 2008; Elliott et al., 2004, 2013), the creative arts therapies (Baker et al., 2018; Feniger-Shaal & Orkibi, 2020; Malchiodi, 2020), and the body- and movement-oriented interventions (van de Kamp et al., 2019).

Because CPTSD is an add-on diagnosis to PTSD, we may assume that the research on PTSD and psychodrama is also applicable to CPTSD and psychodrama. However, CPTSD includes three extra symptom clusters related to emotional dysregulation, relationship difficulties, and negative view of self. Most psychodramatists (and clients) would argue that psychodrama is particularly helpful in these three areas.

As I am finishing writing this book, I am also finishing preliminary data analyses on what appears to be the first study of psychodrama's effectiveness for CPTSD. This forthcoming study (Giacomucci, Marquit, Gupta, & Roldan, in preparation) has a sample of about 175 participants from inpatient substance use treatment and demonstrates a significant decrease in CPTSD symptoms after participating in the trauma-focused psychodrama program within the inpatient rehab. After just two or three weeks of treatment, patients experienced a 56.28% decrease in CPTSD, 56.42% decrease in PTSD, 50.42% decrease in anxiety, and 58.36% decrease in depression. At the same time, participants demonstrated increases in various measures of well-being, including 19.14% in addiction recovery capital, 36.97% in posttraumatic growth, 18.56% in resilience, and 34.98% in spontaneity. This study establishes a foundation of empirical evidence to support the use of trauma-focused psychodrama as a treatment for CPTSD.

Validation and Community Witnessing

One of the simplest, but most overlooked aspects of healing in psychodrama seems to be the simple validation and witnessing that the process provides for the protagonist and other group members. As psychodramatists, we are often more focused on dramatic, aesthetic, and action-based components of roles, interventions, and scene development. However, at a foundational level, one of the healing components of psychodrama is that it offers an experiential validation of the protagonist's story through a communal group experience. This process of being listened to and affirmed is at the heart of all psychotherapy approaches for trauma. In a trauma-focused psychodrama session, the client has the opportunity not only to share their story but also to enact aspects of their story and experientially accomplish a goal with the group's explicit support. Psychodrama is focused on the client's subjective experience, which is inherently validating. Trauma so often leaves survivors with a sense of shame, isolation, and aloneness. The experience of being supported by the group in enacting a goal related to the trauma provides a significant dose of support and affirmation.

The very process of sociometrically selecting a protagonist provides validation for the protagonist that they are not alone in their experience. Furthermore, the permission to engage with their memory, issue, and goal with the support of the director and group offers another layer of validation. The intervention of doubling effectively helps the protagonist to deepen their expression of feelings and thoughts while receiving emotional validation from other group members and the director with each accurate doubling statement. For many protagonists, one of the most powerful moments of their psychodrama has been looking around the room mid-psychodrama and seeing every other group member on the edge of their seat and emotionally engaged in their process – bearing witness to their pain, their work, and their growth. While trauma can leave one feeling insignificant, the collective witnessing that happens naturally in psychodrama can help the protagonist feel a sense of significance. At the end of the psychodrama, the sharing phase also offers considerable validation for the protagonist in that they have an opportunity to hear from other group members about their connection to the topic, trauma, and elements of recovery in the session.

Exposure, Desensitization, and Reconsolidation With New Emotional Context

One of the symptom clusters of CPTSD is avoidance. Many times, this avoidance and dissociation prevent individuals from facing their trauma and organically desensitizing and reprocessing the associated traumatic memories and triggers. There seems to be an element of exposure therapy within psychodrama that is implicitly important for trauma-focused psychodrama. In volunteering to be the protagonist of a psychodrama, the protagonist is facing their avoidance, facing the trauma, and engaging with roles, emotions, and other aspects of the traumatic memory. This willingness to face the trauma and expose oneself to it, with the support of the group, offers an avenue for desensitization. The fear loops that become established in PTSD lead to a re-experiencing of terror, fear of the memory, and fear of triggers associated with the trauma. This pattern of avoidance and fear of triggers and the memories must be interrupted and renegotiated.

Memory is a funny thing. Research seems to suggest that we do not recall memory from the original experience of it – instead, that we recall memory from the last time we recalled the memory (Cozolino, 2017). This process means that we can change our relationship to our memories over time; we can become more afraid of the memories, or we can extinguish our fear toward the memories. One of the foundational healing components of any type of therapy is the accessing of painful memories within the emotional context of safety, care, and validation that is provided by the therapist or group (Cozolino, 2017). This component of healing is also present within the trauma-focused psychodrama process. Each time the traumatic memory is activated with a feeling of safety, it reduces the negative affect associated with it and replaces some of it with positive or neutral feelings. When a memory is avoided for years or decades, it does not have the chance to be renegotiated by new experiences, information, and perspectives that are gained by the client throughout those years or decades. In many cases, the fragmented and avoided traumatic memory is spontaneously reconsolidated and reprocessed simply by consciously activating it, which can result in the integration of all the new adaptive information within the brain, mind, and self since the time of the trauma. This is the foundational component of the theory of change in EMDR therapy, which is called the Adaptive Information Processing Theory (Shapiro, 2018).

Role reversing the protagonist into strengths-based roles facilitates a path for reconsolidation of the memory in that the protagonist is tasked with speaking to themselves about the trauma from a position of strength.

The inclusion of resources within the scene offers a source of spontaneity (new responses), goodness, and reconsolidation throughout the entire process. The strengths-based and supportive roles enrolled in the scene allow for the protagonist to interface with the trauma from a position of strength, safety, and adaptive information. This effectively facilitates role expansion or role creation for the protagonist in developing new perspectives, feelings, and behaviors in their relationship to the traumatic content. This infuses the old, stagnant, re-experienced, and reoccurring traumatic memory with new energy, strength, safety, and adaptive information, leading to a reconsolidation of the memory. Activating a traumatic memory is one thing – but activating the traumatic memory with supportive roles such as courage, supportive friends, and a double provides the protagonist with a new experience related to activating the traumatic memory. Role reversing the protagonist into strengths-based roles facilitates a path for reconsolidation of the memory in that the protagonist is tasked with speaking to themselves about the trauma from a position of strength (e.g., speaking as "courage," speaking as "God," or speaking as "your future self" about the trauma). Beyond the interactions with strengths-based roles, trauma-focused psychodrama often also involves revisiting interactions with trauma-based roles and the provision of a new corrective emotional experience or an undoing and redoing of the experience. These new psychodramatic experiences, although they are not "real," seem to be experienced as real by the brain and help to reconsolidate the old traumatic memory with a newly experienced ending (Giacomucci & Stone, 2019).

Corrective Emotional Experience

The most important finding of the century in neuroscience has been the discovery that the brain maintains its neuroplasticity, or its ability to change, throughout the entire lifespan (Cozolino, 2017). The brain changes based on new experiences. Although past traumatic experiences have had a major impact on our brain and our self, this also means that new experiences can reverse and change how the past has impacted us. Of course, corrective emotional experiences can be cultivated in any form of therapy, but psychodrama allows us to explicitly create them. Many have used these findings to advocate for experiential therapies as the treatment of choice for trauma due to their capacity to provide new emotionally corrective experiences rather than simply sitting and talking or thinking.

> Psychodrama's use of surplus reality provides unlimited possibilities for corrective emotional experiences.

Psychodrama's use of surplus reality provides unlimited possibilities for corrective emotional experiences. Most trauma survivors crave for an experience of closure, empowerment, amends, justice, protection, or nurturing related to their past trauma but are unlikely to experience it in real life due to the lack of opportunity, the other individual(s) refusal to change, the lack of safety, or impossibility of creating the circumstances that the client craves for. Psychodrama makes all of that possible. If the client wants to revisit the traumatic memory and be protected instead of traumatized, we can make that happen. If the client wants to confront their perpetrator and be empowered to yell at them or reclaim their power from them, we can do that. If the protagonist has an emotional need for closure from a loved one who died, we can bring them back to live in psychodrama to say and hear the things that were not articulated before their death. Here is a memorable example from an article I wrote on the topic with a colleague a few years ago (Giacomucci & Stone, 2019):

> Claire had to choose between being present for her mother's funeral or her daughter's court sexual assault court case. She ensured her daughter was supported and chose to go to the funeral but felt like a bad mom for years. The guilt and shame contributed to her drinking, which landed her in inpatient

treatment. Her goal was self-forgiveness, and she shared about wishing she could go back in time to be there for her daughter. As the facilitator, I suggested that we do just that in the psychodrama. Claire set the scene of the courtroom with her daughter, daughter's support, the judge, jury, lawyers, and the perpetrator (represented by an empty chair). The scene emerged with Claire by her daughter's side offering support throughout the legal deliberations. The role player in the role of the daughter was emotional throughout the process (later sharing that she had also been a sexual assault survivor), which made it feel even more real for Claire and the group. The judge facilitated the process with the jury reenacting the decision to sentence the perpetrator – all with Claire by her daughter's side offering words of encouragement. The scene ended with the perpetrator being escorted to prison and Claire offering her final messages of validation to her daughter.

This psychodrama offered Claire the experience that she craved for in real life but was impossible to actually have. Claire shared that she could now think of the court case 8 years ago without crying for the first time and that she felt a newfound sense of lightness and gratitude. This is just one example of corrective emotional experience through psychodrama; some of the most common uses of it (many of which will be depicted in other chapters of this book) include creating scenes where the trauma survivor is protected during the trauma, standing up to their perpetrator to defend themselves, offering themselves nurturing at a time when they felt neglected or abandoned, or a discussion for closure with someone else.

I suggest that we update this classic psychodrama sequence for trauma-focused psychodrama to – "Resource, Undo, Redo."

Resource, Undo, Redo

One of psychodrama's classic dramatic structures is that of "Do-Undo-Redo." In this sequence, the protagonist is invited to use role-playing to demonstrate and re-experience something that they are struggling with and would like to further explore (Do). Then, in another scene, they are invited to Undo the situation by intervening or changing it. A final scene emerges where the protagonist then Redoes the scene with a different ending that allows them to feel more complete and resolved about the situation that was causing them stress. This general structure works quite well for life stressors but may need to be modified to prevent retraumatization and keep protagonists (and the group) within their window of tolerance when it comes to traumatic experiences. Asking someone to reenact a trauma scene right from the start is not advisable. Instead, I suggest that we update this classic psychodrama sequence for trauma-focused psychodrama

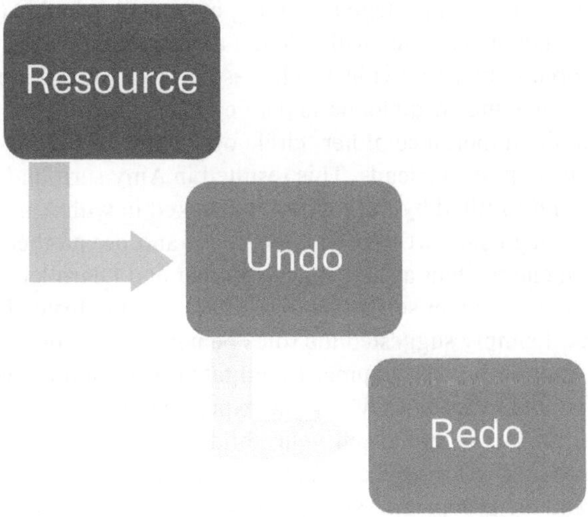

Figure 4.1 Resource, undo, redo sequence

to – "Resource, Undo, Redo" (see Figure 4.1). This process offers a baked-in recipe for community witnessing, desensitization, reconsolidation, and corrective emotional experience.

If a protagonist has expressed a desire to address a traumatic memory, the memory is likely already activated – re-experiencing is one of the symptom clusters of CPTSD. Reenacting it in the room is unlikely to be necessary and carries some risk of harm. First, we need to resource the protagonist with supportive roles or strengths that can help them undo the trauma – which is already being reenacted within them. In the resourcing of a psychodrama, it is important that the resources be specific to the trauma and the contract of the psychodrama. We want to help the protagonist find specific strengths or supportive figures that can help with this specific situation. Usually, I will just ask the protagonist, "what strengths or supports do we need to face the trauma?" After resourcing has been adequately addressed, then we can move toward the trauma scene with the intent of undoing and redoing it. When working with trauma, this updated framework is recommended instead of the classical Do, Undo, Redo approach. The following is an example from my most recent psychodrama, which coincidentally used this structure:

> Amy is chosen as protagonist with the issue of childhood physical abuse and the goal of letting go of her hate and anger towards her mom and to stop blaming herself for the abuse. In naming the topic and being chosen, she has already begun to access her emotions related to the traumatic memory.

I initiated the resourcing stage by having her enroll a double (I usually call it an inner supportive voice with clients) and a strength that could help her with the topic – she chose vulnerability as the strength. After enrolling both roles and engaging in dialogue and role reversals with the strength, she mentioned the importance of her 'circle of friends' so I invited other group members to step in as friends. This resulted in Amy surrounded by most of the group and fortified by the support. I checked in with Amy who said she now had enough support to revisit the abuse and her mother. I invited her to enroll an empty chair as her abusive mother and I enrolled another group member as her younger self at the time of the trauma. Instead of reenacting the trauma, I simply suggested the roles be next to each other – almost like a frozen sculpture of the trauma. I facilitated Amy in a conversation with her mother about the abuse where she expressed her anger and pain. "How could you do this to me? I am your child, and you are supposed to love me, not hurt me!" Amy yelled and cried. With encouragement and doubling from me and the group, she expressed what she needed to say to her mother about how hurtful the abuse has been and how much this hate and anger has been impacting the rest of her relationships in her life. In doing so, she realized that her mom had also been a victim of abuse and articulated that the hate and the anger may have even been passed down to her from someone else. I invited Amy to concretize the hate and the anger with two different scarves and to physically give the hate and the anger back to her mom. There was a white scarf on the floor in the scene so I asked Amy what it represented and what she felt like her mom took from her that she wanted to take back to replace hate and the anger. She said it was her innocence, and took it back from her mom. This was the psychodramatic undoing of what had happened.

Next, we turned our attention to the Amy's younger self who had experienced the abuse and blamed herself for it. Amy was able to talk to herself as a child and offer the validation, support, and perspective needed to affirm her worth and innocence. "You are such a good girl, and you didn't deserve or cause any of the hurtful things mommy said to you." I knew that Amy was a loving mother to her own young kids so I asked her to speak to herself with the same instinctual motherly love that she offers her kids every day. In this encounter, Amy had the chance to offer her younger self what she didn't get at the time of the trauma – validation, nurturing, love, and an affirmation of her innocence. She effectively stepped in to mother herself in the way she wished she could have been mothered by her own mother. This provided Amy with the opportunity to not only undo the trauma and stop it psychodramatically, but also to redo and correct the absence of what she needed in the past. The scene ended with Amy and her younger self playing and sharing the newfound innocence.

Changing How Complex Trauma Lives Within – Externalize, Reorganize, and Internalize

> The psychodramatic process could be summarized as 1) externalize, 2) reorganize, and 3) internalize.

The psychodramatic process could be summarized as (1) externalize, (2) reorganize, and (3) internalize (see Figure 4.2). We cannot change the fact that the trauma happened. But we can change how the trauma lives within us today. In psychodrama, we are working to renegotiate our relationship to the trauma. The technique of concretization and role-playing provides an avenue for symbolically representing the internalized trauma within the surplus reality of the enactment. Throughout the action, we explore and change relationships between parts of self, examine the internalized trauma, add in strengths, remove roles as needed, facilitate role transformations, and reorganize the role dynamics and positioning. At the end of the psychodrama, the protagonist integrates the externalized roles back into their self in a new way.

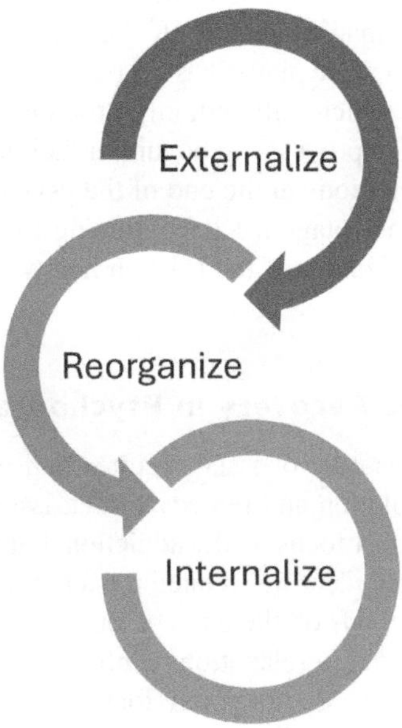

Figure 4.2 Process for externalizing, reorganizing, and internalizing in psychodrama

A lot has been written about the externalization and reorganization of roles in psychodrama, but much less has been written about the process of how the protagonist internalizes the new role dynamics and structure at the end of the psychodrama. It seems that this process is happening throughout the entire psychodrama on some level, as it is an outward representation of an inward reality. After the climax of a psychodrama scene, it seems important to promote integration of the change for the protagonist. There are different interventions that can be used for this integrative process. The mirror position is a very useful tool to facilitate the protagonist stepping out of the scene and seeing it from another angle to further consolidate the gains. It can also be useful to use the future projection to enroll the protagonist into the role of themself in the future, having achieved their goal. This gives them a fuller embodiment of the change integrated over time. Another option is to help the protagonist anchor the change within their body. For example, in the earlier depiction of Amy reconnected with innocence, I could take a moment and ask her to check in with her body to see where she feels the innocence somatically. There are various other interventions that could be employed, including artmaking, writing, doubling, and soliloquy. Integration will be more fully covered in Chapter 14 of this book.

The process of de-rolling would seem to be another logical moment of internalizing the role. Sometimes this is more explicitly depicted in de-rolling by having the role player imagine taking off the role and handing it back to the protagonist. Now that the role player has de-rolled, there is no externalized representation of the role, which will certainly promote internalization of the role from the protagonist. This process can be further facilitated with a thoughtful and conscious de-rolling ceremony at the end of the psychodrama before sharing. It also seems true that the protagonist is continuing to integrate their experience and solidify the internalization of the roles in a new way during the sharing of the psychodrama.

Cultivating Trauma Recovery in Psychodrama

The treatment of any disorder or issue requires that we focus not only on that issue but also on the solution and remedy to that issue. In addiction treatment, for example, we do not just focus on the addiction, but we also focus on cultivating habits, behaviors, and identities related to addiction recovery. When treating anxiety, we do not just focus on the anxiety, but we also offer interventions and suggestions that are related to relaxation, confidence, and peace of mind. In the treatment of depression, we do not solely focus on the hopelessness and stuckness; we help the client to find hope, empowerment, and motivation for life. The same approach must be applied to trauma. In trauma treatment, we do not just focus on the trauma – we must spend just as much time focusing on trauma recovery.

In trauma treatment, we don't just focus on the trauma – we must spend just as much time focusing on trauma recovery.

Psychodrama enables participants to move beyond the trauma into trauma recovery. The action-oriented methodology permits clients to experiment with new identities related to recovery and to personify the embodiment of trauma recovery. One simple way that this is often concretized is through the role of a future self in recovery (which will be further highlighted in Chapter 14). In my work, I find it useful to anchor my conceptualization of trauma recovery to the five domains of posttraumatic growth and use it as a template for helping each client envision their own personalized trauma recovery. One of the most direct ways of bringing trauma recovery into any psychodrama scene is to simply enroll it as a role. Having the "voice of trauma recovery" present in a scene will help the protagonist to build a relationship with it and start to see trauma recovery as a part of their self.

Conclusion

Trauma-focused psychodrama enables clients to heal from trauma and overcome their traumatic stress. The power of the group lends itself to a sense of belonging and validation for trauma survivors. The act of touching upon the trauma in psychodrama is similar to exposure techniques in other therapies and can help promote desensitization and a reconsolidation of the traumatic memory with new positive or neutral emotion. The surplus reality of psychodrama provides opportunities for corrective emotional experiences. In trauma-focused psychodrama, the classical psychodrama sequence of do, undo, redo can be updated to resource, undo, redo to mitigate the risks of retraumatization. The psychodramatic process essentially results in the externalization, reorganization, and internalization of inner trauma in a new way that promotes trauma recovery.

The psychodramatic process essentially results in the externalization, reorganization, and internalization of inner trauma in a new way that promotes trauma recovery.

References

Avinger, K., & Jones, R. (2007). Group treatment of sexually abused adolescent girls: A review of outcome studies. *American Journal of Family Therapy*, *35*, 315–326.

Baker, F. A., Metcalf, O., Varker, T., & O'Donnell, M. (2018). A systematic review of the efficacy of creative arts therapies in the treatment of adults with PTSD. *Psychological Trauma: Theory, Research, Practice, and Policy*, *10*(6), 643.

Benish, S. G., Imel, Z. E., & Wampold, B. E. (2008). The relative efficacy of bona fide psychotherapies for treating post-traumatic stress disorder: A meta-analysis of direct comparisons. *Clinical Psychology Review*, *28*(5), 746–758.

Bucuţă, M. D., Dima, G., & Testoni, I. (2018). "When you thought that there is no one and nothing": The value of psychodrama in working with abused women. *Frontiers in Psychology*, *9*, 1518.

Cowden, R. G., Captari, L. E., Chen, Z. J., De Kock, J. H., & Houghtaling, A. (2022). Effectiveness of an intensive experiential group therapy program in promoting mental health and well-being among mass shooting survivors: A practice-based pilot study. *Professional Psychology: Research and Practice*, *53*(2), 181.

Cowden, R. G., Chapman, I. M., Houghtaling, A., & Worthington Jr, E. L. (2021). Effects of a group experiential therapy program on the psychological health of military veterans: A preliminary investigation. *Person-Centered & Experiential Psychotherapies*, *20*(2), 119–138.

Cozolino, L. (2017). *The neuroscience of psychotherapy: Healing the social brain (Norton Series on Interpersonal Neurobiology)*. W.W. Norton & Company.

Damra, J. K. (2022). The effects of psychodrama intervention on intimate partner violence and quality of life: Trial of Syrian refugee abused women. *Journal of International Women's Studies*, *23*(1), 33.

Elliott, R., Greensberg, L., & Lietaer, G. (2004). Research on experiential psychotherapy. In M. Lambert, A. Bergin, & S. Garfield (Eds.), *Handbook of psychotherapy and behavior change*. Wiley.

Elliott, R., Watson, J., Greenberg, L. S., Timulak, L., & Freire, E. (2013). Research on humanistic-experiential psychotherapies. In M. J. Lambert (Ed.), *Bergin & Garfield's Handbook of psychotherapy and behavior change (6th edition)* (pp. 495–538). Wiley.

Feniger-Schaal, R., & Orkibi, H. (2020). Integrative systematic review of drama therapy intervention research. *Psychology of Aesthetics, Creativity, and the Arts*, *14*(1), 68.

Giacomucci, S., & Marquit, J. (2020). The effectiveness of trauma-focused psychodrama in the treatment of PTSD in inpatient substance abuse treatment. *Frontiers in Psychology*, *11*, 896.

Giacomucci, S., Marquit, J., Briggs, H., & Gupta, R. (2025). Psychodrama's effects on PTSD, depression, anxiety, traumatic grief, prolonged grief disorder, and spontaneity: A mixed methods study in inpatient addiction treatment. *The Arts in Psychotherapy*, *93*, 102293.

Giacomucci, S., Marquit, J., Gupta, R., & Roldan, N. (in preparation). *A mixed methods study on psychodrama in inpatient substance use treatment: Effects on CPTSD, PTSD, depression, anxiety, addiction recovery, resilience, posttraumatic growth, and spontaneity*.

Giacomucci, S., Marquit, J., & Miller Walsh, K. (2022). A controlled pilot study on the effects of a therapeutic spiral model trauma-focused psychodrama workshop on post-traumatic stress, spontaneity and post-traumatic growth. *Zeitschrift für Psychodrama und Soziometrie*, *21*(1), 171–188.

Giacomucci, S., Marquit, J., Saccarelli, R., & Briggs, H. (2023). Psychodrama group psychotherapy as an effective treatment for PTSD and depression in inpatient substance use treatment: A mixed methods study. *Social Work with Groups*, 1–16.

Giacomucci, S., & Stone, A. M. (2019). Being in two places at once: Renegotiating traumatic experience through the surplus reality of psychodrama. *Social Work with Groups*, *42*(3), 184–196.

Hamidi, F., & Sobhani Tabar, S. (2021). Effect of psychodrama on post-traumatic stress disorder symptoms in primary school students living in earthquake-stricken areas. *Iranian Journal of Psychiatry and Clinical Psychology*, *26*(4), 400–417.

Malchiodi, C. A. (2020). *Trauma and expressive arts therapy: Brain, body, and imagination in the healing process*. Guilford Publications.
Mondolfi Miguel, M. L., & Pino-Juste, M. (2021). Therapeutic achievements of a program based on drama therapy, the theater of the oppressed, and psychodrama with women victims of intimate partner violence. *Violence against Women*, *27*(9), 1273–1296.
Orkibi, H., & Feniger-Schaal, R. (2019). Integrative systematic review of psychodrama psychotherapy research: Trends and methodological implications. *PloS One*, *14*(2), e0212575.
Perry, R., Saby, K., Wenos, J., Hudgins, K., & Baller, S. (2016, Spring). Psychodrama intervention for female service members using the therapeutic spiral model. *Journal of Psychodrama, Sociometry, and Group Psychotherapy*, *64*(1), 11–23.
Ron, Y., & Yanai, L. (2021). Empowering through psychodrama: A qualitative study at domestic violence shelters. *Frontiers in Psychology*, *12*, 1017.
Seppälä, K. M. (2020). *A thematic analysis: How dramatic techniques can be applied in therapy to facilitate clients in regaining an integrated sense-of-self after experiencing interpersonal trauma*. Doctoral Dissertation. FCHS (DCPC) – Dissertações de Mestrado, Repositório Institucional da Universidade Fernando Pessoa.
Shapiro, F. (2018). *Eye-Movement Desensitization and Reprocessing (EMDR) therapy (3rd edition)*. Guilford Press.
Tabar, S., Hamidi, F., & Tahmasebipour, N. (2020). Effectiveness of psychodrama in reducing the psychological nervous problems of students with post-traumatic stress disorder. *Neuropsychology*, *6*(1), 121–146.
van de Kamp, M. M., Scheffers, M., Hatzmann, J., Emck, C., Cuijpers, P., & Beek, P. J. (2019). Body-and movement-oriented interventions for posttraumatic stress disorder: A systematic review and meta-analysis. *Journal of Traumatic Stress*, *32*(6), 967–976.

Chapter 5

Sociometry Group Processes for Trauma Therapy

This chapter contains content from my previous books (Giacomucci, 2021a, 2023) with updated material throughout. Reprinted with permission.

Most of the other chapters of this book focus on psychodrama interventions, but this chapter orients on sociometric interventions. It is important to note that every psychodrama case example in this book takes place after a warming-up process utilizing sociometry or other group warm-ups (such as described in Chapter 7). Without sociometry and a warming-up process, there is no psychodrama.

There are numerous commonly used experiential sociometric group processes that are employed in clinical settings, including dyadic or triadic sharing, spectrograms, locograms, floor-checks, step-in sociometry, and hands-on-shoulder sociometry (Dayton, 2005, 2015; Giacomucci, 2021a; Giacomucci et al., 2018). Each of these processes can be modified with content appropriate for any population or chosen topic. In terms of clinical uses of sociometry, these sociometric tools often stand on their own as multi-dimensional action-based group processes that provide the group with an avenue to discover and enrich their connections with each other. Sociometry can also be employed with an objective of recognizing shared identity between group members, including membership to privileged or oppressed groups (Nieto, 2010). These same sociometric action structures frequently serve as a group warm-up exercise before conducting a psychodrama but can be used in the beginning, middle, or ending stages of a group. Each of these experiential sociometry structures can be used for group assessment, exploration, intervention, and evaluation.

Regardless of which sociometry tool is being utilized, it is useful for both the group and the facilitator if a clinical map is employed. To cultivate an experience of safety, vulnerability, containment, and warming-up, it can help to select criteria for prompts while adhering to the three clinical maps for trauma previously outlined. Initial prompts would be simple and strengths-based with the goal of facilitating connection. The next prompt(s) invite the group to share deeper with a focus on difficult emotions, defense mechanisms, trauma, loss, addiction, or mental

DOI: 10.4324/9781003639497-5

illness – and to finish, making an offer of prompt(s) that facilitate or engage with meaning-making, integration, future projection, and posttraumatic growth. Essentially, this clinical map starts with *positive* prompts, moves into *negative* prompts, and ends with *positive* prompts again (see Chapter 1 for more on the clinical map). This process reflects the process of slowly moving in and out of difficult emotional content – called pendulation and titration described by trauma experts (Levine, 2010). While providing containment, direction, and safety for the larger group process, this practice may also help clients internalize a sense of containment, self-efficacy, and safety related to their trauma (Giacomucci & Marquit, 2020).

The experiential group processes described in this chapter can be conceptualized as trauma-informed processes as they reflect the six principles outlined by SAMHSA (2014) (see Figure 5.1).

Experiential sociometry is particularly useful in promoting connection within the group and enhancing interpersonal relationships. It cultivates peer support, safety, and trustworthiness while illuminating and making transparent the sociodynamics within a group. Participants are able to see clearly where they fit in within the group on various topics or preferences while reflecting on and articulating their experience. As the connection and group cohesion increases, so too does the felt sense of safety for each participant. Experiential sociometry provides multiple opportunities for choice, indicating preference, and elevating voices within the group while empowering participants with the power to influence the

Figure 5.1 SAMHSA's six trauma-informed principles

Republished with permission from Giacomucci (2021a)

group process – sociometry is most frequently used as a warm-up to psychodrama during which the director tunes into the warm-up of the group and channels it into a psychodrama enactment. This process is inherently collaborative as the group-as-a-whole is seen as co-responsible for the group process. A sense of mutuality and universality is inherently rooted in these exercises as they position participants as therapeutic agents for each other, honoring their capacity to promote healing, education, and support for one another. Experiential sociometry promotes a less hierarchical group structure in that, instead of positioning the facilitator as the primary source of education or healing, the group-as-a-whole is elevated to this position. These action-based group processes are fundamentally anti-oppressive in the way that they disrupt traditional power-dynamics in a group setting and promote co-creation (Giacomucci, 2021b).

Not only do they offer trauma-informed and action-based processes, but they can also be adapted for trauma-focused or trauma-informed content. For example, a facilitator could ask spectrogram prompts related to gender issues, safety, or trustworthiness. A locogram or floor check can easily be employed using the six trauma-informed principles as the locogram/floor check options, which allow the group to explore their relationship with them. This floor check is particularly useful for organizational workshops or meetings, as it helps the organization-as-a-whole reflect on how they already incorporate these principles and where they have room to grow in this regard. Step-in sociometry can be used with clients, communities, staff, or students to explore their shared experiences related to trauma recovery or aspects of identity/experience. Sociogram prompts can be generated to help a group explore how the principles are experienced within interpersonal relationships in the group or organization. The Circle of Strengths process can be modified to either concretize strengths to support trauma-informed work or to concretize the trauma-informed principles themselves.

Dyads, Triads, and Small Groups

Jacob Moreno often wrote of the importance of dyadic connection within groups and suggested that group cohesion was a function of the number of reciprocated mutual choices within the group (Hale, 2009; J. L. Moreno, 1934). Consequently, the use of dyadic sharing and breaking the larger group into smaller pairs can help facilitate interpersonal connection, mutual aid, and overall group cohesion (Giacomucci, 2021a). Using dyads, triads, or small breakout groups seems to be especially useful at the early stages of groups and when working with larger groups. Many clients do not feel comfortable sharing in front of large groups – using smaller groups allows for participants to feel safer as they are invited to share with one or two others. This process also mitigates the chances of one participant monopolizing the group discussion and preventing the more reluctant or introverted group members from actively engaging (Olesen,

Campbell, & Gross, 2017). The process of a traditional talk-based group only permits one discussion to take place at a time, but using dyads or small groups allows for multiple discussions to take place concurrently. The nature of small group discussions, especially dyads, invokes a role demand for each participant to respond, attend to, support, and share with their partner – thus engaging in mutual aid. The process of utilizing small group discussion frees up the facilitator to move around the room and listen to or check in with each group. This allows the facilitator to take a less active role and indirectly reveals the facilitator's confidence, trust, and faith in each participant's ability to serve as a therapeutic agent for each other.

The method of choosing configurations of small groups or dyads can be modified depending on the facilitator's intention or the nature of the group. Partners or small groups can be assigned randomly, intentionally chosen by the facilitator, self-selected by participants, or chosen based on prompts. When inviting participants to self-select a partner or break into triads, participants are likely to choose the person(s) physically closest to them. Often, they are already sitting next to the group members that they feel most connected to, so this may lead to already cohesive small groups and few new connections. Prompting participants to "partner with someone you don't know well" is a simple way to facilitate dyads ripe with new opportunities to connect.

In terms of the content of the discussion within the small groups, it helps to offer directed prompts related to the nature of the group or the therapeutic goals of the session, guided by the aforementioned three-stage clinical map. Generally, three to five prompts seem to be sufficient for small group discussions in terms of adequately warming up the group without losing the interest of participants. The following are some examples of prompts following the aforementioned clinical map based on different topics for clinical groups:

Topic: Relationships

1. Share about one of your favorite relationships.
2. Share about a person who has helped you in some way recently.
3. Share about a relationship that you have difficulty or conflict in.
4. Share how you would change a difficult relationship to be different in the future.
5. Share about one way you would like to change your behavior in relationships.

Topic: Emotions

1. Share a memory that gives you a positive feeling.
2. Share about the emotion that you have the most difficulty with.
3. Share about ways you could respond to difficult emotions differently in the future.

Topic: Mental Illness

1. Share about the tools you have to cope with symptoms of mental illness.
2. Share about one role model for living with mental illness (personal, societal, archetypal, historical, religious, or even a fantasy character).
3. Share about how your mental illness impacts you.
4. Share about what you imagine your life would look like in the future without mental illness.

Topic: Trauma

1. Share about one strength you have that can help you work through your trauma.
2. Share about one step you have already taken toward healing from trauma.
3. Share about one way your trauma has negatively impacted you.
4. Share about one way you would like to grow from your trauma.
5. Share about one step you plan to take in the future toward healing from trauma.

Another method for facilitating dyadic connections within groups is to place cards, objects, or images in the center of the group space and ask participants to choose one based on a guiding prompt. Some prompts might include inviting participants to choose a card that can represent "your strength," "the next step on your journey of healing," "defense mechanism," "your spirituality," "your goal for today," or "your ideal self in the future." Once chosen, group members are instructed to share in dyads about their choice of cards and the symbolic representation. Sharing can be extended with new prompts and/or new partners to facilitate increased connection. This process can be done with any set of cards and used as a warm-up to any topic with various prompts.

The Therapeutic Spiral Model (TSM) utilizes this process of choosing cards to represent the role of the *observing ego* – sometimes called the *compassionate witness* or *caring observer* (Hudgins & Toscani, 2013; Lawrence, 2015). The observing ego is a concept, borrowed from Freud (1932), which, in this context, refers to the part of self that can accurately observe self and others without shame, blame, or judgment (Giacomucci, 2018b). In TSM groups, the cards are then placed on the walls of the group room to provide a conscious reminder of this role and its importance. The use of cards to concretize the observing ego, a strength, or any other positive role provides an anchor of safety for the group experience going forward (Giacomucci et al., 2018). The presence of the cards on the walls behind the group offers a sense of being contained as well as an already defined strengths-based role for the psychodrama director to utilize during the group if extra grounding is needed. TSM practitioners primarily use this process to concretize a psychodramatic role, but it is important to note here for the sociometric aspect of using cards or objects to cultivate dyadic sharing at the beginning of a group process. The experience of using small groups or dyads offers participants the opportunity to create new connections, deepen relationships, enhance their sense of belonging, warm up to a topic, and increase overall group cohesion.

Spectrograms

The spectrogram is essentially a group-as-a-whole assessment tool that allows the facilitator to efficiently gather information about the group while providing participants with the chance to see where they fit in within the group and to connect with each other. A spectrogram is an action-based self-assessment along a spectrum within the room. Facilitation of a spectrogram is done by designating two different objects or two opposite walls of the room to represent the beginning and end of the spectrum. Generally, one side is designated as a 0/10 or 0% and the opposite side as a 10/10 or 100% while emphasizing that the imaginary line between the poles includes every possibility between 0 and 10 or 0% and 100%. Participants are invited to physically place themselves on the imaginary line based on where they believe that they belong when considering the prompt(s).

The following video depicts the use of Spectrograms with a live group http://www.phoenixtraumacenter.com/spectrograms/

Some examples of spectrogram prompts following the aforementioned clinical map are depicted in the following:

Topic: Connection and Loss

1. How many supportive relationships do you have in your life today?
2. How much loss have you experienced in your life?
3. How well do you think you handle grief?
4. How resilient do you judge yourself to be?

Topic: Addiction and Recovery

1. How many resources (supports, coping skills, tools, etc.) do you have to help in your recovery?
2. How motivated are you today for your recovery?
3. How much has addiction impacted your life?
4. How hopeful are you for your future in recovery?

Topic: Inpatient Treatment Experiences

1. How many days have you been in inpatient treatment?
2. How connected do you feel to the inpatient community of clients?
3. How difficult has it been for you to remain in treatment?
4. How much progress do you feel you have made since the day of your entered treatment?

Topic: Stress and Self-Care

1. How many tools for self-care do you have?
2. How often do you find yourself stressed out?
3. How much tolerance for stress do you judge yourself to have?
4. How many new strategies for coping with stress have you learned from the group?

Topic: Psychoeducation of Trauma

1. How curious are you to learn more about trauma?
2. How familiar are you with the common ways that trauma impacts people?
    a. How aware are you of how trauma has impacted you or your loved ones?
3. How knowledgeable are you in the different treatments and approaches to healing from trauma?

With each new prompt, it is helpful to change the axis of the spectrogram, using different areas in the room. This facilitates more physical movement and prevents participants from staying in the same physical place. Each prompt results in a new configuration of participants along the spectrogram. There are multiple ways to facilitate sharing. The simplest form of sharing is to have the group sharing in groups of two to three based on whoever is physically closest to them on the spectrogram. The use of dyadic sharing allows for everyone to share about why they are standing on the spectrogram at the point they are at without taking up too much time. Similarly, participants could be invited to share in clusters of larger groups about where they have chosen to stand on the spectrum. Another option is to ask for group members to share aloud to the group about their placement on the spectrogram. Other non-verbal ways to facilitate spectrogram sharing include body posture, movement and gestures, or sound.

It is important to consider that the spectrogram is a self-assessment and how that may impact one's choices in the process (Giacomucci et al., 2018). There are spectrogram prompts where it would be advantageous to change the spectrum to a 1–10, or even a 5–10 spectrum. For example, when using the prompt "how resilient do you judge yourself to be?" with a group of trauma survivors, it may be empowering to limit the spectrogram to a 5–10 while indicating the belief that everyone in the room is at least of 5/10 in resilience whether they believe it or not. Most of the clients that we work with are struggling with trauma, loss, addiction, oppression, mental illness, or other forms of suffering and may have distorted judgments about themselves, which will impact their self-assessment in the spectrogram process. When the facilitator notices this happening with a group member, it can be helpful to gently challenge the individual to reconsider or to reflect back to the group member where the facilitator would assess them to be on the spectrum. Another option would be to ask the group to share with the individual about where on the spectrogram they would assess that person to be based on the prompt – thus creating an opportunity for mutual aid.

A spectrogram prompt results in a distribution of group members along a continuum, sometimes with participants spread out, sometimes with clusters of participants in different places, and occasionally with isolates on the high or low end of the spectrum. When a prompt results in an obvious isolate on the spectrogram, it can be helpful to explore that person's experience at the group level. If they are an outlier on the higher end of a strengths-based prompt, they likely have important information that they could share to help the rest of the group. If they are an outlier on the lower end of a positive prompt, they might have questions about how to gain more understanding or competence related to the criteria. It can also be helpful to invite group members to raise their hands if they can remember a time in the past when they were at that point on the spectrogram and offer suggestions or identification with the person who is currently an outlier. A psychodramatist might also direct role reversals between group members on the spectrogram to have them explore what it is like to be at various spots. When participants have mobility limitations, the process can be modified by using an object to represent participants on the spectrogram or by having participants raise their hands to varying degrees (10/10 is as high as you can raise your hand; 0/10 is placing your hand on your lap) (Simmons, 2017). Spectrograms can also be easily modified for use during teletherapy or online teaching sessions by using the top and bottom of each participant's video feed as the top and bottom of the spectrum. Participants are simply instructed to place their hand along the vertical spectrum of their camera window to indicate where on the spectrogram they are.

Spectrograms allow the facilitator to meet the group where they are at in terms of their warm-up to a specific topic or their understanding of the topic. They are especially useful in psychoeducational sessions, training workshops, classrooms, and supervision groups to assess the knowledge level of participants at the start of the session. This gives the facilitator the chance to change the content of the session to meet the learning needs of the group (Giacomucci, 2018a). Spectrograms are also useful for evaluation in that the same spectrogram prompt could be asked at the beginning and end of a session or program, or pen-to-paper assessments can be modified into experiential spectrograms (Giacomucci, 2020).

Locograms

The locogram is a sociometry tool that offers a quick visual group assessment or democratic group vote in an experiential format based on different options or categories. As suggested by the prefix of the term *loco-gram*, this process is an exploration of choices using places in the room. While the spectrogram orients itself upon a spectrum, the locogram is oriented based on designated locations in the room. One of the simplest ways to facilitate a locogram is to use the four corners of the room to each represent a different choice and ask participants to physically indicate their preference by standing at the corresponding location (Giacomucci, 2020). Other styles of directing a locogram involve using objects or chairs to represent the various choices. Most locograms offer at least three options, which usually include an option for "other" – this invites other suggestions from the group. Locograms are useful for quick assessments or group choices in action. They can be used for many purposes including choosing a topic, discerning when to take a break, making a group decision, assessing group preference, uncovering similarities, and exploring a group's warm-up.

Here are some examples with the bullet points representing the different locations in the room (represented by the corners of the room or objects):

Purpose: Choosing a Topic in an Outpatient Group

- Anxiety
- Depression
- Trauma
- Other

Purpose: Discerning What the Group Is Warmed Up for Next

- Discussion
- More sociometry
- Psychodrama
- Writing activity
- Other

Purpose: Outpatient Group Decision About Holiday Scheduling Conflict

- Schedule the session on the holiday
- Cancel the session on the holiday
- Meet on a different day that week
- Meet twice as long as the following session
- Other

Purpose: Uncovering Shared Experiences in School

- I hated school
- I loved school
- I had mixed feelings about school
- Other

Purpose: Exploring Religious/Spiritual Beliefs

- I am religious
- I have a belief in a higher power
- I am uncertain about spirituality
- I do not believe in God or a higher power
- Other

The locogram can be used for a quick group-as-a-whole assessment and group choice, or for an exploration of shared perspective, experience, or identity. When facilitating a locogram, it helps to limit or expand the number of options based on the size of the group. The facilitation of a locogram may or may not include sharing. If the goal is to make a quick group choice, then sharing is likely unnecessary. But if the goal is to facilitate connection and explore shared experience, then sharing is likely to be helpful.

A locogram can also be used in teletherapy groups and online teaching sessions. This could be done in a variety of ways, including using a poll feature, instructing participants to write their choice/preference in the chat box, or assigning numbers to each locogram choice and instructing participants to indicate their choice/preference by showing the number of fingers that corresponds with their choice. If the technology platform utilized allows for breakout rooms, the facilitator can initiate breakout rooms, which will allow for participants to talk about their shared preferences/choices. This method of adapting the locogram for teletherapy or online sessions is identical to how the floor check is modified for online groups. The floor check, a similar sociometry tool that evolved from the locogram, is outlined in the next section.

Floor Checks

The floor check is an experiential psychosocial process in the Relational Trauma Repair Model created by Tian Dayton (2014, 2015). It was inspired by the locogram process of using various places in the room for different options – the primary difference is that with the floor check, the facilitator utilizes printed pieces of paper to label the options and offers a series of prompts, each involving sharing. The floor check expands choice-making potential with increased options that transcend here-and-now prompts into past or future-oriented questions. The floor check expands the process with continual groupings and clustering, which offer exponentially more chances for individual reflection, choice-making, group connection, education, and healing. The floor check was developed, based on evolving research on trauma, grief, mental health, addiction, and posttraumatic growth, to meet the pressing needs within addiction treatment centers which were faced with shorter group times, larger group sizes, varying degrees of client vulnerability, and therapists with different levels of psychodrama training. When employing the floor check process, it is advantageous to construct prompts or floor check options with research-based content. This can be done by simply choosing floor check options that correspond to the recognized symptomology of a diagnosis or evidence-based research findings, theories, or practices (as described by Dayton, 2014, 2015). Thus, the floor check offers a psychoeducational and therapeutic healing avenue for addressing symptomology in an engaging and dynamic process involving intrapsychic and interpersonal explorations. The multiple, focused prompts in a floor check sociometrically align participants based on the content while providing a progression of spontaneous connection and healing.

With each prompt, participants physically place themselves at the paper that corresponds to their preference or response. A floor check prompt results in group members clustering in small groups based on shared experience for verbal sharing about their choice. The process, similar to the locogram, provides a group-as-a-whole assessment but also cultivates a deepening of sharing and connection between group members in small groups. Floor checks "put healing in the hands of the process itself rather than exclusively in the hands of the therapists" (2015, p. 10) while empowering participants to become therapeutic agents for each other and quickly activating the mutual aid within a group (Giacomucci, 2019, 2020, 2021a, 2021b).

Once a floor check is put into action, and group members have physically indicated their choices, they are invited to share with whoever is standing with them. When participants are standing alone at a choice, the facilitator simply directs them to join others nearby to share about their choice. This process creates sociometrically configured small groups, opening up opportunities for social-emotional learning and healing. Similar to the use of dyads or small groups, it allows the director to take a passive role in the process and move around the room listening or checking in on each cluster of clients. Floor checks are versatile and can be used in any group context with nearly any topic.

The following video depicts the use of Locogram and Floor Checks with a live group

http://www.phoenixtraumacenter.com/floor-check/

Some useful examples are listed in the following (more detailed prompts available in Dayton, 2014), including prompts following the previously described clinical map:

Feeling Floor Check – Anger; Sadness; Fear; Guilt/Shame; Happiness; Other

1. Which feeling best describes your experience today?
2. Which feeling most characterized your experience last week?
3. Which feeling do you most try to avoid?
4. Which feeling is hardest for you to tolerate in others?
5. Which feeling have you gotten better with?

Relationships Floor Check – Family; Friends; Self; Groups/Communities; God/Higher Power; Other

1. Which relationship do you feel most supported by today?
2. Which relationship has the most conflict in it for you?
3. Which relationship has improved the most since you started therapy?
4. Which relationship would you like/need to work on today?

Defense Mechanisms Floor Check – Humor; Denial or Minimization; Rationalization or Intellectualization; Acting Out; Passive Aggression; Dissociation; Fight; Flight; Freeze; Other

1. Which defense do you feel you are most aware of using in your life today?
2. Which defense do you feel you have used the most in this group?
3. Which defense is most difficult for you to tolerate when someone else uses it?
4. Which defense do you no longer use as much as you used to?

CPTSD Symptom Cluster Floor Check – Avoidance; Arousal and Reactivity; Re-Experiencing and Intrusions; Negative Mood and Cognitions; Emotional Dysregulation; Relationship Difficulties; and Negative View of Self

1. Which would you like to learn more about?
2. Which best describes how trauma has impacted you?
3. Which describes symptoms you previously experienced but now have effective coping skills for?

Domains of Posttraumatic Growth Floor Check – Personal Strength; Appreciation of Life; Relationships; Spiritual/Religious Growth; New Possibilities

1. Which domain do you feel you have grown in the most?
2. Which domain do you feel you struggle with the most?
3. Which domain do you feel you could help someone in this group with?

The floor check can be modified for any group topic or theme that can be sectioned down into categories or choices. Other useful examples include the stages of change, the stages of grief, the tasks of resilience in ambiguous loss, mental health diagnoses, treatment themes, and strengths. This process is also valuable in educational spaces and can be used as an experiential teaching tool promoting reflection and the integration of concepts into personal experience (Giacomucci & Skolnik, 2021). The floor check is a holistic instrument that effectively warms people up physically, emotionally, socially, and to the chosen topic. It can be utilized alone as a group process or as a warm-up to another group process, such as a psychodrama, art therapy piece, or writing process.

Step-in Sociometry

The next sociometry process that we will explore is *step-in sociometry* – sometimes called the *circle of similarities*. This experiential process is effective at quickly identifying shared experience or similarities in the group-as-a-whole (Archer, 2016). Buchanan (2016) notes that step-in sociometry is a newer addition to the sociometry toolbox in the 1970s from the New Games Movement (Fluegelman, 1976). Step-in sociometry is facilitated with the group stand in a circle. Prompts are offered with the instruction to step into the circle if you identify with the prompt. Prompts can be offered spontaneously, or the facilitator can ask participants to offer step-in prompts one at a time by going around the entire circle. It is helpful to encourage group members to make their statements broad and general rather than specific, as it creates a more inclusive experience and prevents individuals from making statements so specific that they end up stepping in alone. If a prompt does result in one person alone in the circle, it is helpful to reframe the prompt in a more general way – for example, the prompt "I enjoy water color painting" could be generalized to "I enjoy creating art," which would result in more participants stepping in.

Either the facilitator offers prompts asking participants to physically step in if they identify, or group members take turns stepping in while making statements about themselves, while others who identify also step in. Buchanan (2016) describes the latter as the *democratic approach* and the former as the *totalitarian approach* to step-in sociometry. This writer has discovered that the democratic approach is favorable in nearly all contexts. One exception where the totalitarian approach may be useful is when offering trauma-related prompts in a group where it could be harmful if the process goes too far into the trauma. The totalitarian approach would allow the facilitator to intentionally choose very broad trauma-related prompts that ensure the largest number of participants identify. In this context, the facilitator providing all of the prompts would contribute to group safety and containment. Another facilitation consideration is the facilitator's decision to participate in the process or not. The choice to participate or not, or participate in some rounds but not others, would come back to the facilitator's style, the goals for the group, the group population, and the group context. In some groups and with some prompts, it may be advantageous for the facilitator to participate, which allows the group to connect with them, while in other groups and with other prompts, it may be best for the director not to participate (Buchanan, 2016; Giacomucci, 2017).

In facilitating this process, it is also important to inform participants that they can choose whether they want to self-disclose or not on any given criterion, as there may be prompts offered that some participants are willing to self-disclose while others may not be ready to do so (Buchanan, 2016). When a group member offers a prompt and other participants step in, it allows the group to visually see others who have a shared experience. Step-in sociometry makes the invisible connections and similarities within the group visible and conscious – thus increasing overall group connection and cohesion (Giacomucci et al., 2018). Once participants have stepped in, concretizing their connection to the prompt, the facilitator invites them to quietly acknowledge others who have stepped in and then step back into the larger circle. This process seems to be appealing to introverted clients and young adults who find it to be an opportunity for peer identification without much verbal sharing (Giacomucci, 2017). Alternative ways of facilitating include inviting participants who have stepped in to briefly share why they stepped in or to use sound or movement to express their connection to the prompt.

Step-in sociometry can be facilitated with multiple rounds, each with a larger theme, or as a single open-ended process without a theme. Both options have benefits. An open-ended step-in sociometry experience allows the group to choose any prompts, which is likely to be revealing of the group's overall warm-up and allows the group to control the process (Archer, 2016). The method of using multiple rounds of step-in sociometry, each with themes, allows the facilitator to create a more directed and intentional group warm-up, which may be most useful in clinical settings. When using multiple rounds of step-in sociometry, it is useful to follow the clinical map referenced previously.

The following video depicts the use of Step-in Sociometry with a live group http://www.phoenixtraumacenter.com/step-in-sociometry/

The following are some examples of different themes for step-in rounds:

Group: Inpatient Addiction Treatment

1. Step in and name something you like to do that is not related to your addiction.
2. Step in and name a consequence of your addiction (medical, emotional, social, legal, etc.).
3. Step in and share a hope or goal for your future in recovery from addiction.

Group: Immigrant Families

1. Step in and name something that is important to you about your family or culture.
2. Step in and label something that has been difficult for you related to immigration.
3. Step in and share a hope you have for your family going forward.

Group: Grief and Loss Group for Parents

1. Step in and share one thing that has helped you in your grief and loss.
2. Step in and share one difficult aspect related to your grief and loss.
3. Step in and share one goal for yourself and your family going forward in the grief process.

Group: Hospital-Based Cancer Support Group

1. Step in and share something about yourself beyond your medical condition.
2. Step in and share one difficult aspect of your cancer diagnosis.
3. Step in and name one goal for yourself going forward.

Group: High School Group

1. Step in and share something about yourself.
2. Step in and share one thing you find difficult about high school.
3. Step in and share something you would like to accomplish by the end of high school.

Group: New Social Work Graduate Students

1. Step in and share one thing that influenced your decision to get a graduate degree in social work.
2. Step in and name one fear you have about the graduate program.
3. Step in and name a professional role that you would like to have in the future.

Step-in sociometry cultivates universality, curiosity, connection, and inclusion with the group experience and can be adapted for any topic or group setting (Buchanan, 2016; Giacomucci, 2020). Archer (2016) provides an in-depth exploration of various ways to adapt step-in sociometry with groups that consist of participants with physical limitations, including group members who are visually impaired, wheelchair bound, or on crutches. In larger groups or group spaces where creating a circle is not possible, the step-in sociometry process is often modified to utilize standing up or raising hands instead (Archer, 2016).

Similar to the previously described experiential sociometry processes, step-in sociometry can be used as a warm-up or as a group process on its own. Furthermore, the utilization of step-in sociometry for closure, processing and integration after a psychodrama enactment or other group process has been described (Giacomucci, 2017). This may be most useful in the context of large groups or when time is limited, and a quick, efficient method for sharing is called for.

Hands-on-Shoulder Sociograms

The sociogram was one of the first sociometry instruments that Moreno developed through his sociometric tests (J. L. Moreno, 1934; J. D. Moreno, 2014). A sociogram shows the number of times group members choose each other based on specific criteria. Using pen-to-paper sociometric tests, Moreno collected the written choices of participants and drew complex sociograms to depict the distribution of choices within the group. The hands-on-shoulder sociogram, sometimes called an action sociogram, moves this process from paper into the room as an experiential process. The action sociogram makes the unseen choices within a group conscious, revealing the invisible web of attractions, and repulsions within a group (Korshak & Shapiro, 2013). Hale (1981) refers to this as enhancing the sociometric consciousness of the group. While the previously described sociometry processes are all based on self-assessment, the sociogram is oriented on the assessment of others and the group's overall assessment of itself (Giacomucci, 2018a).

The experiential sociogram process prompts participants to put their hand on the shoulder of one other group member based on a specific prompt, simultaneously revealing the distribution of choices and preferences within the group. This process uses physical touch, so it is important to check in with the group about their comfort level with physical touch and obtain their consent – especially when working with trauma survivors. Sometimes, the aforementioned sociometry processes are used to explore comfort with physical touch, such as a spectrogram, locogram, or step-in sociometry. If participants are not comfortable with others putting their hand on their shoulder, the process can be amended by having participants indicate their choices by touching their shoe to the shoe of another, standing next to another, pointing at their choices, or holding a scarf or string to indicate their choice (Hudgins & Toscani, 2013; Olesen, Campbell, & Gross, 2017; Simmons, 2017). While some may find the experience of physical touch uncomfortable or intolerable, others may find it soothing and comforting (Giacomucci et al., 2018). Moreno wrote of the power of physical touch and highlighted the practice wisdom from the field of nursing in this area (McIntosh, 2010; J. L. Moreno, 1972).

The sociogram often helps participants become aware of their own tendencies around choosing, waiting to be chosen, and prioritizing their first choice. When one has difficulty with making a choice, they are encouraged to choose with their intuition or to trust their tele. Once each participant has indicated their choice by putting their hand on the shoulder of one person in the room, the facilitator may offer a brief interpretation of the sociometric constellation – for example, noting the prevalence of mutual choices, the equal distribution of choices, or the choices being highly concentrated with social stars and social isolates. The sociogram quickly depicts the distribution of criteria-specific social wealth within the group, thus highlighting the presence of tele and the sociodynamic effect. Then, participants are invited to share briefly with the person they chose about their reasoning for choosing them. This effectively increases interpersonal relationships within the group while enhancing overall group cohesion. The following are some examples of prompts tailored to different groups using the prescribed stages of the clinical map:

Group: Veterans Support Group

1. Place your hand on the shoulder of someone who you experienced taking a significant step in their growth last month.
2. Place your hand on the shoulder of someone who has said something related to your identity as a veteran, which was meaningful to you.
3. Place your hand on the shoulder of someone whose experience you would like to know more about.
4. Place your hand on the shoulder of someone whom you could see yourself connecting with outside of the group.

Group: Substance Use Relapse Prevention Group

1. Place your hand on the shoulder of someone who inspires you.
2. Place your hand on the shoulder of someone who has said something that worries you.
3. Place your hand on the shoulder of someone whom you could call if you had a craving to use drugs.
4. Place your hand on the shoulder of someone whom you could call for relationship advice.

Each of the given examples demonstrates the use of hands-on-shoulder sociogram criteria that is reality-based and sociometric-based. Another option is to offer prompts that are surplus reality and psychodramatically oriented. The difference between reality-based sociometric prompts and surplus reality-based psychodrama prompts is depicted in the following:

Sociometric Reality-Based Prompts:

A. Place your hand on the shoulder of someone whom you experience as courageous.

B. Place your hand on the shoulder of someone whom you look up to as a role model.
C. Place your hand on the shoulder of someone who reminds you of yourself.
D. Place your hand on the shoulder of someone whom you would call for spiritual guidance.
E. Place your hand on the shoulder of someone whom you experience as motherly.

Psychodramatic Surplus Reality Based Prompts:

A. Place your hand on the shoulder of someone whom you would choose to play the role of your courage.
B. Place your hand on the shoulder of someone whom you would choose to play the role of one of your role models.
C. Place your hand on the shoulder of someone whom you would choose to play the role of yourself.
D. Place your hand on the shoulder of someone whom you would choose to play the role of God.
E. Place your hand on the shoulder of someone whom you would choose to play the role of your mother.

Some find that psychodramatic prompts provide more distance and thus more safety for group members when choosing and being chosen. Psychodramatic prompts also have the benefit of getting participants warmed up to choosing roles in a psychodrama. Many practitioners employ both sociometric and psychodramatic prompts in their use of sociograms in groups. The following are some examples of mixed prompts:

Group: Depression Support

1. Place your hand on the shoulder of someone who you would have helped you feel comfortable in the group.
2. Place your hand on the shoulder of someone whom you would choose to play the role of your resilience.
3. Place your hand on the shoulder of someone who has helped you understand depression better.
4. Place your hand on the shoulder of someone whom you could call if your depression increased.
5. Place your hand on the shoulder of someone whom you would choose to play the role of yourself in the future no longer experiencing depression.

Group: Healthy Relationships for Couples

1. Place your hand on the shoulder of someone whose sharing has helped you understand yourself better.

2. Place your hand on the shoulder of someone whom you would choose to play the role of your willingness to work on your relationship.
3. Place your hand on the shoulder of someone whose love for their partner has inspired you.
4. Place your hand on the shoulder of someone whom you would choose to play the role of your honesty or vulnerability.
5. Place your hand on the shoulder of someone whom you would call if you needed support in the future.

While these are examples of prompts that could be offered in groups, it is important for the facilitator to remain attentive to the group process and to offer new prompts when needed to create a more inclusive experience. For example, if a facilitator notices that a participant repeatedly is unchosen, it would be important to spontaneously offer a new prompt that makes this person highly chosen. Group facilitators have a responsibility to be aware of the sociodynamic effect and to reverse its impact within the group to create an inclusive experience. While one may be unchosen in this group based on this criterion, they are almost certainly a social star when it comes to other criteria and in other groups. Korshak and Shapiro (2013) note that reversing the sharing in a sociogram is another method of reversing the sociodynamic effect. Rather than having participants *share their reason for choosing* another, the person chosen *shares their experience of being chosen* with the person choosing them. Zerka Moreno (2006) writes that the "essential reason for doing sociometric investigations is not just to make relationships visible and available for interpretation, but to reconstruct groups to maximize sociostasis and find some resolution to the problem of the unchosen and rejected" (p. 296).

At this point, it is important to note that of all of the experiential processes described in this chapter, the action sociogram has the most risk. Unless conducted attentively, spontaneously, and skillfully, the group may have a negative response to the hands-on-shoulder sociogram. This process is best utilized in higher functioning groups where participants are familiar with each other and have demonstrated a capacity for tolerating vulnerability and discomfort.

Circle of Strengths

The circle of strengths is a safety structure that originates from the TSM (Hudgins & Toscani, 2013). It is an experiential process of concretizing the collective strengths of the group and strongly compliments trauma-informed care's strengths-based approach (Saleebey, 2012). Generally, this exercise begins with a large pile of scarves or other fabric in the center of the group room (though it can also be done with objects in the room or with pen/paper). As group members enter the room, the scarves spark their curiosity, playfulness, and creativity. One simple way of facilitating the circle of strengths is to have the group break up into dyads; if there are an odd number, the facilitator can join – this method of using dyads prevents anyone from being chosen last (Giacomucci et al., 2018). Participants are provided with psychoeducation on the importance of strengths and various types of strengths (intrapsychic, interpersonal, and transpersonal strengths). Participants are then asked to choose a scarf to represent a strength that they see in their partner and to present the strength to their partner one at a time while reminding their partner of examples of how they have demonstrated the strength. This provides a ritual for group members to practice healthy risks and vulnerability with each other based on positive criteria. The rest of the group witnesses the individual exchanges of strengths. As each strength is concretized (with scarves), they are placed on the floor of the group room, creating a large circle of strengths. This process can be repeated in new dyads or spontaneously between group members. The facilitator may choose to do one round in dyads, then a round where everyone identifies one of their own strengths, and finally a round where everyone concretizes a strength they experience in the group-as-a-whole.

The resulting circle of strengths on the floor serves as a conscious reminder of the individual and collective strengths within the group. They can be utilized by the facilitator later in the process if a group member becomes overwhelmed and might benefit from a reminder of their strengths. Symbolically, the circle is representative of the unity of the group and the ability of the collective group's strengths to contain any participant's stories, experiences, trauma, or feelings. Logistically, the circle of strengths can serve as a stage for a future psychodrama in the group (Hudgins & Toscani, 2013).

The exercise was initially developed through the process of having group members choose scarves to symbolize their own personal strengths that they bring to the group. As TSM became utilized around the world, especially in Asia, this process evolved to become more culturally sensitive, and new methods were developed, including having group members choose scarves to concretize the strengths they see in each other (Hudgins & Toscani, 2013). Novel methods for creating the circle of strengths continue to be developed, including using short enactments of strengths, inviting group members to ask for reminders of specific strengths, and concretizing the strengths of an organization or program. The experience of engaging in this process seems to significantly increase connections in the group, cultivate mutual aid, renegotiate one's sense of self, enhance group cohesion, and establish an "all in the same boat" mentality (Giacomucci, 2019, 2021a, 2021b; Giacomucci & Ehrhart, 2021; Shulman, 2010).

The following video depicts the use of Circle of Strengths with a live group http://www.phoenixtraumacenter.com/circle-of-strengths/

Some examples of statements from clients engaging in this process are provided in the following.

Interpersonal Recognitions of Strengths

- "I chose this for your courage because it is a strong and bold scarf. I have seen you demonstrate courage in the times you are vulnerable with us and in the stories you have shared about your childhood."
- "I chose this scarf to represent the compassion and kindness that I experience from you each time we are together. You always are friendly and are quick to offer support whenever anyone needs it – I know I can count on your support."
- "I picked this scarf to be your spirituality and the sense of purpose it gives you. It is clear that your spirituality is important to you and gives meaning to your life in the way you help others and maintain faith through uncertainty."

Acknowledging Personal Strengths

- "I chose this one to symbolize my resilience. Even though I have experienced hardship, I keep bouncing back and I survive no matter what."
- "This represents my relationship to my family. I believe family is the most important thing in life and they are always there to support me."
- "I chose this scarf for my ability to ground myself. I have learned breathing techniques and meditation which allow me to center myself internally even when things get chaotic."

Strengths in the Group-as-a-Whole

- "I chose this to represent our willingness to change. Everyone here demonstrates this strength each time you show up to group. Regardless of our failures or successes, we continue to be willing to change and grow."
- "I chose this colorful scarf to symbolize the diversity in this group. We all come from different walks of life and various backgrounds which gives us each a unique perspective that we bring to the group. I always learn new ways of looking at things because of you all."
- "I picked this scarf to represent the safety of this group. I usually don't trust people, but I know that this is a safe place and this group of people are worthy of my trust."

The circle of strengths process can be quite powerful for participants and has the potential to tap into strong emotions for some. As group therapists and organizational leaders, we often work with traumatized, oppressed, and disenfranchised populations. The process of taking the time to recognize strengths can be incredibly restorative, especially for those who have been marginalized within society, dehumanized in their interpersonal relationships, or stuck in self-loathing. This process could be employed as a warm-up for a psychodrama or as its own group process. The circle of strengths can also be facilitated in online groups by having participants choose objects in their own room to concretize the strengths of others and themselves. It can also be adapted for use in community groups, supervision groups, student groups, and organizational settings to increase confidence and cohesion in a meaningful and strengths-based process.

Conclusion

Experiential sociometry processes offer strengths-based and trauma-informed methods for engaging groups.

Experiential sociometry processes offer strengths-based and trauma-informed methods for engaging groups. These approaches intrinsically embody trauma-informed principles and can be used to further explore the six trauma-informed principles with clients, communities, students, and staff. Each of the aforementioned group processes can be adapted for use with any community and any topic, making them valuable tools for group workers, psychodramatists, and leaders. While these exercises are often used as warm-ups for a psychodrama enactment, they can also be utilized on their own for group-as-a-whole assessment, engagement, intervention, and evaluation. These processes are also invaluable tools for organizational leaders as they offer avenues for active engagement, assessment, and intervention within organizational culture and the relational dynamics between staff.

References

Archer, M. (2016). Who, like me, loves to use the step-in circle? *The Journal of Psychodrama, Sociometry, and Group Psychotherapy*, *64*(1), 79–82.

Buchanan, D. R. (2016). Practical applications of step-in sociometry: Increasing sociometric intelligence via self-disclosure and connection. *Journal of Psychodrama, Sociometry, and Group Psychotherapy*, *64*, 71–78.

Dayton, T. (2005). *The Living Stage: A step-by-step guide to psychodrama, sociometry, and experiential group therapy*. Deerfield, FL: Health Communications Inc.

Dayton, T. (2014). *Relational Trauma Repair (RTR) therapist's guide (Revised edition)*. New York: Innerlook, Inc.

Dayton, T. (2015). *NeuroPsychodrama in the treatment of relational trauma: A strength-based, experiential model for healing PTSD*. Deerfield Beach, FL: Health Communications, Inc.

Fluegelman, A. (1976). *The new games book*. San Francisco, CA: New Games Foundation.

Freud, S. (1932). The dissection of the psychical personality. In *Standard edition 22* (pp. 67–80). London: Hogarth Press.
Giacomucci, S. (2017). The sociodrama of life or death: Young adults and addiction treatment. *Journal of Psychodrama, Sociometry, and Group Psychotherapy, 65*(1), 137–143.
Giacomucci, S. (2018a). Social work and sociometry: An integration of theory and clinical practice. *The Pennsylvania Social Worker, 39*(1), 14–16.
Giacomucci, S. (2018b). The trauma survivor's inner role atom: A clinical map for post-traumatic growth. *Journal of Psychodrama, Sociometry, and Group Psychotherapy, 66*(1), 115–129.
Giacomucci, S. (2019). *Social group work in action: A sociometry, psychodrama, and experiential trauma therapy curriculum*. Doctorate in Social Work (DSW) Dissertations. 124. https://repository.upenn.edu/cgi/viewcontent.cgi?article=1128&context=edissertations_sp2
Giacomucci, S. (2020). Addiction, traumatic loss, and guilt: A case study resolving grief through psychodrama and sociometric connections. *The Arts in Psychotherapy, 67*, 101627.
Giacomucci, S. (2021a). Experiential sociometry in group work: Mutual aid for the group-as-a-whole. *Social Work with Groups, 44*(3), 204–214.
Giacomucci, S. (2021b). *Social work, sociometry, and psychodrama: Experiential approaches for group therapists, community leaders, and social workers*. Springer Nature.
Giacomucci, S. (2023). *Trauma-informed principles in group therapy, psychodrama, and organizations: Action methods for leadership*. Routledge.
Giacomucci, S., & Ehrhart, L. (2021). Introduction to psychodrama psychotherapy: A trauma and addiction group vignette. *Group, 45*(1), 69–86.
Giacomucci, S., Gera, S., Briggs, D., & Bass, K. (2018). Experiential addiction treatment: Creating positive connection through sociometry and therapeutic spiral model safety structures. *Journal of Addiction and Addictive Disorders, 5*, 17.
Giacomucci, S., & Marquit, J. (2020). The effectiveness of trauma-focused psychodrama in the treatment of PTSD in inpatient substance abuse treatment. *Frontiers in Psychology, 11*, 896.
Giacomucci, S., & Skolnik, S. (2021). The experiential social work educator: Integrating sociometry into the classroom environment. *Journal of Teaching in Social Work, 41*(2), 192–202.
Hale, A. E. (1981). *Conducting clinical sociometric explorations: A manual for psychodramatists and sociometrists*. Roanoke, VA: Royal Publishing Company
Hale, A. E. (2009). Moreno's sociometry: Exploring interpersonal connection. *Group, 33*(4), 347–358.
Hudgins, M. K., & Toscani, F. (2013). *Healing world trauma with the therapeutic spiral model: Stories from the frontlines*. London: Jessica Kingsley Publishers.
Korshak, S. J., & Shapiro, M. (2013). Choosing the unchosen: Counteracting the sociodynamic effect using complementary sharing. *The Journal of Psychodrama, Sociometry, and Group Psychotherapy, 61*(1), 7–15.
Lawrence, C. (2015). The caring observer: Creating self-compassion through psychodrama. *The Journal of Psychodrama, Sociometry, and Group Psychotherapy, 63*(1), 65–72.
Levine, P. A. (2010). *In an unspoken voice: How the body releases trauma and restores goodness*. Berkeley, CA. North Atlantic Books.
McIntosh, W. (2010). Walking with Moreno: A historical journey of psychodrama and nursing'. *Australian and Aotearoa New Zealand Psychodrama Association Journal*, (19), 30.

Moreno, J. D. (2014). *Impromptu man: J.L. Moreno and the origins of psychodrama, encounter culture, and the social network*. New York: Bellevue Literary Press.
Moreno, J. L. (1934). *Who shall survive? A new approach to the problems of human interrelations*. Washington, DC: Nervous and Mental Disease Publishing Co.
Moreno, J. L. (1972). *Psychodrama and group psychotherapy: First Volume (4th edition)*. Beacon House.
Moreno, Z. (2006). The function of "tele" in human relations. In T. Horvatin & E. Shreiber (Eds.), *The Quintessential Zerka: Writings by Zerka Toeman Moreno on psychodrama, sociometry and group psychotherapy* (pp. 289–301). New York: Routledge.
Nieto, L. (2010). Look behind you: Using anti-oppression models to inform a protagonist's psychodrama. In E. Leveton (Ed.), *Healing collective trauma using sociodrama and drama therapy* (pp. 103–125). New York: Springer Publishing Company.
Olesen, J., Campbell, J., & Gross, M. (2017). Using action methods to counter social isolation and shame among gay men. *Journal of Gay & Lesbian Social Services, 29*(2), 91–108.
Saleebey, D. (2012). *The strengths perspective in social work practice (6th edition)*. Boston: Pearson Education.
Shulman, L. (2010). *Dynamics and skills of group counseling*. Belmont, CA: Cengage Learning.
Simmons, D. (2017). Implementing sociometry in a long-term care institutional setting for the elderly: Exploring social relationships and choices. *The Journal of Psychodrama, Sociometry, and Group Psychotherapy, 65*(1), 85–98.
Substance Abuse and Mental Health Services Administration. (2014). *SAMHSA's concept of trauma and guidance for a trauma-informed approach*. HHS Publication No. (SMA) 14-4884. Rockville, MD: Substance Abuse and Mental Health Services Administration.

Chapter 6

Basic Psychodrama Directing Elements and Interventions for Trauma

Psychodrama is unique in that it is not a manualized treatment, and it can include a variety of interventions employed by the director in any given session. As a director, I might use some psychodrama interventions in one session but not in another. I might rely more on one intervention in one psychodrama and less in another psychodrama. We modify our use of interventions depending on the presentation of the protagonist, the group dynamics, the issue at hand, the contract or goal of the session, and the nature of the setting where the psychodrama is taking place. In a 2018 review of psychodrama practice (Cruz et al., 2018), 56 different interventions were discovered in the literature and 11 core interventions – most of which are outlined in this chapter or Chapter 7.

Phases and Elements of a Psychodrama

Every psychodrama session is structured into three phases while including five core elements. The first phase of a psychodrama is the warm-up, then we have the action, which is followed by sharing. These three phases, depicted in Figure 6.1, initiate an important structure and pacing for the session. We cannot skip any of these phases. There is no adequate action without a warming-up process. A warming-up process that skips the action and goes directly to sharing is anticlimatic. A session with warm-up and action, but no sharing, prevents integration and consolidation of gains, which is essential to the process of having lasting change. Proper time must be devoted to each of these three phases.

There are five core elements within a psychodrama – the director, the stage, the protagonist, auxiliary egos, and the audience. In psychodrama, the therapist or facilitator is referred to as a director – a term borrowed from the theater. The stage is simply the space within which the psychodrama session takes place. In the past, it was more common for psychodrama to take place on an elevated stage, but most psychodrama today is simply facilitated in the empty space in the center of a group room. The protagonist is the person who is issue and goal we are putting into action in the psychodrama. Auxiliary egos are the other roles that are being embodied within the surplus reality of the scene and role played

DOI: 10.4324/9781003639497-6

Figure 6.1 The three phases of a psychodrama session

by other group members. In individual therapy with psychodrama, the other roles are typically held by an empty chair or concretized with an object. And the audience is made up of the other participants in the group who have not been cast in any roles. While minor adaptations are made to these five elements at times (such as having two co-directors, multiple protagonists, or enrolling all participants in roles to avoid inactive audience members), these five elements are foundational to all psychodrama practice (Giacomucci, 2021).

Protagonist Selection

After a warming-up process has been initiated and the group is ready to move toward the psychodrama, we must discern who will be the protagonist. There are multiple different strategies for eliciting a protagonist from the group – (1) the director's choice, (2) a volunteer from the group, (3) schedule a protagonist, or (4) sociometric selection. I often avoid the first two options in clinical settings as they are uniformed by the sociometry of the group and prone to being influenced by bias or impulsivity. The scheduling of protagonists is often utilized in longer-term treatment settings or multi-day workshops, where everyone is going to have a chance to be the protagonist. Scheduling protagonists might initially seem like it would stunt spontaneity (and it could), but it also offers some predictability and time for the protagonist to internally warm up to their work. I have been part of a men's group for over a decade, where we made a decision a few years ago to begin scheduling protagonists each session. This was one of the best decisions our group made, as it pushed us into doing deeper work each session and gave each man time to warm up to a topic and an issue to work on when it was their turn. It effectively led to us arriving to the group more prepared to work.

The preferred method of choosing a protagonist is through sociometry. In a sociometric protagonist selection, group members are invited to volunteer themselves and a topic as a protagonist. Then the rest of the group are instructed to choose which of the volunteered topics would help them the most personally.

It is important to emphasize that we are choosing solely on the content of the topic, not the person who proposed the topic. This process results in the group identifying the topic that best represents the entire group and thus is most likely to lead to helping the majority of group members. The sociometric selection process prevents psychodrama from turning into individual therapy with a group audience and keeps its focus as a group-as-a-whole approach. Traditionally, a sociogram is used for a protagonist selection, which means that each participant puts their hand on the shoulder of the person whose topic they most relate to. Usually, the volunteer protagonists also participate, which frequently results in complicated sociometric constellations and the director having to figure out what to do next. Sometimes, a protagonist volunteer gains most of the group choices, but, in turn, chooses someone else's topic that did not receive any other group choices. Traditional sociometric teaching would suggest that the sociometric chain ends with the least chosen volunteer protagonist, and thus, they become the protagonist, even though nobody else in the group chose their topic. I find this to be faulty. Instead, I suggest the use of a locogram for protagonist selections without the protagonist volunteers having the option to choose a different topic. A locogram with the psychodrama topic choices is much cleaner and simpler. Sociometric protagonist selection is likely to contribute to further engagement from the group, less guilt from the protagonist about taking up too much space, more tele and emotional involvement from role players, and richer sharing at the end of the psychodrama. For these reasons, I recommend sociometric protagonist selections as the best option for discerning a protagonist if there is enough time to do it.

> The sociometric selection process prevents psychodrama from turning into individual therapy with a group audience, and keeps its focus as a group-as-a-whole approach.

Contracting and Setting a Goal

After discerning a protagonist for the psychodrama, it is essential to discern a contract for the session. This is typically done during a "walk and talk," where the director and protagonist walk in a circle around the room (originally, it was done on the lower circular level of the psychodrama stage) and make an agreement about the goal of the psychodrama together. In my own experience, I have found that the contact can be more efficiently obtained earlier when topics are proposed. I ask protagonists to state both their issue and their goal when volunteering as protagonists. This saves me time later with contracting and prevents the psychodrama that was chosen from morphing into something different than what the group selected during the walk and talk – which often happens. If the group chose a protagonist based on their initially proposed topic, we need to be careful that we do not change to a completely different contract unrelated to the topic, otherwise we risk losing the rest of the group. In establishing a contract with the protagonist, it is important that the contract be clear and achievable in the allotted time frame. Some common errors include having a contract that is too abstract to assess if we have made progress toward it, or choosing a contract that is unrealistic for the amount of time available for the psychodrama.

I believe that the contract is one of my most important aspects of the psychodrama because it gives us a clear direction to move toward throughout the action. Having a contract also provides transparency and autonomy for the protagonist of the direction of the process while mitigating the risks of the psychodrama director's bias from taking over the direction of the session. While directing a psychodrama, I steer each intervention and the interactions with each role back toward the established contract. The contract becomes a beacon for where we are headed in the surplus reality of the psychodrama. Without it, we do not know if we have been successful, and we will not know which direction to go.

The contract becomes a beacon for where we are headed in the surplus reality of the psychodrama.

After contracting with the protagonist for their goal, I also like to take a moment to contract with the protagonist about the process. Usually, this looks like me speaking to the protagonist in front of the group to affirm their control over the action of the psychodrama and inviting them to let me know if it is too fast or slow, too intense or boring, or if they feel like it needs to go in a different direction than we are heading. In the same short conversation with the protagonist, I find it helpful to also name any differences in identity that may impact the process. For example, if the drama is about racial trauma, I would be compelled to acknowledge my whiteness to the protagonist before starting and to approach my role as director with humility. The contracting and goal setting before the psychodrama are an important part of setting up the psychodrama for success. Including options, identity, and transparency in this process is particularly important for complex trauma survivors.

Scene Setting

As we shift from contracting into the surplus reality of the role play, we must consider the scene. Scene setting involves using objects in the room, role players, and the space available to symbolically represent the imaginal scene that is being enacted. Some psychodramas have elaborate scene setting processes, while others involve very little or no explicit scene setting. Initially, I did not place much value in the scene setting process, but over the years, I have come to see its value more and more often – especially in situations where the protagonist (or the group) is struggling to enter into surplus reality and act as if. The setting of the scene can really bring the process to life (Lesnik, 2024). However, if the situation at hand is related to a traumatic memory, I may intentionally avoid scene setting due to the risks involved with bringing the protagonist back to the scene of a trauma.

> Inviting the protagonist to engage in scene setting activates their imagination, helping to stabilize them within the surplus reality.

Inviting the protagonist to engage in scene setting activates their imagination, helping to stabilize them within the surplus reality. Scene setting often provides us with a lot more information about the nature of the situation, which can be invaluable. Furthermore, many times the setting of the scene illuminates new resources within the scene that can be drawn upon to help accomplish the contract or goal that has been established by the protagonist.

> In a psychodrama training group, I had a protagonist whose goal was related to expressing gratitude to a romantic partner. For this psychodrama, I wanted to ensure we that we chose a place that was meaningful for the protagonist and their relationship to their partner. She chose a bench next to a waterfall in a local park that was meaningful to her and her relationship. The waterfall in the scene seemed significant, so I invited her to enroll someone as the waterfall and to dialogue with this waterfall about what it could offer her. The interaction with the waterfall resulted in a deepening of perspective through metaphors related to water and time. In this specific psychodrama, the scene emerged with three separate snapshots of her relationship to her partner, each surrounding the same waterfall, at different stages in their relationship – past, present, and future. The waterfall seemed to core to the entire scene as the center piece that was a constant throughout time and constantly witnessing the growth within the relationship. If I hadn't asked for a setting for the psychodrama expressing gratitude to her partner, we would not have considered enrolling the waterfall from the park and missed out on the richness that if offered.

The scene setting process is useful for many reasons, as it activates the imagination of the protagonist and the group. It also facilitates a useful process of deconstructing the scene after the psychodrama is over, which can further help the protagonist come back from the surplus reality and psychodramatic trance of the enactment.

Enrolling, Prompting, and Interviewing Roles

One of the most essential directing skills in psychodrama is enrolling and interviewing roles within a scene. This becomes even more important when the protagonist and the role players are less familiar with psychodrama and less spontaneous within the process, as the director will likely need to be more active. There are two primary options to choose from when setting up a psychodrama scene in terms of enrolling the roles. We can identify a list of all of the roles that are needed for the enactment and cast all of the roles at the start of the psychodrama, placing them within the scene one by one. Or, we can simply start with one or two roles and let the spontaneity of the psychodrama lend itself to additional roles. I have found both options to have their benefits and their limitations. Here is an example of setting up the scene with all of the roles at the start:

> Jeremy has contracted to do a psychodrama speaking to his family about how his alcoholism has impacted them and how guilty and shameful he feels about his actions. He has set the scene of his family home's dining room table. The roles have already been defined as his wife and three kids. He also stated that he may need the group's support to have this conversation with the backing of other recovery alcoholics who understand. In this psychodrama, I simply had the protagonist enroll each of the roles in his family and invited anyone else in the group to stand behind him in the scene to play the role of support from his recovery community. Fortified by the group's support and encouragement, Jeremy practiced making amends to his family for his behavior in the past while committing to be a better husband and father.

In the aforementioned scene, the roles were already pre-determined based on the contract and the support needed to meet the contract. It made sense as a director to enroll all the roles and start the psychodrama without further delay. However, in other circumstances, the scene and roles may not be as clear, and it may make more sense to start with one role, allowing the other roles to unfold spontaneously within the scene.

> Terry's psychodrama contract is about letting go of self-hate to develop more self-love. He stated that his self-hate is not specific to any one example or past trauma but has been a constant throughout his life. He also started to quickly become emotional when talking about his self-hatred which left me concerned with keeping him within his window of tolerance. As the director of this psychodrama, I opted to start with one role to assess his responsivity to the process and see where it took us. I invited him to start by enrolling a double to help provide grounding, expression, and labeling of what he was experiencing internally. The double offered statements that Terry repeated such as "I have beat myself up for too long, it is time to stop," "I am a good man and

a good father," and "I have a good heart, and I deserve to love myself." The final statement about his heart seemed to deepen his emotional resolve as he repeated it, so I invited him to enroll his heart into the scene. He dialogued with his heart and explored his relationship to his heart. In the role reversal with his heart, I instructed Terry (as his heart) to tell himself about the goodness and love within his heart – "Terry's heart, can you tell us about the goodness within you?" "tell Terry about how much love you have to offer instead of self-hate," and "tell Terry what he needs to do to let go of self-hate and fill himself with self-love." These prompts deepened the process further and led Terry (in the role of his heart) to mention allowing God into his heart. Next, I enrolled God into the scene to talk to Terry about self-hate and self-love. From the role of God, Terry was able to see how painful it is for God to see Terry hating himself. This led to Terry as God encouraging him to love himself and offer additional love.

In the conversation with God, an important idea emerged of listening in for the voice of self-love while protecting your heart from the voice of self-hatred. After hearing this from God in the scene, I asked Terry to enroll self-love and self-hatred into the scene and to hear both of them speak to him at the same time to practice listening for one while quieting the other. This process involved back and forth dialogue with the voice of self-hatred while protecting his heart from it. Terry had the chance to tell self-hatred how much it has held him back throughout his life and how it has impacted his relationships. After role reversing Terry with self-hatred, I interviewed him in the role – "how long have you been with Terry and where did you come from?," "what does Terry need to do to quiet your voice and messages?," and "can you tell Terry what your purpose is – why did you keep showing up?." These questions challenged Terry to really consider the nature of his self-hatred and its relationship to him. He was able to access new action insights in the role reversal through this process, such as the understanding that self-hatred is composed of messages he adopted from bullying, the media, and verbal abuse. He also learned that his self-hatred was coming from a place of hurt and that if he healed the hurt, the self-hatred would quiet down. This conversation brought us back to his heart, carrying the hurt from the past, and his newfound self-love which had been enrolled earlier. The integrative action in the scene included Terry offering love to his wounded heart and strengthening his connection to self-love.

This example is quite different from the prior example in that scene was not explicitly defined, and we enrolled one role at a time into the scene rather than starting the drama with all (or most) of the roles already chosen. The latter option leaves much more room for spontaneity but may also limit the protagonist's (and the group's) ability to enter surplus reality as an imaginal scene has not been established, and, other than the contract/goal, we do not know exactly where we are headed. The first option of enrolling all of the roles early on allows for a faster transition into the surplus reality of the scene and more structure for the enactment. Additional roles can always be added as needed, even if they were not originally named at the start of the psychodrama. In my work with trauma-focused psychodrama, I tend to do more of the latter types of scenes as I do not want to enroll antagonist or perpetrator roles into a scene until I am sure that the protagonist can tolerate the intensity of the process with strength-based roles first. After the protagonist demonstrates their ability to access spontaneity with resources in the scene, I feel that I can confidently bring in an antagonist role without overwhelming the protagonist.

Interviewing roles is a foundational aspect of psychodrama directing and something that every director must learn. Once the role is enrolled, the director must prompt dialogue between the roles – otherwise, there is likely to be no action. I often liken this process to the experience of having two friends who have never met and you have finally gotten together, and you want to prompt as much dialogue between your two friends without you being involved in the discussion. This is what it is like to direct a psychodrama. You are there prompting and inviting discussion, suggesting topics, but trying to stay out of the conversation as much as possible. The healing comes in the interaction between the protagonist and the other roles, not the director. The interviewing of the role can only take place after it has been enrolled and the protagonist has been role reversed with the role.

The healing comes in the interaction between the protagonist and the other roles, not the director.

When enrolling roles into a psychodrama, there is a question of whether or not to have the protagonist first speak to the role or to first have the protagonist role reverse and speak as the role. For any perpetrator or antagonist roles, we need the protagonist to speak to the role first and demonstrate their capacity to interact with the role while in their window of tolerance before we can consider a role reversal. For strength roles (such as courage, resilience, or wisdom), I find it best to immediately role reverse and prompt the protagonist as the strength to speak to themselves. When working with interpersonal or transpersonal roles, I find it works best to ask the protagonist as themself to speak to the other role first before role reversing. Usually, there is a question or request to be made to the other role, which is a signal to reverse roles so the protagonist can then answer the question as the other role.

If there are nuances in the relationship that suggest that it would not be best for the role to speak to the protagonist, then it is okay to commence the role interview between the director and the role (with the protagonist role reversed into that role). For example, in the aforementioned scenario with Terry and his self-hatred, if Terry's self-hatred was volatile in the scene toward him and overwhelming, then it may be a good time to interview the role directly rather than have it continue to speak to Terry. Here is what that could look like:

> Terry steps into the role of his self-hatred and begins berating himself with harsh attacks. It becomes clear that Terry is struggling to soften in the role of self-hatred and continues to approach himself with strong energy, even after other interventions. As the director, I could shift the discussion away from Terry and talk between me and self-hatred (or even tell self-hatred to come with me to another part of the room to interview it). "Self-hatred, why are you so angry at Terry?," "Terry is offering you peace, but you continue to attack him, what is going on?," "can you tell me what you need to step back from Terry?," "if you and Terry continue like this, you are going to kill him – is that what you want?." These types of questions would offer more insight to me as the director, as well as to Terry playing the role of self-hatred, about the nature of his self-hatred and how to loosen up its hold on him.

Generally, it is best that the psychodramatic dialogue be between the protagonist and the role player, but there may be times, such as the aforementioned example, when it would be most helpful clinically to shift the dialogue between the director and the role.

One of the most frequently asked questions that I get from newer psychodrama directors is "how do I know questions to ask the roles in the psychodrama?" This is where the spontaneity of the process comes into play, but also the thoughtfulness of the director. There is not a script for the director to follow, but here are some general types of questions or prompts that may be helpful in directing and interviewing roles:

- Geared toward the contract or issue of the psychodrama
  - Can you tell the protagonist how you can help with the goal today?
  - Speak to the protagonist about how you can help with the issue they are struggling with.
- History of the relationship
  - How long have you been a part of the protagonist's life?
  - Remind the protagonist of the first time you showed up in their life.
  - What is a recent example of how you showed up with the protagonist?
  - How are you related to the other roles in the scene?
- Emotionally focused
  - How do you feel about the protagonist struggling with this issue today?
  - How can you help the protagonist with their feelings?

- What do you want to tell the protagonist about letting themself express their emotions?

- Somatic or body-oriented
  - Where do you show up in the protagonist's body?
  - Can you remind the protagonist how they can connect with you within their body?
  - Describe what that feels like within the protagonist's body.
  - Describe what it feels like the protagonist's body wants to do.

- Cognitive or belief
  - What do you think about the protagonist?
  - What beliefs can you see are holding the protagonist back?
  - Tell the protagonist what you want them to believe about themselves.

- Purpose, intent, and effect
  - Tell the protagonist what your purpose is for them.
  - Can you explain what your intent is for the protagonist?
  - When the protagonist connects with you, what changes?

- Future and recovery
  - Can you tell the protagonist how you can support their recovery?
  - What do you want for the protagonist going forward into the future?

- General questions
  - What else do you want to say to the protagonist, or what do they need to hear from you?
  - What is the most important thing to say to the protagonist?

These are certainly not an exhaustive list of questions or prompts for directing and interviewing roles, but these are often the types of questions I tend to use while directing. As a director, I am always trying to get to the most important messages and the messages related to the issue and goal of the psychodrama.

Psychodrama's Core Interventions

There are various interventions employed within a psychodrama; some of the core interventions include doubling, mirror position, role reversal, soliloquy, and concretization. Other foundational psychodrama interventions, which are described elsewhere in this book, include sculpting, social atom, games, and sociometry exercises.

The Double

Doubling is a core psychodrama intervention that can be employed by the director, by an audience member, or by a role player in the role of the double. The mechanics of doubling are quite simple but profound. Someone positions themselves next to the protagonist and places a hand on their shoulder (with consent) and then offers a one-sentence statement attempting to articulate something that has been unspoken for the protagonist thus far but may be true. The protagonist is invited to repeat the sentence if it is accurate for them or to change it and state what is true for them. Either way, doubling offers the protagonist a chance to deepen their expression in the moment and work at finding the words to label their experience. Badis and colleagues (2025) suggest a framework for decolonizing doubling to include statements related to strengths, ancestors, collectives, social rank, and social action. They also recommend the use of open-ended doubling statements rather than closed statements. For example, instead of doubling "I am going to call my local politicians and encourage others to vote in the election," one could double, "One social action that I'm ready to take is. . . ." This leaves it open for the protagonist to find what is true for them rather than using the content someone else provided as a reference point for their inner truth. Doubling helps the protagonist feel supported and understood by the group and the director. Doubling is also often used in conjunction with the role reversal intervention, where the protagonist assumes the role of another person or part of self and then receives doubling. This use of doubling can really help the protagonist expand their perception of the role and thus their sense of the situation and of themselves.

Doubling is important for trauma survivors in that it helps to find words for the sensations, experiences, and emotions related to the trauma.

Doubling is important for trauma survivors in that it helps to find words for the sensations, experiences, and emotions related to the trauma. Enrolling a double into a scene can be a stabilizing intervention for trauma work as it ensures that the protagonist has an ally by their side throughout the entire psychodrama. There are various types of double roles in psychodrama, which focus on different functions of doubling – cognitive double, expressive double, containing double, body double, somatic double, and others. Doubling is also the first phase of Moreno's child development theory (Moreno, 1952). When working with clients who have experienced inaccurate doubling, neglect, or trauma early in life, we may need to emphasize the use of doubling to try to satisfy some of the important functions of this unmet developmental need. Without sufficient doubling, there will be a lack of emotional awareness, accurate labeling, expression, and stability within the self.

The Mirror

The mirror intervention is an under-utilized technique in psychodrama but proves to be quite helpful in trauma-focused psychodrama and a core aspect of psychodramatic sculpting (see Chapter 7 for more on sculpting). The mirror phase is the second developmental phase in Moreno's child development theory and describes the child's newfound awareness of themself as a differentiated individual (1952). The mirror position is used by simply having the protagonist step out of the psychodrama scene, choose someone to stand in as themselves in the scene, and observe the scene from a distance. This intervention helps to titrate the intensity of trauma-based scenes and can effectively help a protagonist regulate emotions, develop new insight, and more accurately see themselves or others. I have seen entire trauma-focused psychodramas be facilitated with the protagonist in the mirror position to help desensitize them to the scene before having them enter the scene. I also find this intervention useful when the protagonist is in their defenses, in denial or minimizing something, unaware of how they are experienced by others, or really stuck in a repetitive behavior or response. The mirror takes them out of the first-person perspective and puts them into a third-person perspective to see things more objectively. Doubling can also be employed while the protagonist is in the mirror position to help with regulation, awareness, expression, or insight. The mirror position is also very useful as an integrative process at the very end of a psychodrama after the abreactive catharsis but before de-rolling. The protagonist can take the mirror position to reposition the roles in the scene one final time and further integrate, experience, and internalize the change that has taken place.

The Role Reversal

Role reversal is the linchpin of psychodrama (Moreno, 2012) and perhaps one of the most important interventions. We could argue that one of the fundamental differences between role-playing and psychodrama is the use of role reversal in psychodrama. The role reversal involves the protagonist physically and psychologically swapping places with another role in the scene. The other role player also engages in the role reversal to become the protagonist. The role reversal allows the protagonist to show the group how others in the scene behave toward them, effectively role training the other group member to accurately play the role. However, the role reversal also allows the protagonist to see things through another person's point of view and develop new insight, catharsis, integration, and an expansion of self. Role reversal can be combined with doubling or the director interviewing the role to deepen the experience. In my work with strengths-based roles and complex trauma, I often find it helpful to keep the protagonist role reversed for longer periods of time with a strengths-based role and continue to offer doubling or interviewing questions to them to help them access a state of spontaneity and further internalize the strengths-based role within the psyche. This embodied process of stepping into the shoes of another person can be quite transformative, emotional, and/or exciting. Role reversal can help to cultivate expression, awareness, spontaneity, insight, empathy, awareness, new social skills, integration, and closure (Dayton, 2005; Kellermann, 1992). It is important that the role reversal is completed by having the protagonist reverse roles back into the role of themself. The full circle process helps to consolidate the gains and integrate the new perspective back into the self.

Role reversal is the third child developmental stage in Moreno's system (1952), which describes the ability of a child to recognize that everyone else has their own perspectives, experiences, feelings, and internal worlds. If a client is struggling to engage in a role reversal, it may be an indicator that the interventions associated with earlier developmental stages (doubling and mirror) may need to be revisited before a role reversal will be successful. When working with trauma-based roles (especially perpetrators and wounded child roles), there are important guidelines to consider when using role reversal. These safety guidelines will be described in detail in Chapters 12 and 13. Essentially, these guidelines instruct us to approach role reversal with trauma-based roles differently from other roles. Traditionally, when a new role is brought into a psychodrama scene, it is common to immediately have the protagonist reverse roles to help show the role player how to play the role. However, with trauma-based roles, we want to see that the protagonist can first interact with the role in an adult ego state before we role reverse them due to the increased risks present.

Soliloquy

The intervention of soliloquy is one that comes from the theater world. With this technique, the protagonist is invited to articulate an internal monologue, acting as if nobody else were listening. The soliloquy is used to promote new insight, expression, or to slow down the psychodrama scene. This intervention is often used while the protagonist is role reversed with another role to help them develop a new perspective from that role. Practically speaking, I frequently find myself and other directors using the soliloquy intervention when we are not fully sure about what the protagonist is thinking or feeling. If a director is struggling to assess or track the protagonist's emotions or experience, the soliloquy can help provide transparency for the director and the group to better understand the internal experience of the protagonist.

Concretization

Psychodrama relies on symbolic representation. Concretization is when we use a physical object (often a scarf, empty chair, or role player) to symbolically represent another person, object, or part of self. In Chapter 4, we explored Amy's psychodrama where she concretized the hate and anger as two separate scarves and physically gave them back to her mom in the psychodrama scene. Charles' psychodrama on traumatic loss in Chapter 11 will depict using concretization to represent the forgiveness that he craves to stop blaming himself for his grandmother's death. In my previous book (Giacomucci, 2023, p. 80), I described it as "the psychodrama stage becomes a bridge between the inner reality of the client and the external reality emerging on the stage." Concretization and acting as if are the vehicles that allow us to move across that bridge into the inner reality of the client. Through concretization, the client and the group can experience physically what the protagonist has been experiencing psychologically (Watersong, 2011). Concretization becomes an important vehicle that allows the protagonist to convey their inner experience to the director and the group through a three-dimensional representation beyond words. Concretization is also particularly important for trauma survivors in that it offers a non-verbal alternative to telling the story of the trauma or trying to articulate the impact of the trauma for which there may be no words. Trauma often results in fragmentation and a confusion from undifferentiated affect, all of which can be explored, reorganized, and integrated through concretization in psychodrama. This effectively affords the trauma survivor with the opportunity to take back a sense of power and control over their inner experience and how the trauma has been internalized. Concretization is often used in phase 1 of trauma work to integrate a stronger awareness of resources, strengths, and supports (e.g., the Circle of Strengths in Chapter 5).

The psychodrama stage becomes a bridge between the inner reality of the client and the external reality emerging on the stage.

De-Rolling and Coming Back From Surplus Reality

At the end of a psychodramatic enactment, we must facilitate the group returning from surplus reality. This process includes the de-rolling of roles and the deconstruction of the scene. Often, this is a very quick process without much thought given to it. Role players are instructed to approach the protagonist, physically wipe off the role, and verbally state that they are not the role they played while affirming their real name. Then the protagonist is invited to physically deconstruct the scene, which further assists them in returning from the surplus reality.

However, in some cases, additional de-rolling is necessary due to the emotional intensity or involvement of the scene. Other ways to facilitate a more involved de-rolling can include utilizing more movement, playfulness, and physicality in the de-rolling. One fun option is to use a "scarf wash" where audience members each swirl a scarf in two rows facing each other – creating a station resembling a tunnel or car wash that role players playfully move through. When there are concerns that the protagonist or the group might not fully be able to de-role a role player, or the role player may have emotionally over-identified with the role, we can invite the role player to state multiple reasons why they are different from the role they played. This process can be further deepened by having the role player put the role they played into an empty chair in front of the group and speak to the role they played to differentiate themselves from it. After the de-rolling process has taken place, we move into the sharing phase of the psychodrama session.

The Sharing Phase

Sharing is the third phase of a psychodrama group. It is equally important to the warm-up and the action phases. The sharing provides a time for cooling down from the psychodrama and integrating the experience together. At its simplest level, group members each take a turn to share with the protagonist how they related to the psychodrama, what emotions emerged for them, and how they benefited personally from being a part of the process. The sharing is explicitly a time for group members to talk about themselves, not to analyze the drama, not to congratulate the protagonist, and not to give advice or feedback. The sharing is important for the group as it brings the focus off of the protagonist and back to the group-as-a-whole. The sharing also shows the protagonist that their work has helped other people and gives them an opportunity for role relief and time to consolidate the gains from the experience.

With more experienced psychodrama groups, the sharing process can be enriched by inviting role players to share from the role they played, as well as to share from themselves as group members. Often, there are experiences, feelings, thoughts, or perspectives that a role player may be aware of related to the role they are playing and the scene that they do not have a chance to articulate in the actual scene. Giving them the chance to share those insights may be valuable for the protagonist and the group. For example:

> Maria played the role of the protagonist's dog in a psychodrama scene. The dog was a source of comfort, grounding, and affection but wasn't given much time to speak in the drama because the contract focused the scene on a dilemma the protagonist was in where they had to choice between two options. Maria in the role of the dog, noticed a feeling of certainty that the protagonist would find their way through things emotionally and that she would love them no matter what. As the dog, Maria felt like the choice the protagonist had to make in the issue didn't matter in the larger scheme of things. When invited to share from the role, Maria shared her perspective – "as your dog, I noticed that I cared deeply about you and that it didn't matter to me which choice you made in your dilemma. I would be there and excited to see you no matter what." This sharing from the role helped the protagonist to see that the choice

they are confronted with, although a stressful one, wasn't going to change everything in their life and was likely to be a miniscule moment in the grand scheme of their life and the world. This new perspective helped to reduce the anxiety about making the "right" choice.

Sharing from the roles is a useful way to enrich the sharing phase of a psychodrama and often results in unexpected insights and perspectives.

Another consideration within the sharing phase of the process is the question of whether or not the director should share how they relate to the psychodrama. Traditionally, in psychodrama, the director shares how they relate, instead of trying to maintain emotional distance from the group. Each director must discern what is right for them in terms of sharing, vulnerability, and professionalism based on their comfort level, what would help the group, the populations they are working with, and the treatment setting. Furthermore, the nature of what is shared must be considered – should we share about our own past trauma or keep our sharing to more here-and-now experiences? In my client groups, I often am short on time, so I will not share and instead prioritize the sharing of the other group members. However, if there is time and I have something personal that I feel comfortable sharing that I think would help the group, then I will take the time to share that.

At the end of sharing, I find it helpful to give some short recommendations around self-care and, sometimes, will facilitate a short 5-minute improv or spontaneity game to ensure that all participants are emotionally grounded before ending. I remind clients to seek help if the psychodrama elicits difficult emotions or memories over the next few days and to take care of themselves physically with adequate rest, hydration, and nutrition. I let participants know that it is common to be tired or exhausted after a psychodrama and that it is a sign that they did some emotional work during the group. I also inform the group that it can take hours, days, or weeks to fully digest and integrate the experience from a psychodrama. I encourage everyone to try to reinforce the work that they did rather than undoing the work internally. For example, at the end of Terry's psychodrama, which was described earlier in this chapter, I may insist that each group member intentionally connect with the goodness within their heart, their higher power, and self-love – rather than reverting into old patterns of self-hatred.

At the end of the group, it is ultimately the director's responsibility to assess that each person is emotionally stable after the session. Sometimes, the sharing can destabilize group members, and additional time may be needed for closure and grounding. This is especially common if other group members start to share their own trauma stories after the psychodrama to relate to the protagonist. The director needs to be attuned to the needs of the group throughout the sharing and utilize interventions as needed to ensure that it is emotionally safe to end the group.

Conclusion

Facilitating a psychodrama is a complex process that emerges differently from session to session and is influenced by the presentation of the group, the preferences of the protagonist, the nature of the topic, the setting of the treatment, and the style of the director. Psychodrama's five elements and three phases provide a structure for the facilitator to employ a variety of interventions as needed. The action phase of the session commences with a protagonist selection and contracting with the protagonist, followed by scene setting and enrolling of roles, interaction between protagonist and roles, de-rolling, and sharing.

References

Badis, D., Hernandez, C. L., Nieto, L., Ruiz Esparza, M. P., & Tkachuck, C. (2025). A world with many worlds: Decolonizing education with action methods. In S. Giacomucci, H. Fleury, & D. Altinay (Eds.), *Psychodrama in education: Creativity and experiential teaching around the world* (pp. 137–161). Springer Nature.

Cruz, A., Sales, C. M., Alves, P., & Moita, G. (2018). The core techniques of Morenian psychodrama: A systematic review of literature. *Frontiers in Psychology*, *9*, 1263.

Dayton, T. (2005). *The living stage: A step-by-step guide to psychodrama, sociometry, and experiential group therapy*. Health Communications Inc.

Giacomucci, S. (2021). *Social work, sociometry, and psychodrama: Experiential approaches for group therapists, community leaders, and social workers*. Springer Nature. https://doi.org/10.1007/978-981-33-6342-7

Giacomucci, S. (2023). *Trauma-informed principles in group therapy, psychodrama, and organizations: Action methods for leadership*. Routledge.

Kellermann, P. F. (1992). *Focus on psychodrama: The therapeutic aspects of psychodrama*. Jessica Kingsley.

Lesnik, P. (2024). An exploration of scene setting in psychodrama: The sociometry of place. *Journal of Psychodrama, Sociometry, and Group Psychotherapy*, *70*(1), 1–15.

Moreno, J. L. (1952). Psychodramatic production techniques. *Group Psychotherapy, Psychodrama, & Sociometry*, *4*, 273–303.

Moreno, Z. T. (2012). *To dream again: A memoir*. Mental Health Resources.

Watersong, A. (2011). Surplus reality: The magic ingredient in psychodrama. *Journal of the Australian and Aotearoa New Zealand Psychodrama Association*, *20*, 18–27.

Chapter 7

Psychodrama-Like Interventions, Sculptures, Structures, and Empty Chairs

It is possible to do psychodrama without doing a full psychodrama. I recommend that anyone new to psychodrama start by learning to facilitate sociometry exercises first, then psychodrama in individual settings and psychodrama-like interventions or psychodrama structures, and then full psychodramas. Psychodrama-like interventions and psychodrama structures offer more contained and prescriptive group processes that utilize psychodrama techniques without engaging in a longer and fully spontaneous psychodrama enactment. There are countless psychodrama-like interventions and psychodrama structures, so this chapter is certainly not a comprehensive list. A full psychodrama often requires two to three hours of time, which is simply not possible in many treatment settings. As such, the method needed to be modified to meet the changing times of managed care and shorter group lengths. For anyone leading groups that are less than 2 hours in length, it will make more sense to utilize psychodrama vignettes, psychodrama-like interventions, or psychodrama structures instead of full dramas. In my trainings, when utilizing these types of methods instead of full psychodramas, I am often reminded of just how powerful and helpful these techniques can be without needing to create a longer and more complicated psychodrama scene. Shorter psychodramatic structures may be a good alternative for groups with complex trauma survivors to ease into full psychodramas later.

Psychodrama methodology includes a variety of psychodrama interventions, which are outlined in Chapter 6. These interventions can also be employed outside of full psychodrama enactments. For example, doubling can be easily incorporated into talk therapy sessions or any sociometry exercise. Role reversal is another tool that can be easily utilized during sociometry warm-ups – especially during spectrograms when exploring who are at the opposite ends of the spectrum. An empty chair can be brought in during a powerful moment of sharing during a floor check to shift into a short psychodrama vignette for a few minutes. The mirror position can be employed during hands-on-shoulder sociometry to help a group member see how they are chosen by others in the group, even if they sometimes feel like an isolate. Incorporating psychodrama interventions into sociometry exercises can feel intimidating at first, but it is actually quite

DOI: 10.4324/9781003639497-7

simple and can be done very seamlessly. This allows the group process to transition back and forth between sociometry and psychodrama rather than treating them as two distinctly separate parts of the group process.

Incorporating psychodrama interventions into sociometry exercises can feel intimidating at first but is actually quite simple and can be done very seamlessly.

Improv Games and Spontaneity Exercises

Many psychodramatists utilize a variety of improv games, spontaneity exercises, or drama games. These types of exercises vary in complexity, scope, and involvement. The commonalities between most of these exercises seem to be that they are short and provoke a sense of excitement, spontaneity, and playfulness within the group. I recommend using these types of exercises as ice-breakers to loosen up the group, as well as keeping them in mind at the end of the group session if the group needs some extra grounding after an intense psychodrama process. I will frequently employ one of these exercises to help the group reconnect with a sense of playfulness, spontaneity, and here-and-now presence after an emotionally tough session.

Some of my favorite simple exercises of this nature include the sound ball, near and far, evil twin, and what are you doing? In the sound ball game, participants stand in a circle, and the facilitator holds up an imaginary ball while explaining the instructions – "I'm going to throw this ball to someone and make a sound. Whoever I throw it to must catch the ball while repeating the same sound." Then that person throws the ball to someone new while making a new sound. This exercise results in a playful process of making spontaneous sounds, while group members throw and catch an imaginary ball. I sometimes modify it to involve strengths that group members see in each other rather than only the sound. This deepens the process and makes it a bit more emotionally stimulating and vulnerable.

The near and far game involves each person secretly choosing someone else in the room whom they will try to stay physically close to while also choosing someone else whom they will try to physically avoid. I often give these prompts one at a time to create multiple rounds of the game. Then I like to combine them together to have everyone moving around the room simultaneously while trying to avoid one person and trying to stay near another person.

Evil twin has become my favorite game for more spontaneous and experienced groups. It involves two volunteers stepping forward to become the two main characters of a scene. Then two more volunteers emerge to become the evil twins (or, in psychodrama, I call it the evil double) for each of the main characters. The rest of the group spontaneously co-creates the roles, the scene, and the objective that the two main characters are trying to accomplish (e.g., person 1 is a car salesman and person 2 is trying to buy a new car). The catch is that the evil twins can offer doubling statements to the main characters at any time to sabotage the scene, and the main characters are required to repeat the doubling statement and roll with it in the scene. I find it helps create a sense of urgency to set a timer for two or three minutes to keep the scenes short and focused.

"What are you doing?" is another favorite improv game. It involves everyone standing in a circle. The facilitator begins by acting something out, and the person next to them is instructed to ask them, "What are you doing?" However, the facilitator acting something out tells them that they are doing something completely different from what they are actually acting out. Then, that person has to act out what was said. The next person asks them what they are doing, and they say something completely different than what they are actually acting out. They then have to act out what was said. This continues around the circle until everyone has taken a turn.

Entire books have been devoted to these types of group processes (Dayton, 1990; Hall, 2014; Wiener & Axelrod, 2024). I encourage every psychodrama practitioner to have a few improv games and spontaneity exercises in their back pocket for when groups are in need of an icebreaker, some movement after lunch, or a playful cool-down exercise.

I encourage every psychodrama practitioner to have a few improv games and spontaneity exercises in their back pocket for when groups are in need of an icebreaker, some movement after lunch, or a playful cool-down exercise.

Psychodramatic Letter Writing and Journaling

Psychodramatic letter writing and psychodramatic journaling are two simple alternatives to full psychodramas, both of which keep the process contained to pen and paper (Dayton, 2005; Giacomucci, 2021). These tools can be used in a group setting, an individual setting, or even assigned as homework in between sessions. When writing psychodramatic letters, the client is instructed to write a letter to someone, a part of self, to themselves at a different point in time, or to something else. This letter is often written for the purpose of expression or catharsis. For example, they could write a letter expressing anger to a parent, expressing sadness to a deceased loved one, or expressing gratitude to a friend. The psychodramatic letter writing process can be deepened by instructing clients to then write a response letter from the other role to themselves. For example, write an apology letter you wish you could receive from someone you are angry at, write a letter from a deceased loved one that you wish you could receive to have closure, or write a letter of forgiveness from a higher power to yourself. This effectively facilitates a psychological role reversal in a simple, contained way. Psychodramatic letters are often written to pets, depression, addiction, God, ancestors, future children, inner children, future selves, family members, friends, body parts, defenses, or other parts of self.

Psychodramatic journaling is similar to letter writing; however, the client is writing a journal entry instead of a letter to/from someone. Psychodramatic journaling could be thought of as a role reversal and soliloquy on paper. For example, we might ask a client to write a journal entry from themselves in the future no longer impacted by the trauma, or from themselves as a child at the time of the trauma, or from the perspective of their parent witnessing them experience something difficult, or from the perspective of a fly on the wall during an event. Psychodramatic journaling helps to promote expression, catharsis, and a deepened insight into one's experience.

Role Wheel and Short Role Plays

The role wheel is a simple but dynamic exercise that is generally used with a mix of psychodramatic and sociodramatic roles and scenes (Giacomucci & Ehrhart, 2021). The group is split into two groups, creating concentric circles with each person having a partner in front of them. The facilitator assigns a role to each group, and partners are instructed to spontaneously enact a scene with their partner in the roles that they have been assigned. Each scene is about two to three minutes in length to keep it short. There is no audience to avoid performance anxiety and focus more on the process of the role play. After each scene, the director instructs everyone to de-role, say bye to their partner, and the outer group rotates one person – resulting in everyone having a new partner for the next scene. With this exercise, I find it helpful to start with playful and easy roles and scenes before moving into more difficult roles and scenes. I also find it particularly important to ensure that most of the roles and the scenes are grounded in the clients' actual experience so that the exercise does not feel useless or just silly. Here are some of the more common roles and scenes that I use in my client groups when facilitating the role wheel:

Role 1: A client in detox trying to avoid attending the required therapy group
Role 2: A staff member at the detox who is required to ensure everyone is at the group session
Role 1: A long-term, motivated member of a trauma therapy group welcoming a new member
Role 2: Someone joining a trauma therapy group for the first time with many defenses, fears, and insecurities about joining the group

Role 1: A client completing treatment successfully and expressing their gratitude to someone who supported them
Role 2: Someone receiving gratitude for how they supported their partner throughout their treatment
Role 1: A client in early recovery trying to set a boundary with someone who they know isn't healthy for them
Role 2: Someone who is not living the healthiest lifestyle trying to convince their partner to do something unhealthy with them (such as engage in drug use or something illegal)
Role 1: A person in long-term recovery who is making amends to someone that they hurt during their addiction
Role 2: Someone receiving amends and offering forgiveness to their partner
Role 1: Yourself a few years from now in recovery from trauma, catching up with your group member you have not seen in years
Role 2: Yourself a few years from now in recovery from trauma, catching up with your group member you have not seen in years

In this last scene, I often present it as "we are fast forwarding time a few years and you are each yourself in recovery a few years from now." This gives each of them a chance to become their future selves and reflect on what their life would be like having maintained their trauma recovery work and completed some of their treatment goals.

The role wheel exercise can be done with more sociodramatic roles to give clients more emotional distance from the scenes. Or, it can be done with more psychodramatic prompts to encourage more emotional experiencing. For example, the amends scene is much more emotionally involved if the clients are practicing making a real amends to someone they actually hurt in the past, compared to making an imaginary amends as a character in a random scene. The role wheel is often a very fun, meaningful, and emotional experience for participants and can easily stand alone as the primary group exercises for a session. It can also be used as a warm-up for a psychodrama enactment.

Beyond the use of the role wheel as a structure, short role plays can be utilized with a group audience to explore collective or personal themes. These can be short and playful or can be longer, more elaborate, and touch on deeper emotions. One memorable example of using short role plays came from an event I attended in Philadelphia about youth and police conflicts (see longer write-up in Giacomucci, 2021). During this event, a moderator elicited short stories from youth and from police about their difficult encounters with each other in the community. Both groups felt dehumanized and disrespected by the other group. Then the stories were spontaneously enacted in front of the group, but the youth played the role of the police officers, and the police played the roles of the youth. These enactments ranged from routine traffic stops to noise complaints at the park. The role plays were short but led to a more embodied understanding of each other and the difficult aspects of each other's roles.

Small Group Skits or Sculpts

Another psychodrama-like intervention is the use of short skits – sometimes called "sculpts," but not to be confused with psychodramatic sculpting, which will be described later in this chapter. These short skits tend to involve a larger group being split into smaller groups based on a sociometric similarity. The smaller groups are tasked with generating a short skit or enactment to play back in front of the larger group. They are usually very short, perhaps between 10 seconds to 1 minute in length, and are mostly non-verbal but do sometimes include some speaking. To be honest, I was never a big fan of this exercise as a participant because it felt performative and superficial to me most of the time. However, in 2024, I attended the Brazilian Psychodrama Conference and, to my surprise, nearly every workshop included this exercise as a warm-up. Every time I have seen it in the USA, the small groups each took their turn to play back their skit, and that was it. In Brazil, the facilitators employed other psychodrama interventions during the skits to deepen the experience for the group. For example, a small group did a short enactment about someone grieving the loss of a family member. Instead of simply letting the small group act it out, clap for them, and move on to the next one, the facilitator paused the small group enactment and initiated doubling for the grieving person in the scene. This very quickly dropped the group into a deeper emotional experience of the scene. In another small group skit about grief within the same workshop, the facilitator used role reversal to invite audience members to step into the scene and offer one sentence to their own loved one who had died. Another skit involved audience members offering messages to console the grieving person in the scene. After seeing and experiencing how these small group skits or sculpts could be deepened with some simple psychodrama interventions, I have a newfound appreciation for them and have begun to use them more often.

One of my recent workshops was focused on archetypal and spiritual roles. During this workshop, I had group members break into smaller groups and share about a spiritual or archetypal role that they felt connected to. Next, I tasked them with summarizing the story of that character into three sentences that follow the arc of a traditional storyline – (1) set the scene, (2) encounter difficulty, and (3) grow from the adversity. Then they collectively chose one story from their own group and created a short three-part skit to enact the storyline. Various characters were mentioned, including superheroes (spiderman and batman), religious or spiritual figures (such as Our Lady of Guadalupe), archetypes (the rebel and the wounded healer), and other mythological creatures (a dragon and a phoenix). Each group enacted their three-scene skit, during which I paused it at climactic moments and invited doubling, role reversal, or opportunities for audience members to interact with the roles and the scene. This exercise, when combined with psychodrama interventions, offers a nice warm-up to role-playing and helps to cultivate a space for creative co-creation and collaboration within the group process.

Empty Chairs as Sociodramatic or Psychodramatic Structure

The empty chair technique can be modified for an unlimited number of group topics and processes. A single empty chair or multiple empty chairs can be employed as a psychodramatic structure or vignette. One of the simplest structures is to place an empty chair into the center of the group room and invite any group member to approach the empty chair and speak to someone that they have unresolved business in the empty chair. This simple empty chair process can be modified to focus on messages of gratitude, anger, grief, forgiveness, boundaries, or any other clinical issue. The empty chair process in a group can be contained to a specific role – such as God, younger self, future self, addiction, depression, or any other role. Containing it to a single role would help focus the group process and help participants warm up in a more specific way. The empty chair technique can be employed with additional psychodrama interventions such as doubling and role reversal to deepen the process and provide more integration.

The empty chair technique can be modified for an unlimited number of group topics and processes.

One of my favorite uses of the empty chair is to place multiple empty chairs in the center of the room and define them as different sociodramatic roles. For example, I might use the roles of "a patient in residential treatment" and "a family member" and then invite patients to come and double for what each role might be thinking or feeling based on different prompts or at different milestones in the treatment process. Or, I might put out empty chairs in a line along a timeline and label each chair as a different point in the recovery process – "during trauma," "starting trauma therapy," "during trauma processing in therapy," and "at the end of trauma therapy having completed one's goals." Another simple structure using empty chairs is to have one chair represent "the part that wants to" and another empty chair for "the part that doesn't want to." Then I could give various situations, such as "getting out of bed in the morning," "entering treatment for the first time," "setting a boundary," "telling a trauma story in therapy," and so on. With each new situation, clients can step into either role and articulate what they imagine that part would be thinking or feeling based on the situation. These exercises can easily shift from sociodramatic to psychodramatic by having clients imagine themselves in the roles and speaking from their own parts of self in the roles. This process can transition smoothly into a protagonist-based vignette with someone exploring two parts of self in conflict in more detail with doubling and role reversal.

Timelines With Sociometry, Sociodrama, or Psychodrama

Timelines are versatile interventions that can be employed through pen-to-paper instructions, sociometry, sociodrama, and/or psychodrama interventions (Dayton, 2014). It is even possible to utilize all four approaches in a single timeline group exercise. When working with complex trauma, however, it is important to be sensitive about timeline exercises as the timeline is more likely to be emotionally overwhelming for complex trauma survivors. Asking someone with CPTSD to make a trauma timeline in early recovery may lead to dysregulation, dissociation, or relapse. Instead, I would recommend diversifying the timeline to include various themes instead of only trauma, and I would recommend starting in the future to use the future self as a stabilizing resource on the timeline before getting to the trauma. Wells (2018) describes the use of a resiliency timeline to plot the development of support, resources, and personal strengths within one's life. I often will start a timeline exercise on paper and then shift it into sociometry by having the group imagine a life-size timeline in the room from wall to wall (similar to a spectrogram). Then I would offer prompts to the group, inviting them to stand at different ages on their timeline – "how old were you when you felt most connected in your life?," "how old were you when you experienced a difficult loss?," "how old were you when you experienced a trauma that you know you need to revisit to heal from?," and "how old will you be 3 years from now?" With the last prompt, I would initiate discussions about each person's goals for the future and vision of one's self in recovery.

The timeline could be used sociodramatically in various ways (one of which is described above in the empty chair subsection). Another sociodramatic timeline structure could be to have the group co-create a story about a character's life experiences (positive and negative) as they move through each developmental stage in their life, experience trauma/loss, and cultivate a life of recovery. Using sociodrama, this story would be spontaneously generated while being acted out by the group as the character walks their timeline. The timeline could also be walked psychodramatically with clients narrating major events in their life, as they walk the life-sized timeline in the room. As they offer a soliloquy of major life events, other interventions can be employed to enrich the process, such as doubling, enrolling roles, role reversal, concretization, and the mirror position. With complex trauma, the psychodramatic timeline exercise can be quite difficult, so I would urge facilitators to first resource the protagonist with supportive roles. For example, the last time I used this intervention, the protagonist picked

God as a resource, and they walked their timeline with God next to them at all times to support them.

Psychodramatic Sculpting

Psychodramatic sculpting is another useful method when a full psychodrama is not possible, time is limited, and/or the facilitator is new to directing psychodramas. Psychodramatic sculpting differs from a full psychodrama in multiple ways – (1) the protagonist is in the mirror position most of the session (and not in the role of themselves in the center of the scene), (2) the roles are enrolled quickly with minimal lines, and (3) the scene is more static with a focus on proximity, posture, and non-verbal expression (with some talking) but not as much movement as a psychodrama. Psychodrama sculpts are often more prescriptive in that they tend to have a theme or set roles already, rather than being more spontaneous in enrolling roles along the way, like in some psychodramas. For example, we might sculpt a meaningful memory with a client, a social atom, a constellation of personal strengths, a family of origin scene, a frozen moment of trauma (Dayton, 2014), or an internal scene with parts of self (Giacomucci, 2021). Sculpting tends to be a much slower-paced version of psychodrama, which can be advantageous for working with complex trauma where there is a higher risk of overwhelming group members. The use of the mirror position throughout the psychodramatic sculpting process helps to titrate the intensity of the process by keeping the protagonist distant from the scene or sculpture.

Psychodramatic Structures

Psychodramatic structures (or structured psychodrama as Bill Coleman describes it) are essentially short psychodrama processes that are replicated with the same roles or mechanics. There are countless psychodramatic structures, and each year more continue to be created. The purpose of this section is not to outline or list all psychodramatic structures, but to provide an introduction to the nature of psychodramatic structures (see White, 2002, or Dayton, 2014 for resources with various psychodramatic structures described). Most psychodramatic structures include a few pre-selected roles, a theme or topic, and an already established goal or contract. Many psychodramatic structures have an established beginning, middle, and end, which helps keep the process contained (Coleman, 2012). Trauma expert, Bessell van der Kolk, popularized the use of psychodrama structures through his 2014 book, *The Body Keeps the Score*, and his psychodrama workshop offerings. However, his approach seems to be more from the lens of the Pesso-Boyden System Psychomotor than from psychodrama theory and practice.

Psychodramatic structures are essentially short psychodrama processes that are replicated with the same roles or mechanics.

One example of a psychodramatic structure is the recovery courtroom structure, which has a template of roles (defendant/protagonist, judge/therapist, the prosecuting attorney, the defense attorney, and the jury), an already established theme of exploring a protagonist's recovery plan, and a goal of helping to strengthen a protagonist's aftercare plan. The courtroom scene is set up in the room with roles cast and the therapist taking on the judge's role. The protagonist, with the help of their defense attorney, attempts to defend the protagonist's recovery plan and aftercare plan. The prosecuting attorney attempts to poke holes in the plan and challenge the integrity of the plan. Doubling and role reversal can be employed to deepen the experience. After both parties have said their piece, the audience/jury votes on whether or not the protagonist's aftercare plan is solid enough to maintain recovery. Sometimes, it can help to modify the defense attorney role into more of an emotional support role, as it impacts the jury if the defense attorney is speaking for the protagonist the entire time. After the jury votes on the soundness of the client's recovery plan, it can be helpful to elicit constructive feedback from those who voted against the protagonist – while also asking for positive feedback from those who voted in favor of the protagonist's recovery plan. Another role that can be included is the scribe or stenographer who can write down the main components of the plan, as well as the feedback group members provided on which aspects of the plan were strong and how they could be improved.

Another simple psychodramatic structure is called "P.S. Letters," where a chair is placed to represent the protagonist role, another chair across from them to represent another person in their life, and a third chair next time them for the P.S. messages. The offer is made by the director for a protagonist to volunteer and take the first chair. Their task is to articulate a message that they need to express to someone in their life (the empty chair across from them). Once they have said what they need to say, group members take turns stepping into the third chair to offer "P.S.'s" to add to the end of the message (essentially, this is a simplified version of doubling). The protagonist is instructed to repeat the P.S. if it is true for them or change it to make it true. This exercise lends itself to multiple short psychodrama vignettes, each with multiple P.S. statements added at the end. In facilitating this exercise with trauma groups, I have found that it often will go quickly into perpetrator work unless the director contains it with specific prompts. For example, I might start by inviting someone to offer a message of gratitude. Then allow one to three vignettes that involve expressions of anger, guilt, shame, sadness, or fear. Then end with a final vignette that focuses on a hopeful message.

Bill Coleman (2012) describes a psychodrama structure that he named the Denial Buster (Rebecca Walters teaches it with an updated name of the Angle of Choice). This involves setting up eight chairs in the center of the room in the shape of a "V." The protagonist chair is the chair at the apex of the "V," and across from them is the chair for the issue they are struggling with. The first line of three chairs is designated as a timeline of the problem getting progressively worse every six months (though this can be modified in the number of chairs and designated time). The protagonist transitions through each of the three chairs, articulating from each place how the problem has evolved into a bigger problem every six months. Role players from the group take on each of the three additional roles. Next, the remaining three chairs are designated as a timeline of the problem getting progressively better every six months. The protagonist role reverses with each of the remaining three chairs, articulating how things have gotten better at each stage. Three more role players assume the three new roles. From this experience, the protagonist is able to work through any denial about the need for change and muster more motivation to change their relationship with whatever the issue is. This structure results in the protagonist exploring the potentials of their issue escalating and becoming progressively worse or better while considering the action steps they may need to take to affect change in their life. I find it helpful to also include two chairs behind the protagonist for two resources to help them with this change. For example, I used it in a training recently where the protagonist wanted to change their relationship to dissociation. They chose mindfulness and a close friend as resources that could help them with this change. The resources sat behind the protagonist and supported them as they faced the two timelines and their dissociation in front of them. The protagonist experienced a catharsis when enrolling the roles. I then had all roles speak at the same time and instructed the protagonist to practice using their mindfulness rather than dissociating with the chaos. Then they asked to move dissociation (and the timeline of dissociation getting worse) further away to the other side of the room. After doing so, I used the supportive roles for an integrative moment at the end to hear a final message from each before de-rolling.

Coleman (2011) describes another psychodramatic structure called The Little Willingness, which reflects the stages of change in action. This structure starts with the protagonist enrolling the role of something that they want to change, such as shame. The protagonist reverses roles with the shame and is interviewed by the director. A group member takes on the role as the protagonist reverses roles back. Next, three chairs are placed in the room to represent three stages of change – (1) "I am not willing to give up my shame because . . . .," (2) "I might be able to give up my shame if . . .," and (3) "I am now completely willing to give up my shame because. . . ." The protagonist is facilitated through each of these three stages, while the director continues to interview them in each place and deepen their insight. At the end, the protagonist enrolls resources into the scene that can help them make the change that they want to make (in this case, letting go of shame). The protagonist gives a supportive line from each resource to themselves about the shame or longer role reversals can be employed if there is time. At the end, the protagonist listens to all of the supportive messages from the supportive roles to motivate them to create the change they hope to make in their life.

Another simple structure is a three-chair structure focused on ambivalence, inner conflict, or role conflict. The protagonist takes the middle chair and places the two conflicting parts of self in opposing chairs on either side of them. Role reversal, mirror positions, and doubling are used to explore both parts and gain clarity on which part to move closer or further away. This could be done with inner parts of self, such as "the part that wants to be in trauma therapy" and "the part that doesn't want to be in trauma therapy." This can also be employed with other roles in conflict (or seemingly in conflict) with each other such as trauma and trauma recovery, addiction and addiction recovery, self-blame and self-forgiveness, self-love and self-hate, denial and acceptance, life and death, angel and devil, fear and courage, shame and self-worth, victim and survivor, vulnerability and guardedness, closeted self and out self, burnout and compassion satisfaction, vicarious trauma and VPTG, and so on. Any one of these three-chair psychodramatic structures could be utilized psychodramatically or sociodramatically (or with a combination of both, as described in Chapter 15's section on psychosociodrama). The aforementioned examples for this three-chair structure could be short 5–10 minute processes (with one more or more protagonists) or drawn out into a longer 45-minute process with additional roles enrolled as needed. When working with some of the tougher roles listed above, or less resourced groups or protagonists, it is advised to enroll an extra supportive role or two to help stabilize the protagonist. This could be the role of the double, a strength, a spiritual role or wisdom figure, an interpersonal support, or even group members stepping in as themselves to support.

Conclusion

Full psychodrama enactments are not always possible due to limitations in time, warm-up, willingness, containment, stability, or the director's level of competence. In these situations, it is advantageous to employ psychodrama-like interventions such as psychodramatic letter writing, psychodramatic journaling, the role wheel or short role plays, sociodramatic empty chairs, or psychodramatic vignettes. Timeline exercises can be employed with pen-to-paper instructions, sociometry prompts, and sociodramatic or psychodramatic processes. Psychodramatic sculptures can be used to keep the process contained and keep the protagonist in the mirror position for slower-paced psychodrama scenes. Furthermore, psychodramatic structures offer a pre-packaged but adaptable structure for using psychodrama techniques with an already developed set of roles, objectives, or themes.

Psychodramatic structures offer a pre-packaged but adaptable structure for using psychodrama techniques with an already developed set of roles, objectives, or themes.

References

Coleman, B. (2011). The willingness exercise structured psychodrama: An illustrated description. *The Journal of Psychodrama, Sociometry, and Group Psychotherapy, 60*(1), 79–86.

Coleman, B. (2012). The Denial Buster, A structured psychodrama: An illustrated description. *The Journal of Psychodrama, Sociometry, and Group Psychotherapy, 60*(2), 31–35.

Dayton, T. (1990). *Drama games: Techniques for self-development*. Health Communications Inc.

Dayton, T. (2005). *The living stage: A step-by-step guide to psychodrama, sociometry, and experiential group therapy*. Health Communications Inc.

Dayton, T. (2014). *Relational Trauma Repair (RTR) therapist's guide (Revised edition)*. New York: Innerlook, Inc.

Giacomucci, S. (2021). *Social work, sociometry, and psychodrama: Experiential approaches for group therapists, community leaders, and social workers*. Springer Nature. https://doi.org/10.1007/978-981-33-6342-7

Giacomucci, S. (2023). *Trauma-informed principles in group therapy, psychodrama, and organizations: Action methods for leadership*. Routledge.

Giacomucci, S., & Ehrhart, L. (2021). Introduction to psychodrama psychotherapy: A trauma and addiction group vignette. *group, 45*(1), 69–86.

Hall, W. (Ed.). (2014). *The playbook: Improv games for performers*. Fratelli Bologna.

van der Kolk, B. A. (2014). *The body keeps the score: Brain, mind, and body in the healing of trauma*. New York: Viking Press.

Wells, J. (2018). Psychodramatic resiliency timeline. *The Journal of Psychodrama, Sociometry, and Group Psychotherapy, 66*(1), 131–140.

White, L. (2002). *The action manual: Techniques for enlivening group process and individual counselling*. YWCA Life Skills Publications Department.

Wiener, D. J., & Axelrod, A. (2024). *The rehearsals for growth practitioner manual (1.5 edition)*. W.W. Norton & Company.

Chapter 8

Strengths-Based Roles and Resourcing in Psychodrama

Sometimes, the problem is the absence of the solution. Moreno argues that anxiety is caused by the absence of spontaneity (1978). Perhaps many of the other common psychosocial problems are also caused by the absence of spontaneity or the absence of the solution. Resourcing is an essential component of any and all trauma-focused modalities. Helping trauma survivors connect to new resources within themselves, within the group, and within the community allows for the establishment of safety and a platform for healing from the trauma. The safety provided by resources offers trauma survivors a sense of stability and assurance as they continue in their healing process. There are many different types of resources, including internal, interpersonal, and transpersonal resources. In psychodrama practice, we often unconsciously leverage the double, the group, and the director as additional resources within the process. Resourcing is primarily approached as an essential first step in the trauma recovery process before trauma processing, but, in many cases, resourcing alone can promote spontaneous healing. When it comes to complex trauma and CPTSD, resourcing needs to be prioritized and may require more time devoted to it than in other groups.

Sometimes the problem is the absence of the solution.

The Importance of Re-source-ing

A quick Google search on the etymology of the word "resourcing" brings back results such as "to rise again," "a means to supply a deficiency or need," and "an action or strategy that can be called upon during difficulty or an emergency situation." At its core, "resourcing" is a process of reconnecting clients to their *source*. To the source of what? Perhaps it is a reconnecting to the Source (God), the source of life, or the source of spontaneity. In Morenean philosophy, these are all the same, but we can simply expand our thinking to be inclusive for agnostic

DOI: 10.4324/9781003639497-8

and/or atheist thinkers. The process of re-source-ing then is the process of helping the client or the group reconnect to spontaneity.

At its core, "re-source-ing" is a process of reconnecting clients to source.

Spontaneity is the most important factor in psychodrama (as described in Chapter 3) and the element that makes any kind of change possible. The process of enrolling strengths, safety, and support within the psychodramatic process facilitates the protagonist (and the group) reconnecting to the source of spontaneity. This spontaneity allows for a new response to the old trauma or an adequate response to a new situation. Operating from a state of spontaneity affords the protagonist and the group with the opportunity to change their relationship to the trauma.

Enrolling resources within the psychodrama scene offers another opportunity to further warm-up the group and the protagonist to the intensity of the action that is yet to come with more complex roles. For participants newer to psychodrama, the use of strengths-based roles first helps familiarize everyone with the process of role reversal, doubling, and role-playing. At the same time, the use of supportive roles for resourcing offers the director with an important opportunity to assess the protagonist and the group in action. If I am directing a protagonist who is on the edge of their window of tolerance from interacting with a supportive role, then I will not enroll any trauma-based roles into the scene as there are indicators that it will be too much. If my protagonist is rejecting the supportive roles or unable to access adaptive information or a spontaneity state in the supportive roles, then I am not going to move forward with trauma-based roles, as the protagonist is likely to get stuck in the trauma vortex without allowing support in. The resourcing part of the psychodrama also gives the director information about the group's participation and engagement level.

Resources provide safety and stabilization within the psychodrama scene and within the self. A protagonist speaking alone to a trauma-based role is a very different experience than a protagonist speaking to a trauma-based role with a team of supportive roles surrounding them. In many of the trauma-focused psychodramas that I have facilitated over the years, the protagonist has commented on the psychological impact of having more supportive figures than antagonist figures in the scene. The inclusion of strengths-based roles offers an anchor for us to pendulate back to if the protagonist is becoming overwhelmed later in the psychodrama scene. Strengths-based roles provide the protagonist with another angle to look at themselves from and to perceive the trauma from which can initiate new action insights. Furthermore, the presence of resources within the psychodrama scene affords an opportunity for more group members to be involved in the process as active participants rather than observers.

Strengths-based roles provide the protagonist with another angle to look at themselves from and to perceive the trauma from which can initiate new action insights.

Here is a simple example of a strengths-based psychodrama scene with a young man in inpatient treatment.

Dimitri is a 20-year-old client in rehab for substance abuse and complex trauma, who also lives with mild autism. He shares about his psychodrama goal of working through his resistance to growing up and being an adult. He says that being an adult seem boring, full of complicated rules, and expectations. We start to create a scene with supportive roles to help him with his goal. He enrolls courage as the first role and chooses a group member to play it. In back-and-forth dialogue with his courage, he explores the bravery needed to step into adult responsibilities and social expectations that feel overwhelming for him due to his neurodiversity. Next, I ask Dimitri if there is any kind of role model, spiritual or superhero role that could help with the topic today. Without hesitation, he says Peter Pan! So, we enrolled a group member into the scene as Peter Pan (he happened to pick a FDNY firefighter to play the role) and he instructed him to fly around the room throughout the psychodrama. He begins sharing with Peter Pan – "I feel like I'm failing as a person. I can't seem to do all the things everyone else does and I get overwhelmed easily by too many people or noise. How am I supposed to become a man when I can't even be like the other kids?" I asked him to reverse roles and become Peter Pan to speak to himself about growing up. As Peter Pan, he says to himself, "Dimitri, you can't be a kid forever – I tried it already and it doesn't work for everyone. Growing up doesn't mean that you have to be like everyone else or pretending that you aren't different. You will have to grow up soon and become a man, but you can always have fun and hold onto some fun childhood things like playing games, laughing, and your imagination! You don't have to be an adult like all the adults in your life – you can still be you as an adult."

At this point, as the director, I started to remember themes in the Peter Pan movies, so I had Dimitri role reverse back to himself and suggested that we enroll The Lost Boys from Peter Pan into the scene to talk to them about what it was like for them when they went to Neverland to try to avoid growing up. He chose group members to take on the roles and began talking to them – "well, what do you think Lost Boys, is it possible to avoid growing up like Peter Pan? Growing up seems to mean doing all sorts of hard things like having a job and pretending to like things you don't like." I ask Dimitri to reverse roles with one of the Lost Boys to respond – "well Dimitri, we went to Neverland to try to avoid growing up and it isn't really possible. It seems like a good idea but there are some real dangers of not growing up – like pirates and alligators and missing your family! Plus, there was a part of each of us that wanted to become men too." I ask Dimitri as one of the Lost Boys to tell Dimitri what it was like to be lost in Neverland and to find his way back to the real world to become an adult. He responds, "It was really scary and painful to be lost and chased by creepy characters like Captain hook and his pirates. I thought I wanted to be young forever but then I realized that I had to let go of my childhood to become an adult. But even as an adult, I can still revisit Neverland every so often to have fun going on adventures. Being an adult doesn't mean that you have to give up your childhood or having fun or going on adventures. Becoming a man was one of the coolest adventures I've ever been on." Dimitri reverses roles back to himself to hear these messages from the Lost Boys. Next, I invite the men in the group to step in the scene as themselves and share with Dimitri about their own experiences of transitioning into manhood while feeling different. One man said, "being a man means learning how to live in your own skin" to which Dimitri smiled and nodded. Afterward the psychodrama, we moved onto de-roling and into sharing.

Dimitri's psychodrama highlights the adaptability of the psychodramatic method, which can be used with various themes and modified for neurodiverse clients. I have found many neurodiverse clients really appreciate certain aspects of psychodrama, such as the visual cues, use of imagination or play, and flexibility to incorporate their favorite characters or self-soothing techniques. I find it important to slow the process down and allow more space for processing while being sensitive to noise, chaos, and eye contact, which could make the process tougher for a neurodivergent client. This psychodrama highlights the possibilities of change through supportive roles and resources in psychodrama, but it also shows the power of metaphor and archetypal stories, which can be embodied through the dramatic process for any client.

Resourcing as Healing

The utilization of resources within a psychodrama scene is often approached as a means to an end. The resources are enrolled to help the protagonist face the trauma and accomplish the goal or contract. However, in many cases, the engagement with resources in a psychodrama can be healing and restorative by itself – without having to enroll any trauma-based roles into the scene. I have directed countless psychodrama scenes in inpatient, outpatient, and training settings that only involved supportive roles but were still quite cathartic, moving, and healing. The majority of my inpatient psychodramas over the past 10+ years have involved mostly resources, while many of them included only resources and excluded any antagonist or trauma-based roles. This group has several years of outcomes data demonstrating its effectiveness and an average reduction in PTSD by over 50%, depression by 60%, anxiety by nearly 55%, and traumatic grief by over 30% (Giacomucci et al., 2023, 2025).

The facilitation of trauma-focused psychodrama without trauma-based roles or antagonist roles does not mean that the trauma is avoided entirely. It simply means that the trauma is not enrolled within the scene. When directing a trauma-focused psychodrama with all strengths-based and supportive roles, I am still prompting and interviewing every role to speak about the trauma from their perspective. This offers the protagonist with the opportunity to renegotiate their perspective, feelings, and sensations associated with the traumatic memory. Much of trauma involves harm caused by inaction rather than action. The experience of connecting with resources in a psychodrama scene often provides the protagonist with what was missing at the time of the trauma and a corrective emotional experience. The internalization of these resources after the psychodrama can promote lasting change without the need to re-experience or tell the story of the trauma again (Giacomucci, 2023).

The experience of connecting with resources in a psychodrama scene often provides the protagonist with what was missing at the time of the trauma and a corrective emotional experience.

Strengths-Based Roles for Safety, Stabilization, and Spontaneity

There are many different types of strengths, but this multitude of qualities can be categorized into three primary categories – internal strengths, relational strengths, and transpersonal strengths. Many strengths include components of more than one category and also overlap with other strengths. There seems to be an entire sociometric constellation of strengths within each person and each group. As a director trained in the TSM, one of the things I was taught to look for is the presence of all three types of strengths before moving explicitly into traumatic content with the protagonist (see Figure 8.1). These three types of strengths also mirror and reflect three of the five domains of posttraumatic growth.

Intrapsychic Strengths

These are strengths that exist within an individual, such as courage, willingness, intelligence, wisdom, and so on. Internal strengths are important in that they promote a sense of autonomy, self-efficacy, and ego strength. Intrapsychic strengths provide an individual with the confidence and capacity to face relationships and

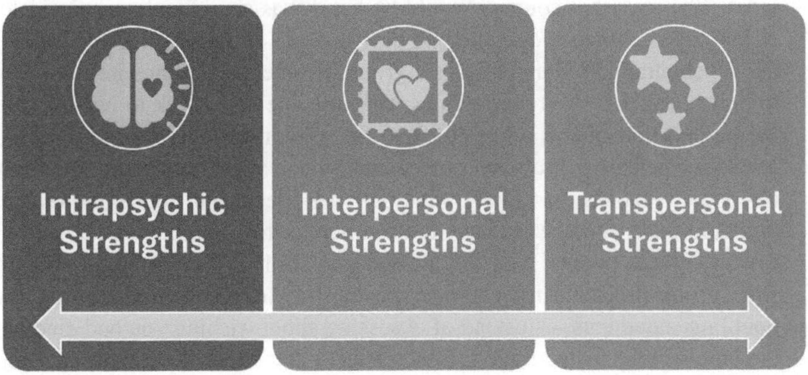

Figure 8.1 Three categories of strengths

the world. Of course, internal strengths alone are not enough, as no individual can recover from trauma alone.

Integrating intrapsychic strengths into a psychodrama is quite simple. It is usually how I start my trauma-focused psychodrama enactments once a contract has been established. I will simply turn to the protagonist and ask, "what strength do we need to accomplish the goal today?" If I feel that the protagonist may struggle to answer the question, or if the psychodrama goal is related to receiving help or trusting others, then I will start by asking the group to call out the strengths that they see in the protagonist. This leaves us with a list of strengths that the protagonist can choose from to help achieve the contract. Most of the time, the group and protagonist seem to name internal strengths, but sometimes interpersonal or transpersonal strengths are also articulated.

Once a strength has been chosen, then we simply enroll the strength as a role into the scene.

> Jody has established a contract for her psychodrama to work through the self-blame and survivors' guilt that she experiences from being a firefighter during the September 11th, 2001, World Trade Center attacks. From her body language and emotionality, it is clear that this is going to be a tough psychodrama for her. As we begin, I ask her to identify a strength that could help her work through her self-blame and survivors' guilt. She struggles to identify strengths within herself, so I ask the group to help her. Other group members quickly start yelling out strengths – "courage!" "you are so resilient," "empathy," "self-awareness," "more courage," "you have been through so much but are such a kind person," and "you are always willing to help others." I ask Jody which of these strengths seems like it would be most helpful for our goal

> today. She says that courage would be helpful as she is feeling intimidated. "Okay, good choice Jody; who can play the role of courage for you today in the psychodrama?" Jody chooses a group member who jumps into the scene to help. I ask Jody to reverse roles with courage and speak to herself about the trauma, self-blame, and guilt from the role of courage. As courage, Jody speaks to herself – "you are braver than you realize Jody. You could have easily died that day, just like so many of your friends and colleagues did. But you didn't and you need to have the courage to stop blaming yourself for not saving enough people. You did all that you could." Next, I invite doubling from group members for courage speaking to Jody, and I add in my own doubling statements – "instead of obsessing about wishing you had died with the others, have the courage to live for them and honor their memory." Jody repeats the doubling statements. With each statement, her resolve and confidence increase. After reversing roles back, Jody listens to courage repeat the messages as she integrates them within herself and the psychodrama scene.

This is a simple and quite common example of how to integrate a strength into a scene. The use of strengths-based roles helps the protagonist to start the reconsolidation process while cognitively restructuring the memory as they are approaching it from a different role – which carries a new perspective, emotionality, and adaptive information. From a clinical perspective, the addition of strengths-based roles into the scene not only provides stability and support in the scene but also within the self of the protagonist. The process of enrolling, role reversing with, and engaging with the strength is also a process of bringing forth that strength within the protagonist. We are essentially externalizing, reorganizing, and internalizing the presence of the strength within the protagonist's psyche through its involvement in the scene. To effectively accomplish this, we want to ensure that the protagonist reaches a spontaneity state while role reversed with the strength. The presence of the strength alone may help, but the protagonist accessing spontaneity (a new response to the old situation) as the role and in relationship to the trauma is what we are attempting to cultivate.

We are essentially externalizing, reorganizing, and internalizing the presence of the strength within the protagonist's psyche through its involvement in the scene.

Interpersonal Strengths and the Group as a Resource

Relational strengths can come in two primary forms – either strengths that require more than one person (such as empathy, asking for help, altruism, or loyalty) or as supportive people within the scene (such as a helpful friend or a role model).

The process of employing interpersonal strengths into the scene is the same process as outlined above for intrapsychic strengths. With supportive figures, it is important to double-check that the role that has been chosen to be enrolled is not someone that the protagonist has mixed feelings toward. This is quite common, especially when working in higher levels of care. For this reason, in my inpatient psychodrama group, I tend to avoid supportive figures in psychodrama scenes (as resources) and aim for more intrapsychic or transpersonal strengths where it is unlikely that the protagonist has ambivalence.

Often, I will rely on the group members to provide the interpersonal resources necessary in the psychodrama scene. The group is another interpersonal resource that can be leveraged in various ways throughout the scene. I might leverage the group's support by asking them for their guidance during the scene or inviting them to raise their hand if they relate to something meaningful that was said or verbally repeat messages that feel important for the protagonist. Within my psychodrama groups, participants often develop important peer support relationships with each other and may call upon another group member to help in their psychodrama. In these cases, I am apt to enroll that group member (either as themself or have someone else play their role) into the scene. In doing so, I utilize interviewing, prompting, doubling, and role reversal with the other group member to help them deepen their relationship and focus the support on the goal of the drama. Furthermore, I frequently will employ the rest of the group as a resource for the protagonist, especially at the climax of a psychodrama scene when I expect the intensity to rise. I simply turn to the audience and invite them to join the scene as themselves by saying, "whoever would like to support Jody in this conversation, come stand with her in the scene." This intervention helps to fortify the protagonist while engaging the rest of the group. It effectively focuses the entire group energy onto the interaction at the climax of the scene. Having everyone place themselves with the protagonist shows the protagonist that they are not alone and that the entire group has their back. Many of my protagonists stated later that this was one of the most important moments in the psychodrama for them, as it helped them feel like they had momentum, support, and could face whatever was next in the scene.

Transpersonal Strengths

Strengths that go beyond human are called transpersonal strengths – these include roles such as God, angels, archetypes, religious or spiritual figures, existential themes (such as meaning, purpose, life, or death), and for many, this would include art, music, nature, energy, or the universe. Transpersonal roles can be quite powerful when enrolled in psychodrama scenes and often elicit catharsis and meaningful insights. Many of my clients have engaged in psychodramas with God where they gained new acceptance, forgiveness, and peace of mind related to their trauma or loss. Transpersonal, spiritual, and archetypal roles seem to be less complicated than interpersonal roles in that there is often an ongoing idealization with them. This can help allow a trauma survivor to receive support without the baggage that often comes with human relationships. However, this is not always the case, as many trauma survivors have experienced trauma related to religion or spirituality.

The first psychodrama conference workshop that I ever co-presented was on the use of archetypes in psychodrama. Working with archetypes and other transpersonal or existential roles has always been something that I am drawn to as a protagonist and trainer. I find that the surplus reality of psychodrama lends itself well to working with these types of roles, which are also emphasized through Moreno's mystical philosophy.

The Double as Resource

Beyond roles in the scene, the use of doubling can also serve as a sort of resource in that it helps the protagonist connect with support and spontaneity from the group or the director. Of course, a double can also be enrolled within the scene as its own role. A double fortifies the protagonist with an ongoing ally in the scene who stays with them throughout the entire process. Doubling provides assurance to the protagonist that the group has their back and empathizes with their experience. It stabilizes the protagonist within the surplus reality of the scene and nudges them closer to their truth and their goal. Doubling initiates a re-source-ing, in that it helps to promote a reconnection to spontaneity and adaptive information.

Furthermore, Badis and colleagues (2025) highlight the importance of resourcing-related doubling statements as components of decolonizing doubles. Their framework for decolonizing doubling encompasses five types of statements: (1) strengths, (2) social rank, (3) ancestral, (4) collectives, and (5) social action. I would argue that most (and at times, all) of these five categories encompass resourcing through doubling in that they are connecting the protagonist with inner strength, supportive ancestors or collectives, and opportunities for action. They also suggest that open-ended (rather than close-ended) doubling statements be used in decolonizing practice. For example, instead of doubling and saying "I'm overwhelmed with anger towards you," one could double and say, "I'm overwhelmed with emotion towards you right now and what I'm feeling is. . . ." This type of open-ended doubling statement avoids any influence on the protagonist to repeat the content of the double and provides maximum freedom to find and state one's truth.

In many trauma-focused psychodramas, the protagonist provides feedback that the person playing the role of their double throughout the scene was one of the most helpful roles that allowed them to ground themselves, express themselves, and develop new perspectives throughout the session. I frequently have seen protagonists who present as hesitant or unsure in their psychodrama and are able to let go of this hesitancy after a few doubling statements from their peers and/or the director. If a protagonist seems to need more support, doubling from the director and group members is a quick way to provide that support and further resource them.

The Director as Resource

One resource that we might lose sight of in any psychodrama is ourselves! Other times, I have seen psychodrama trainees rely too much on themselves as a resource to the detriment of the group feeling empowered to be involved. As the director, we have a therapeutic relationship with the protagonist that we can leverage to further resource them in the session. As previously mentioned, one way of doing this is through offering doubling statements as the director for the protagonist. Furthermore, we might also engage in the "use of self" at other times in the session, such as during the warm-up, protagonist selection, contracting, during the scene, and in the sharing phase of the session. When I am facilitating, I try to push myself to connect emotionally with participants before the group even begins and to greet each person as they enter the room while asking them how they are doing today. In the contracting, I often will inform the protagonist that we will lead the psychodrama together and assure them that I have a good sense of where we will go in the psychodrama scene, so they feel held as the protagonist. Beyond all of this, however, I find that simple words of encouragement interspersed throughout every part of the psychodrama are most important and often missed opportunities for resourcing the protagonist (or other auxiliary roles or audience members). While directing, I make it a point to say to the protagonist things such as "nice job," "keep going, you are doing great," "you've got this," and "there you go, just like that." These simple words of encouragement help the protagonist feel reassured that they are not "doing it wrong" or second guessing their actions in the psychodrama. These are words of encouragement that I offer all of my clients when engaging in other types of therapy, so it seems to make perfect sense to also incorporate them into psychodrama directing.

The Scene as Resource

Resources exist within the surplus reality of the psychodrama scene. This is one of the most beneficial aspects of scene setting, in that we are apt to uncover unexpected resources that can be called upon within the scene. Within most scenes, there are untapped sources of spontaneity, creativity, strength, and meaning. Many psychodramas begin with scene setting and move very organically into resourcing as the strengths-based roles simply show up and can be concretized in the setting of the scene (Lesnik, 2024). One example of this came in a recent three-day training I led, which was on attachment theory and psychodrama:

> The protagonist established a goal of having a difficult conversation with a loved one. In discerning a scene and place for the conversation, the protagonist chose a grove within a forest. As we concretized and set up the scene, it felt important to check-in about the tress as resources and roles. The protagonist liked the idea and had a strong connection to nature, so we enrolled multiple trees surrounding the protagonist. The dialogue between the protagonist and the trees provided rich support, insight, and metaphors for the complicated conversation that was to come. The metaphors that were uncovered through the support from the trees became a central theme in the difficult conversation at the climax of the drama.

One of the exciting things about psychodrama and surplus reality is that we can simply pull new resources out of thin air if they are needed in the psychodrama. If we need a magic potion to bring someone back to life for a final goodbye, we can do that. If we need a special force field to protect us from an antagonist role, we can set it up in the scene. Anything that is needed can be imagined and integrated to move the scene toward the goal. My psychodrama trainers often shared stories of Zerka Moreno‘s directing and her use of "psychodramatic scissors" that she would pull from her pocket while directing and invite the protagonist to cut their ties to people in their life characterized by trauma bonds, codependency, or other unhealthy relationship dynamics.

Anything that is needed can be imagined and integrated to move the scene towards the goal.

Beyond objects within the surplus reality scene, we can also utilize objects within the room, from the warm-up, or from previous psychodramas. I often will utilize the Circle of Strengths warm-up (described in Chapter 5) before a psychodrama scene, which results in a circle of scarves on the floor. Whenever needed, I can instruct group members or the protagonist to pick up a strength that they may benefit from connecting with further. Another warm-up that I often employ is using art-based cards to concretize different roles or goals at the start of the group. For example, I may put cards on the floor and ask everyone to choose one that can represent themselves in the future, having healed from some trauma and loss. During the actual psychodrama enactment, I could call upon this role for the protagonist, which has already been concretized in the room with the card. Sometimes I use the trashcan in the room within the scene to "throw out" things that the protagonist no longer needs. Or, I once had a protagonist get to the ending of their psychodrama scene. When I asked how they wanted to end the scene, they looked around and picked a marker off the whiteboard, moved it around in the air in a writing motion, and exclaimed, "I get to write my future instead of being defined by my past."

Strengths-Based Psychodrama Scenes

It is possible to provide a healing, transformative, and even cathartic psychodrama experience without any antagonist, perpetrator, trauma-based, or conflictual roles. Strengths-based psychodrama scenes are made up of strengths-based roles and resources. Sometimes referred to as Positive Psychodramas (Orkibi, 2019) or Prescriptive Psychodramas (Hudgins & Toscani, 2013), strengths-based psychodramas are focused on helping protagonists and group members connect with resources to help with their goals (Giacomucci, 2021). Strengths-based psychodramas are a good option for groups new to psychodrama, demonstrations in settings with limitations on emotional experiencing (such as in higher education or organizations), or when working with clients with less emotional or psychiatric stability – such as in higher levels of care and/or in the very early stages of trauma recovery.

Strengths-based psychodrama can include internal strengths, interpersonal supports, and/or transpersonal roles. Strengths-based psychodramas provide an option for group members who may be too intimidated to volunteer as protagonists to engage in a psychodrama with trauma-focused roles. In my trauma-focused psychodrama groups and trainings, I will often start with a strengths-based psychodrama before moving into more intense psychodrama scenes with non-strength-based roles. Not only does this resource the group, but it also helps to familiarize everyone with the psychodramatic process, so there is less fear and uncertainty about the mechanics, interventions, and experience. Some common strengths-based psychodramas include expressions of gratitude, connecting with a higher power, psychodramatic dialogue with one's self in the future, or building up the strengths and supports needed to face one's trauma. I have found gratitude psychodramas to be a great balance of containment, emotion, meaning, and vulnerability for one-time psychodrama demonstrations in professional or academic settings. When I provide guest lectures or conference workshops with students or professionals new to psychodrama, I usually facilitate a gratitude psychodrama. In my trauma-focused psychodrama practice with clients, more frequently, I am facilitating psychodramas with the goal of resourcing the protagonist (and the group) to be able to move into the feelings, defenses, and traumatic content in future sessions. Here is a depiction of a recent strengths-based drama:

> Dakota is chosen as protagonist with the goal of building up the courage and support to address his traumatic childhood. He shares that he often finds himself avoiding dealing with the trauma because it overwhelms him to consider.

> We started by enrolling courage as a role and connecting the protagonist to their courage. "You are more courageous than most people – demonstrated by the fact that you survived your past and are here addressing it." Next, we enrolled resilience. In the role reversal with resilience, Dakota was able to remind himself of times he developed resilience and his ongoing adaptability and strength. The group chimed in doubling for him to further enhance the depth of his connection to resilience. When asked who could support him in addressing his complex trauma, Dakota mentioned his two closest friends. We enrolled his two best friends and facilitated role reversals so that Dakota could see himself through his friends' eyes. Noticing that we have intrapsychic and interpersonal roles in the scene, but no transpersonal supports, I ask Dakota who or what beyond humans could help him with courage to face his trauma. He thinks about it for a minute, then begins to talk about his Native American heritage and ancestry. He shares about a recent dream he had that involved a native elder and spiritual leader. We enrolled this elder from his dream and engaged in a conversation with him about finding the courage to face trauma. The conversation with this spiritual leader proved to be quite meaningful in that it helped Dakota to reconnect with this spiritual lineage. I interviewed Dakota after role reversing him into the transpersonal role – "what can you tell Dakota about finding the courage to face his trauma?" "what does Dakota need to know from you in order to make sense of his childhood trauma?" and "what spiritual teaching can you offer Dakota to help him cultivate more courage in his life and recovery?" Holding Dakota in the role reversal helped him drop further into the role and into his ancestral knowledge that could help him face and heal from trauma. The scene ending with Dakota surrounded by his strengths and support, confiding in this transpersonal role the stories of his childhood trauma and receiving support and validation from the group.

This is a pretty common example of a strengths-based or prescriptive role psychodrama that incorporates a series of resources as roles to build up to addressing a trauma-related issue at the end of the scene – or making a commitment to address the trauma in a future session now that the resources have been tapped.

Conclusion

Strengths-based psychodrama scenes and roles are particularly important in trauma-informed and trauma-focused practice to prevent retraumatization. Strength-based roles are essential when working with complex trauma and CPTSD for stability. Resources help protagonists and groups reconnect to the source of spontaneity, which allows them to create change in their lives and within their self. Resources can include various roles such as intrapsychic, interpersonal, or transpersonal strengths, doubles, the director, the rest of the group, and other objects within the room and/or within the surplus reality of the psychodrama scene. Strengths as the place to begin when directing trauma-focused psychodramas and ensuring that the group is able to stay within its window of tolerance throughout the experience.

Strength-based roles are essential when working with complex trauma and CPTSD for stability.

References

Badis, D., Hernandez, C. L., Nieto, L., Ruiz Esparza, M. P., & Tkachuck, C. (2025). A world with many worlds: Decolonizing education with action methods. In S. Giacomucci, H. Fleury, & D. Altinay (Eds.), *Psychodrama in education: Creativity and experiential teaching around the world* (pp. 137–161). Springer Nature.

Giacomucci, S. (2021). *Social work, sociometry, and psychodrama: Experiential approaches for group therapists, community leaders, and social workers.* Springer Nature.

Giacomucci, S. (2023). *Trauma-informed principles in group therapy, psychodrama, and organizations: Action methods for leadership.* Routledge.

Giacomucci, S., Marquit, J., Briggs, H., & Gupta, R. (2025). Psychodrama's effects on PTSD, depression, anxiety, traumatic grief, prolonged grief disorder, and spontaneity: A mixed methods study in inpatient addiction treatment. *The Arts in Psychotherapy, 93*, 102293.

Giacomucci, S., Marquit, J., Saccarelli, R., & Briggs, H. (2023). Psychodrama group psychotherapy as an effective treatment for PTSD and depression in inpatient substance use treatment: A mixed methods study. *Social Work with Groups*, 1–16.

Hudgins, M. K., & Toscani, F. (2013). *Healing world trauma with the therapeutic spiral model: Stories from the frontlines.* London: Jessica Kingsley Publishers.

Lesnik, P. (2024). An exploration of scene setting in psychodrama: The sociometry of place. *Journal of Psychodrama, Sociometry, and Group Psychotherapy, 70*(1), 1–15.

Moreno, J. L. (1978). *Who shall survive?: Foundations of sociometry, group psychotherapy and psychodrama (3rd edition).* Beacon House.

Orkibi, H. (2019). Positive psychodrama: A framework for practice and research. *The Arts in Psychotherapy, 66*, 101603.

Chapter 9

Honoring Defenses and Dissociation with Psychodrama

Psychodrama is a powerful method that often bypasses defenses due to its experiential nature. I find this to be not only one of the reasons for its effectiveness with clients who have not found other methods to be helpful but also one of the reasons for its capacity for harm and retraumatization. As directors, we must be careful that we are not pushing past our clients' defenses in a way that leaves them outside of their window of tolerance. Working with defenses is underrated in psychodrama but has become highlighted through other experiential modalities, such as IFS. I believe that IFS's emphasis on acknowledging, befriending, and honoring protector parts is something important that we could learn from and integrate into our psychodramatic practice. Of course, psychodrama existed decades before IFS and many psychodramatists have been incorporating work with defenses into their practice at times, but few have emphasized its importance. The TSM may be one of the few psychodrama practices or publications that consistently mention defenses (Hudgins & Durost, 2022; Hudgins & Toscani, 2013). Honoring defenses before engaging with trauma-based roles is important when working with complex trauma and CPTSD (Giacomucci, 2023). If the defenses have not been explored, made conscious, honored, and the relationship to the defense changed, it is very likely that it will show up as soon as we try to go toward the trauma.

Honoring defenses before engaging with trauma-based roles is important when working with complex trauma and CPTSD.

Purpose of Defenses

Defenses are behaviors that we engage in to protect ourselves from anxiety, stress, or threats (real or perceived) in our environment. Defenses help us survive at the time of trauma. Defenses are often unconscious and involuntary. They are our attempts to cope with stressful situations and/or distort reality in a way that makes it feel more tolerable. Essentially, defenses help us to manage our

DOI: 10.4324/9781003639497-9

emotional and psychological experience in a way that keeps us within our window of tolerance from moment to moment.

There are many different types of defenses. Classic psychoanalytic theory articulates the presence of various defenses, including projection, repression, displacement, denial, and others. The idea of defenses can be traced back to Sigmund and Anna Freud (A. Freud, 1946; S. Freud, 1962/1894). When thinking about defenses or providing education on the topic for clients or students, I like to simplify the discussion too easy to understand and identify defenses such as avoidance, intellectualization, rationalization, acting out, humor, dissociation, fight, flight, and freeze. I also find it helpful to consider that most symptoms of PTSD (and perhaps also of many other mental health disorders) could be categorized as defenses – or attempts of our body and mind to protect itself from future trauma and navigate the anxiety or pain of the past trauma. When working with clients or colleagues in 12-step recovery, I often liken defenses to the character defects or shortcomings described in steps 6 and 7.

Everyone, even the healthiest of individuals, utilizes defense mechanisms to navigate the world and relationships. Defenses seem to get a bad reputation and become stigmatized as only something bad when, in reality, there are many good and helpful aspects of defenses. The problem with defenses is that we often get stuck in habits of using defenses long after the trauma is over – or we end up utilizing defenses to navigate our internal experience of trauma responses, which are disproportionate to what is happening around us in the world. Defenses can prevent us from being the best that we can be in our relationships, in work, school, home, and in the world in general. For these reasons, it is important that we address defenses in our work and are aware of them within ourselves and our clients.

Bypassing versus Befriending Defenses

While it may be tempting as a director to bypass the defenses of the group or protagonist by employing psychodrama interventions that move the process along quickly into deeper experiences, we must also remember that our clients' defenses are there for a reason. If there are defenses present, that is an indicator that the defenses are either needed by the client to tolerate their experience or were needed by the client in the past to tolerate similar experiences. Differentiating if the client still needs the defense to cope can be complicated. Using doubling, role reversal, or enrolling difficult roles can push us beyond the defenses but may also push the client beyond their capacity to tolerate the emotions that may emerge. It seems that the best approach would be to help the client (and group) become aware of their defenses, acknowledge their purpose, explore their here-and-now necessity, and consciously letting them go. This honoring of defenses can be done through discussion, concretization, letter writing, or psychodrama scenes.

Many of the clients that I work with are quite frustrated and angry at their defenses for holding them back and disrupting their lives. These feelings toward the defenses can make it more complicated to honor them or befriend them. Some of the other clients that I have worked with are very attached to their defenses for how they have helped them maintain comfort or safety. Regardless of the nature of one's relationship to their defenses, for most, it has been a very long relationship originating in childhood. In navigating change in this relationship, there are a few primary options that one might be drawn toward, including (1) rejecting the defense and attempting to cut it off, (2) ignoring the defense and trying to cultivate a new behavior, or (3) befriending the defense to honor it and renegotiate one's relationship to it or promote a role transformation to turn the defense into something new. The best outcomes that I have seen in working with defenses have been when the client befriends the defense, honors it for its help, and renegotiates their relationship with it – which often results in the defense transforming into something new. For example, "acting out" could be transformed into "bravery," or "avoidance" into "self-preservation." This movement toward role transformation is congruent with psychodrama's role theory, which suggests that we cannot fully extinguish roles once they have been developed (thus rejecting or cutting off a role will not work), but we can transform roles into something new (Giacomucci, 2021).

> Kristina is struggling with hyperarousal that leads to avoidance and running away from relationships in her life. She is clear that this defense and behavioral pattern is related to past trauma and that being hyperaware has helped her prevent additional harm. But she is at a point in her life where she realizes she has been too cautious and avoidant of any relational cue that might signal future trauma. We enroll "hyperarousal" into a role so she can speak to this defense. She says "you have been running the show for too long. I know you have kept me safe, but I'm annoyed that you can't ever just let me be okay and at peace in relationships." Kristina reverses roles and becomes her hyperarousal to respond, "I'm just trying to protect you, so you don't get hurt again. Whenever I notice that something might not be right, I let you know so you can get out of there before it gets dangerous." As the director, I prompt her in the role – "hyperarousal, can you tell Kristina what she would need to do in order for you to feel like you can take a step or two back and be less active in her life?" This resulted in Kristina as hyperarousal telling herself that she needs to develop more support in her life, have people she can reality test with, and to develop more tools for calming herself down. Hyperarousal told her that it would step back if she had more support and protection from other places. We continued the psychodrama scene by enrolling more support and strengths to show hyperarousal that it didn't need to be so active. With additional resources in play, hyperarousal was willing to step back and quiet down. Kristina repositioned roles in the scene to put

hyperarousal further away, but still visible and said that "I want you to keep me alert and let me know when I should be cautious or get more information, but not to make me run away." She continued with a dialogue with the defense in which she renamed it as "alertness" and thanked it for all of its help throughout the years.

This is a simple depiction of a role transformation from "hyperarousal" to "alertness." The action of the psychodrama scene and reorganization of resources led to the defense (or symptomology) transforming into "alertness" as a strength and positive quality.

The very process of enrolling a defense into a scene is helping to make the unconscious defense conscious for the protagonist and the group. Bringing the defense into our awareness allows us to have a more intentional relationship with it compared to involuntarily being overtaken by it. This can also be accomplished in a simpler way through the psychodramatic intervention of concretization where an object is used to represent a defense. For example, if I have a client who habitually uses humor or overtalking to deflect and avoid, I can point it out to them and invite them to choose an object to represent this defense. Each time they use the defense, I gently pick up the object and hand it to them to let them know that they are using it. I invite them to put it down if it is not needed as we continue our individual session or psychodrama scene. After a few cycles of picking up and putting down the defense, the client's self-awareness has already increased significantly.

Addictions and Addictive Behaviors as Defensive Patterns

Substance use, food addiction, gambling, sex, workaholism, self-harm, and other compulsive behaviors can also be conceptualized as defenses. These are behaviors that are fueled by fear, anxiety, stress, pain, anger, grief, or discontent. Engaging in any of these addictive behaviors can provide a sense of relief, avoidance, distraction, numbness, or altercation in one's emotions or perception and experience of reality. When we revisit the definition of a defense as a behavior that helps us avoid discomfort or distorts our reality, then it becomes clearer that addictive behaviors also fit into this category. Addictions are further complicated in that, not only are they defenses, but we also use other defenses to protect the addiction when we feel like someone, or something threatening our access to the addictive behavior.

Similar to other defense mechanisms, it is common for clients to have mixed feelings toward their addictions, as the addiction has often been a source of pleasure, fun, relief, and escape, but also brought additional problems with it, such as legal or medical complications, lost relationships and opportunities, obsession, and further trauma or loss. In the psychodramatic process of working with addictions, we often will enroll the addiction into a role or enroll the substance or other behavior into a role in the scene. Enrolling the addiction allows us to explicitly look at one's relationship to it and the internalized messages from it (Giacomucci, 2017).

> Jim is chosen as a protagonist in a psychodrama with the goal of addressing how his addiction has taken everything from him and developing a strong connection to his recovery. We set up the psychodrama scene by first bringing in supportive roles and resources, then enrolling Jim's addiction as a role. He symbolically places his addiction between himself and his recovery in the scene. As the director, I instruct him to call upon his support and talk back to his addiction because it has been talking to him for quite a while. Jim says to his addiction, "I'm sick of you ruining my life and taking everything from me." As the director, I dump a pile of scarves next to Jim and say, "here are all of the things addiction has taken from you." Then I direct the auxiliary playing the role of addiction to physically take everything from Jim. This symbolic representation pulls Jim deeper into the scene standing up for himself with a fuller voice and motivation. Jim continued exclaiming to his addiction about all the opportunities and things it has taken from him while expressing his sadness, guilt, shame, and anger. With the help of the group, he was able to feel empowered against his addiction and challenge all of its distorted messages. As he demonstrated more and more empowerment, his addiction continued to step back away from him which brought the role of his recovery closer to him. The scene ended with Jim having a conversation with this recovery to affirm his commitment to it and savor the gifts and promises that it offers.

Psychodrama with addiction as a role is quite common in addiction treatment settings. Many clients find it illuminating to hear aloud the negative messages from their addiction, which have become so normalized within their own minds but sound ridiculous when spoken aloud. Personifying addiction through role play also helps clients to concretize their issue and direct their anger or other feelings toward addiction rather than at themselves or other people in their lives. The same process outlined earlier can be facilitated with the role of "eating disorder," "workaholism," or any other addiction or compulsive behavior.

Working With Dissociation

> Dissociation is one of the most common defenses in the aftermath of trauma.

Dissociation is one of the most common defenses in the aftermath of trauma. Dissociation is particularly common for clients who have experienced complex trauma or who also utilize addictive behaviors. It makes sense that if one is experiencing childhood trauma and cannot physically escape, that they would learn to mentally and emotionally escape through day dissociation, dreaming, detachment, depersonalization, and/or derealization. Dissociation is simply a dis-association, or separating ourselves from our experience or feelings. We could also conceptualize any addictive behavior as a type of dissociation. Considering the prevalence of dissociation in trauma-focused work, it is important to know how to work with clients utilizing dissociation in psychodrama.

There are various psychodrama techniques and interventions that can help with dissociation when it emerges in the protagonist or group members. The previous chapter on strengths-based roles can offer us a simple option – that we can enroll a new role into the scene to help with dissociation. Maybe we need "grounding" or "safety" or "protection" to join the scene to help the protagonist stay more fully present in the psychodrama experience without resorting to dissociation. A previous subsection in this chapter discusses the utility of enrolling a defense into the scene directly to renegotiate our relationship with it. This is another approach that is available to us when dissociation is present. We can enroll it in the scene as a role and explore what it needs or why it is showing up. Another common technique is to cultivate a physical space in the psychodrama scene to represent a safe place that the protagonist can pendulate back and forth from when they need some extra support or grounded while addressing other tough roles or scenes in the psychodrama enactment.

Furthermore, there are multiple psychodrama interventions that can help with dissociation including doubling, somatic interventions, and the mirror position. Rather than only being used for expression, doubling can be implemented with a focus on grounding, breathing, and awareness of sensory experiences. This type of doubling is sometimes referred to as a body double (Hudgins & Toscani, 2013) or somatic double (Aaron, 2013). In both approaches, the double is stays next to the protagonist and offers "I" statements for grounding or somatic awareness such as – "I can take a deep breath and feel my chest rise and fall," "I can feel my feet on the floor, look around the room, and know that I am safe," or "I notice my shoulders are tight and tense; I can stretch my neck and let my shoulders drop to see how it feels." This approach to doubling can help the protagonist (or group members playing the other roles in the scene) to further integrate their experience, stay within their window of tolerance, and develop/maintain body awareness throughout the process. Similarly to body doubling or somatic doubling, the director can also employ techniques to promote somatic awareness and grounding during the psychodrama, such as reminding the protagonist to breathe, asking the protagonist to check in with their body, and anchoring in strengths-based roles within the body. Encouraging movement throughout the psychodrama can also reduce dissociation and promote body awareness.

The mirror position is another tool that can be helpful in addressing dissociation, in that it provides a built-in mechanism for dis-association from the scene by pulling the protagonist out from the intensity of it to see the scene from afar. Bringing the protagonist into the mirror position gives them a third-person perspective of the situation and an opportunity to create some distance from it. The mirror position can be used in conjunction with the other grounding interventions or body/somatic doubling previously described to cultivate additional grounding.

Navigating Defenses in the Group, Director, and Co-Facilitators

Defenses are naturally going to emerge throughout the group process – especially when facilitating trauma-focused psychodrama. The presence of defenses may indicate that we are nearing the edge of one's window of tolerance, or that we have not engaged in enough warm-up. In psychodrama, we say that there is no such thing as "resistance" and instead conceptualize it as a lack of warm-up or a warm-up to something else. This new perspective allows us to avoid stigmatizing difficult behavior and instead consider some of the sources of it. The presence of defenses in the group process may suggest a need to return to activities that promote group cohesion and connection, such as sociometry exercises or warm-ups outlined in Chapter 5. Defenses will inevitably be activated if participants do not feel safe in the group, if there is unaddressed conflict in the group, if we are moving too fast in the trauma processing, or if the psychodramatic process has not been gradually moved into. At the same time, we must also assess if the defenses that are showing up are no longer needed by the client(s) and are being used because they have become habitual. This differentiation is tough to make in the moment and must be carefully navigated.

In psychodrama, we say that there is no such thing as "resistance" and instead conceptualize it as a lack of warm-up or a warm-up to something else.

As directors, we must be aware of our own defenses, which are certain to be activated throughout our work. The spontaneous and co-created nature of psychodrama means that we often do not know what the topic of the psychodrama will be until we are halfway through the group. If a topic emerges that relates to our own unresolved trauma histories, it is likely to provide countertransference and defenses from the director. If we are working with co-facilitators or have other staff or interns supporting our psychodrama groups, we must also consider their defenses and emotional responses to the psychodrama scenes. In my psychodrama groups, when I have staff or interns sit in the group to learn or assist, I always first assess for the ego strength of the staff/intern to ensure that the potential intensity of the psychodrama might not overwhelm them. I also find it helpful to give them a heads up on the potential of the psychodrama to activate powerful emotions for us as professionals, and that it is hard to mentally prepare ourselves, not knowing what the topic will be ahead of time. On a few occasions, I have had staff join my psychodrama group to learn, and after observing, they need to leave work early to process their own emotions. It seems that the action-oriented process in psychodrama results in more emotional experiencing for observers, including co-facilitators or assistants. This makes it important to briefly prepare and debrief staff or interns before and after the psychodrama. If we are not aware of our own defenses, we are likely to act on countertransference or bias, which could lead to us avoiding or moving too often into specific topics, emotions, or role interactions.

Psychodramatically Letting Down the Walls

One of the more commonly used metaphors for working with defenses of any kind is the idea of "taking town the wall." This is a metaphor that many of my clients tend to naturally utilize. The idea of considering defenses as a wall is quite accurate in that they tend to keep others out or away but also result in us feeling isolated and disconnected from others. One of the most frequently used symbolic representations of defenses in my psychodrama groups is by concretizing and enrolling "the wall" into the scene. This creative representation of the defenses gives us lots of lee way because the wall can be used as a metaphor for all or multiple defenses at once rather than enrolling them separately.

> Andres is the protagonist of a psychodrama with the goal of working towards trusting others and not being controlled by his past trauma any longer. In the development of the psychodrama, it seemed as though we might set up a scene where Andres would revisit a moment in the past related to his trauma but as we resourced him in the scene, it became clear that his defenses were going to prevent us from going much deeper. As the director, I made Andres aware of the defenses that kept surfacing throughout the psychodrama and suggested that we might need to talk to the defenses before going much further. Andres agreed and referred to them as his "walls" which we enrolled into the scene. In reversing roles with his wall, Andres spoke to himself – "I keep you safe and you need me. If you try to get rid of me, life will be terribly uncomfortable, and you will have to feel all the feelings. I help to numb you and prevent you from caring about things, so it doesn't hurt." In role reversing back to himself, Andres got to hear the messages from his wall repeated back to him by the role player. I reminded Andres of his goal related to trust and not being controlled by his past trauma, which helped to motivate him in

changing his relationship to his wall. Andres continued the conversation with his wall, telling it how it prevents him from trusting others and that although it has protected him in the past, it is also controlling him. As he finished up his message for the wall, he said, "I want to thank you for how you have helped me but I don't need you as much anymore." He then moved the wall back away from himself so that there were space for other roles and relationships, saying "I may still need you at times in the future because the world is not always a safe place, but I don't need you to be so close to me all of the time."

In this psychodrama example, Andres did not want to completely get rid of his walls because he realized that he may need them at times to protect himself in the future. Instead of trying to change the role into something else through a role transformation (such as in the first example in this chapter), Andres opted to simply create space between himself and the walls but to leave them intact.

Conclusion

Working with defenses and dissociation is essential before moving towards complex trauma in psychodrama therapy.

Psychodrama offers an engaging methodology for working with defense mechanisms in action. The catching force of the method has resulted in it developing a reputation for bypassing defenses, which seems to be a cause of both its powerful healing and its capacity to retraumatize. The psychodramatic approach comes packaged with multiple interventions for working with dissociation including doubling and the mirror position. A thoughtful director can use psychodrama to help clients befriend their defenses or addictive behaviors and let down their walls, which have been holding them back from being the best that they can be. Concretizing or enrolling defenses into a psychodrama scene gives us a process for making the unconscious defenses conscious and renegotiating our relationships with them going forward. Working with defenses and dissociation is essential before moving toward complex trauma in psychodrama therapy.

References

Aaron, S. G. (2013). The somatic double – A key role in psychodramatic Bodywork®. *The Journal of Psychodrama, Sociometry, and Group Psychotherapy, 61*(1), 29–41.

Freud, A. (1946). *The ego and the mechanisms of defense*. International Universities Press. (Original work published 1936)

Freud, S. (1962). The neuro-psychoses of defense. In J. Strachey (Ed. and Trans.), *The standard edition of the complete works of Sigmund Freud* (Vol. 3, pp. 45–61). London: Hogarth Press. (Original work published 1894)

Giacomucci, S. (2017). The sociodrama of life or death: Young adults and addiction treatment. *Journal of Psychodrama, Sociometry, and Group Psychotherapy, 65*(1), 137–143.

Giacomucci, S. (2021). *Social work, sociometry, and psychodrama: Experiential approaches for group therapists, community leaders, and social workers*. Springer Nature.

Giacomucci, S. (2023). *Trauma-informed principles in group therapy, psychodrama, and organizations: Action methods for leadership*. Routledge.

Hudgins, K., & Durost, S. W. (2022). *Experiential therapy from trauma to post-traumatic growth: Therapeutic spiral model psychodrama*. Springer Nature.

Hudgins, M. K., & Toscani, F. (2013). *Healing world trauma with the therapeutic spiral model: Stories from the frontlines*. London: Jessica Kingsley Publishers.

Chapter 10

Working With Parts of Self or Body Parts in Psychodrama

Psychodrama is a modality that fundamentally works with parts. These parts might be roles, feelings, beliefs, dreams, defenses, or other people, objects, or entities. On a psychological level, even when we are enrolling other people into a psychodrama, we are enrolling the protagonist's internal version of that person (Hudgins & Toscani, 2013). So, even interpersonal roles are really internal roles on some level. Psychodrama allows us to hone in on specific aspects of self so that we can better understand them, explore them, change our relationships to them, and envision a new future. The core psychodrama technique of concretization is employed to externalize parts of self into the room, so they can be interacted with. Employing psychodrama for parts work goes beyond only the protagonist but can also be utilized for parts of the other roles in the scene, parts of the professional, body parts, parts of a group/organization, or parts of a story or idea – psychodrama can be used to essentially be used to explore parts of anything.

Psychodrama is a modality that fundamentally works with parts.

Working With Parts of Self

The idea of conceptualizing the self or personality into different parts can be traced back in the field of psychology to Sigmund Freud, who outlined the id, ego, and superego. Many others have developed theories that include the use of parts of self, including Jacob Moreno's psychodrama, Fritz Perls' Gestalt Therapy, Eric Berne's Transactional Analysis, Jeffrey Young's Schema Therapy, Richard Schwartz's IFS, John and Helen Watkins' Ego State Therapy, and Janina Fisher's Structural Dissociation Model, among others. Parts work has become popularized through IFS and the Structural Dissociation Model, which have gained popularity in recent years. These more modern approaches seem to have simplified, repackaged, updated, and expanded upon approaches that existed

DOI: 10.4324/9781003639497-10

decades prior but used more complicated terms such as "ego states" or described parts of self as "roles." Many contemporary practitioners are integrating multiple approaches together, such as IFS and psychodrama or transactional analysis and psychodrama. Regardless of what we choose to call them or which theory we use to guide us, the practice of working with parts can be incredibly helpful and a simple way of talking about different aspects of self.

The actual work with parts of self becomes valuable in that we can access a deeper level of differentiation and complexity within the self. Instead of thinking of our personality as a single intact entity, we can reconceptualize the self as a multi-faceted collection of sub-personalities. As noted in Chapter 3, psychodrama's role theory proposes that the self is composed of all the roles that one plays in their life (Moreno, 1953). These different roles or parts often also have sub-roles or sub-parts, which can be further explored in their relationships, conflicts, reciprocities, parallels, and polarizations. With psychodrama, we can externalize or concretize these parts or roles, get curious about each, and reorganize our relationships to them. Complex trauma and CPTSD can leave survivors in an internal state of confusion, disconnection, and fragmentation. Exploring parts of self and internal roles can help promote new insight and harmony within the self (Giacomucci, 2021).

The actual work with parts of self becomes valuable in that we can access a deeper level of differentiation and complexity within the self.

Exploring Ambivalence or Inner Conflict

One of the most helpful uses of psychodrama is to externalize parts of self that are in conflict with each other. Many times, an entire psychodrama enactment revolves around this as the goal. For example, exploring the part of me that wants to write a book and the part of me that does not want to write another book. Or the part of me that wants to apologize to my wife for the fight we had versus the part of me that feels justified in my anger and resentment. A common example in trauma therapy is the part of the client that wants to be in trauma therapy versus the part of the client that does not want to do trauma therapy (see Figure 10.1).

While this process of exploring ambivalent or conflicted parts of self is most frequently done with just two roles, it can also be expanded to include more than two roles involved in the conflict or polarization. Here is an example from one of my outpatient clients:

> Andrew is struggling with his marriage and the abuse he has experienced from his wife. After many years of trying to work through things, he has become less optimistic and moved out of his home into an apartment to create

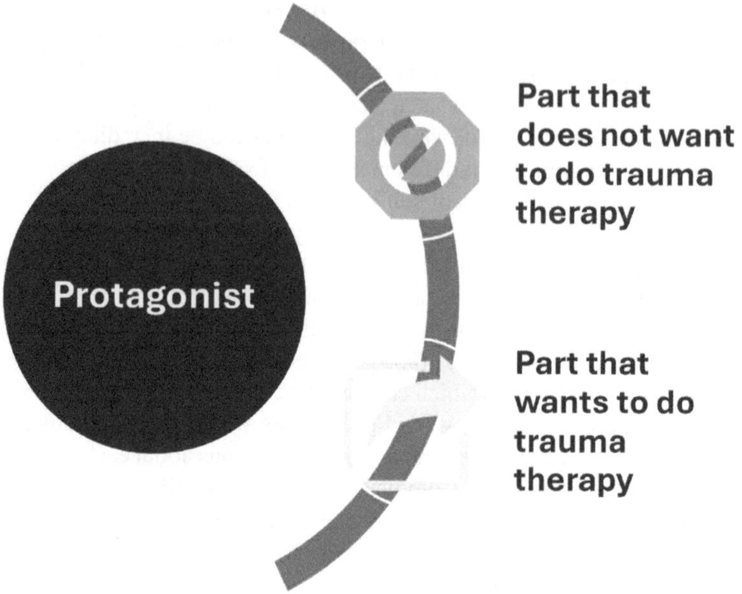

Figure 10.1 Parts of self of the protagonist in trauma therapy

space in his marriage. He is unsure if he should separate or divorce his wife or if he should continue trying to work through things with her. In our individual session, I pulled out two empty chairs and invited Andrew to imagine putting these two parts of himself into the two chairs – the part that wants to leave the marriage and the part that wants to stay in the marriage. In a previous session he had concretized his courage as the picture on my wall and we had done a psychodrama with it. As we warmed up for this psychodrama, I helped him reconnect to his courage through the same picture on the wall. "Andrew, can you reverse roles with your courage? Now tell Andrew, as courage, how you can help him with this decision he needs to make." Courage offered Andrew support and affirmation for the process. After reversing roles back, I brought Andrew to the two parts of self in conflict and took turns becoming each. "As the part of you that wants to end the marriage, I am exhausted. We have tried for years and things have not gotten better, they have gotten worse. Leaving the marriage will be the best thing for you and give you a fresh start." From the other role he said "I can't leave my marriage, I'm afraid of what people will think and I promised her I would be with her until death. There is always a chance that things could get better if we keep working on them." Then I promoted dialogue between the two parts – "you can't give up now. I can't believe you are seriously considering ending the marriage. It would be so

> hurtful to her, the kids, the rest of the family, and to you if you left." Reverse roles. "I can't believe you are considering staying after the abuse you have been through. You deserve so much better than this and shouldn't have to put up with it any longer." After a series of back-and-forth dialogue between the two parts, Andrew couldn't find more clarity. I asked if there was another option between these two choices and he developed a compromise with himself to initiate couples therapy with his wife and give it a few more months to see if things change.

Another example of working through ambivalence comes from my graduate social work course on psychodrama that I teach at Bryn Mawr College.

> A student, Jamie, volunteers as protagonist to explore their ambivalence regarding career paths after graduation. They share about the career path that they originally were pursuing fueled by their own addiction recovery. Then they shared about their current internship site in a medical social work offering them a job which would take their career in another direction. We enrolled both options into a psychodrama scene with other strengths and a mentor to help them with their decision. After connecting with the resources in the scene, they role reversed into each of the other roles. Through doubling and interviewing, we examined the good and bad parts of each career choice. As Jamie the addiction counselor, they offer a soliloquy – "I am comfortable and familiar. I offer you a chance to use your personal experience to help others. You owe it to your recovery community to dedicate your career to help others suffering from addiction. But I'm also something you already know well so you are less likely to learn and grow with me." After role reversing into Jamie the medical social worker role, they responded, "I am a new opportunity to learn and grow. With me you can occasionally help people suffering with addiction but be of service to a much larger population of people. I might be a more scary choice because there are more unknowns, but I also have more potential for career advancement and financial compensation than working in addiction treatment." In this particular psychodrama, the physical proximity of the roles symbolically represented the closeness and distance of the career paths to the student. Jamie placed the addiction recovery career option nearby and the other career path further away. We experimented with moving addiction treatment further away and moving the other career choice closer. The scene culminated with the protagonist directing the roles into a new configuration of closeness vs distance that felt just right.

This scene demonstrates the use of parts of self in psychodrama not only to explore ambivalence but also to explore the different parts of the multiple versions of self. Jamie was able to examine the pros and cons of each future career path, which helped them find new clarity in their career choice. See Chapter 7 for shorter psychodrama structures on working with ambivalence or inner conflict.

Working With Parts of Other Roles

The aforementioned section explored parts of the protagonist, while this section will focus on exploring parts of other roles in the scene. Psychodramatically working with parts of roles allows us to further explore the intricacies within other roles. When we experience emotional charge toward another person or role, it is difficult to fully humanize them or recognize the complexities within them. Instead, we tend to oversimplify them and see things in black and white. Separating out a role into multiple parts can be a useful intervention in psychodrama when the protagonist is getting stuck in the scene due to mixed feelings with the other role. Splitting the role into two (or more) parts can help the protagonist explore their emotions in relationship to different parts of the other role. For example, when doing psychodrama in countries where there is very strong family loyalty and obedience to parents in the cultural norms, I often find it necessary to split the parent role into good and bad parts so the protagonist can honor the good parts while being angry or upset with the bad parts (Lai & Tsai, 2014).

Separating another role into two (or more) parts can also be a helpful intervention if the protagonist is oversimplifying another role, projecting onto another role, or dehumanizing another role. The process of breaking the role into two allows the protagonist to see the role from another perspective.

> One of the most memorable examples of this that I experienced was at a congress of the International Association of Group Psychotherapy and Group Process (IAGP) where a Russian psychodramatist, Pavel Kornienko, facilitated a workshop focused on "Humanizing Your Enemy." In the workshop, he had us reverse roles with someone who we consider to be an enemy (or someone who considers our community to be their enemy) and he interviewed each of us about our beliefs. Then, he had us rewind time to become our enemy as a teenager and proceeded to interview us in the role again. Separating the role of one's enemy into adult and teenage parts allowed each of us to humanize our enemy and develop understanding and even compassion for the life circumstances and experiences earlier in life that may have contributed to their hatred.

Another example of separating a role into two parts that helped a protagonist appreciate the complexity of another person comes from one of my psychodrama training workshops.

> The protagonist, Sam, is angry at her supervisor for being too rigid and conservative. Sam is in the process of expressing anger towards her supervisor – "I'm

> just so annoyed by you and your shit. Whenever I have a new idea, you squash it and want me to do things your way. It feels like you won't let me be myself and I'm so angry!" After Sam had her catharsis, I role reversed her into the role of her supervisor. In the role of her supervisor, she kept attacking herself and was stuck in playing the role through the lens of her projection. I wanted her to humanize her supervisor, so I invited her to step back into another part of the supervisor, the *deepening double* of the supervisor and to articulate what the supervisor might be thinking or feeling as a supervisor. I helped by doubling the role – "sometimes I'm worried as a new supervisor that my license is on the line, and I don't know exactly what my supervisee is saying to their clients." In the role, Sam continues – "my fear can be crippling, and it leads my to squash other people's creativity." Others in the group doubled for this part of the supervisor too – "I feel the responsibility as a supervisor to ensure that the clients are receiving good care," "the organizational leadership keeps pressuring me to keep an eye on the interns," and "I'm not sure if I'm a good supervisor so I get over-involved sometimes." The psychodrama continued to closure and Sam walked away with a deeper sense of empathy for the fear and insecurity that her supervisor may be experiencing that could be fueling the behavior that had been angering her.

The deepening double is a very useful technique to help parse out the underlying feelings, thoughts, and experiences of a role. It helps us get to the inner essence of what might be going on internally for a role, beneath the presenting behaviors. More or less, the deepening double helps us get to the core of the role.

The deepening double helps us get to the core of the role.

Another useful time to separate a role into multiple parts is if the role is a perpetrator role. Some protagonists and groups can tolerate talking directly to perpetrator roles in psychodrama, but sometimes, it can be overwhelming for the protagonist and/or the other group members (Giacomucci, 2023). Splitting the perpetrator role into multiple parts can lower the intensity of the scene or allow the protagonist to go beyond their anger toward the perpetrator for how they were hurt. Here is an example from a recent psychodrama in my trauma group:

> Lydia is the protagonist with the goal of forgiving her sister for all she put their family through. She shares that her sister was a "sociopath" and diagnosed with antisocial personality disorder – and that she had bullied her and hurt her and her other family members consistently throughout her life. Her sister died of an overdose a few years ago. In the psychodrama scene, we first enroll the supportive roles, then bring in an auxiliary as Lydia's deceased sister. Knowing that this was a role that carried many mixed feelings for Lydia,

> and assessing that Lydia was already very emotional, I opted to split her sister into two parts – the human version of her sister and the spirit of her sister. Lydia expressed her anger and frustration towards the human version of her sister then focused her attention towards the role of the spirit of her sister. I help her by differentiating the roles in my directing instructions – "Lydia, now that you have expressed your anger towards the human version of your sister, what do you want to say to the spirit of your sister? This is the part of her that is untouched by mental illness that you never got to see." Lydia takes a sigh of relief and begins to gently cry as she talks to the spirit of her sister, "I craved for you everyday when you were alive. I saw glimpses of you at times, but I know now that you were stuck underneath the mental illness. I wish you and I had more time together." Reverse roles. Now Lydia, as the spirit of her sister responds, "I am so sorry. You are right, I was trapped underneath the mental illness. What I really wanted was to be your sister and love you, but I couldn't. I'm at peace now and I watch over you everyday." I instruct her in the role to tell Lydia what she wanted in a relationship with her sister if the circumstances were different. "I would have wanted to play with you, do our nails together, gossip about boys, and just be normal sisters. I'm so sorry that I took that from you." Reverse roles back. Finally, Lydia hears these messages repeated to her from the role of her sister's spirit and responds with a message of forgiveness and understanding.

This is a good example of how splitting an antagonist or perpetrator role into two parts can be very helpful in moving the protagonist toward their goal or contract (see Figure 10.2). Lydia's goal was about forgiveness. If we had only focused on the part of her sister that had hurt her, the scene would have been likely to get stuck on the anger toward her sister. What she needed was another angle that

Figure 10.2 Depiction of splitting the role of Lydia's sister into two roles

would allow for understanding and compassion. The spirit of her sister provided that angle.

Enrolling Body Parts

Many survivors of complex trauma and CPTSD struggle with their relationship to their bodies. In the same way that we can psychodramatically work with parts of self, we can also work with body parts. The aforementioned example with Lydia's sister highlights the power of working with the spirit of a role. Similarly, the role of one's heart frequently emerges in my psychodrama sessions. Working with the protagonist's or another role's heart or soul as the role can help move the psychodrama along toward the established goal. The role of the heart is one that I often enroll in psychodramas when the protagonist is working toward self-worth or vulnerability. Having the protagonist's heart in the scene makes it easy for us to explore how the protagonist has been protecting their heart after trauma with walls or defenses. It also facilitates a psychodramatic process of validating the goodness within the protagonist's heart, which can be quite moving and affirming. Many of my clients naturally discuss the conflict between their heart and their brain, which makes for a natural psychodrama:

> Dave enrolls his heart and his brain as two roles in conflict with each other. He shares about how he often knows in his heart what the right thing to do is but that his brain talks him out of it and leads him astray. In the role of his brain he talks to himself, "I keep you from getting overwhelmed and stuck in your feelings. I create all sorts of elaborate plans and ideas to keep you safe and out of trouble." As his heart, Dave speaks to himself, "I feel things deeply and help you stay out of your head all of the time. When you connect with me, you are more closely connected with others. I hold your love, hopes, and empathy." I ask Dave to reposition his head and his heart in the room in proximity to himself. He places them on either side of himself and says, "I just realized that my head and my heart are often fighting with each other, but I don't have to fight with them. I can notice the information they each are providing me and ultimately make the final decision on what to do."

Working with body parts can be helpful not only in exploring relationships between heart, brain, and spirit but also with other body parts and even with one's entire body. I have facilitated many psychodramas with clients who struggle with eating disorders or body dysmorphia, where we enroll their body as a role and have a conversation with it. This type of psychodrama can be very simple and help a protagonist to work toward befriending their body and approaching it with more acceptance and love.

I have also found it helpful to enroll body parts when the protagonist has experienced loss of a body part or loss of functionality of a body part. This allows for a grieving process related to the lost body part or its function. I have seen this done with lost limbs, loss of eyesight, loss of a kidney, and even the loss of breasts from a breast cancer survivor. Here is an example from one of my clients:

> Jerome is chosen as protagonist with the goal of making sense of his near-death experience in a motorcycle crash that resulted in the loss of his hand. We set up the scene with strength-based roles and Jerome having a conversation with the grim reaper – "why did I survive the accident and how do I move on?" Reverse roles. As the personification of death, I ask Jerome to respond to himself. He thinks for a moment and says, "most people who meet me don't survive to talk about it. You and I made a deal that I would take your hand in exchange for you keeping your life." I asked Jerome to pick two objects in the room to represent his 'life' and his 'hand' and to hold both with the grim reaper. Death repeated to him that he must choose one or the other. Jerome let go of his hand to hold onto his life. I invited him to say goodbye to his hand which elicited a grief response – "I never could have imagined losing you. You have been with me since the start of my life and every day is difficult without you. It was so painful to lose you and wake up in the hospital without you. I miss you and have had to learn how to live without you, but I had to give you up in order to survive."

Concretizing Jerome's hand in the scene gave him the chance to grieve the loss of his hand while making sense of his loss and near-death experience. While we often think of our body as a complete entity, there are sometimes good reasons to enroll body parts in a scene, so the protagonist can explore their relationship to them.

Conclusion

Psychodrama offers a method for parsing out parts of self, parts of other roles, and exploring one's relationship to various body parts. Splitting the self into multiple roles allows us to work through inner conflict or ambivalence by externalizing one's insides. Enrolling parts of other roles can be a useful strategy when there are mixed feelings, stuck feelings, oversimplifications, projections, or dehumanization present. Working with parts in psychodrama effectively facilitates a deeper understanding of the multiplicity and complexity of one's self and others. Psychodramatic parts work is beneficial for all clients but may be especially helpful when working with complex trauma to help honor and recognize internal states of fragmentation, confusion, and disconnection.

Psychodramatic parts work is beneficial for all clients but may be especially helpful when working with complex trauma to help honor and recognize internal states of fragmentation, confusion, and disconnection.

References

Giacomucci, S. (2021). *Social work, sociometry, and psychodrama: Experiential approaches for group therapists, community leaders, and social workers*. Springer Nature.

Giacomucci, S. (2023). *Trauma-informed principles in group therapy, psychodrama, and organizations: Action methods for leadership*. Routledge.

Hudgins, M. K., & Toscani, F. (2013). *Healing world trauma with the therapeutic spiral model: Stories from the frontlines*. London: Jessica Kingsley Publishers.

Lai, N. H., & Tsai, H. H. (2014). Practicing psychodrama in Chinese culture. *The Arts in Psychotherapy*, *41*(4), 386–390.

Moreno, J. L. (1953). *Who shall survive? Foundations of sociometry, group psychotherapy and sociodrama (2nd edition)*. Beacon, NY: Beacon House.

Chapter 11

Psychodramatic Grief Work with Death, Traumatic Loss, and Complicated Grief

Psychodrama is an ideal approach when working with grief, loss, and traumatic loss. I find that it works quite efficiently and profoundly in helping clients access grief, navigate complex emotions, work through complicated grief, and engage in meaning-making around their loss (Giacomucci, 2020). In my own personal journey of recovery and personal growth, it was a psychodrama about the death of a close friend that convinced me of the power and adaptability of psychodrama as a method and inspired me to later pursue training to become a therapist and psychodramatist. In my work with trauma survivors and clients in recovery from addictions, I find the topic of traumatic loss and complicated grief to emerge at some point with nearly every client. Many of the clients I work with have witnessed gun violence, overdoses, fatal injuries or accidents, war, or medical conditions that lead to death. It seems that the COVID-19 pandemic has only increased the prevalence of traumatic loss in my community and further underscores the importance of practitioners being able to competently work with clients who have experienced traumatic loss.

Psychodrama is an ideal approach when working with grief, loss, and traumatic loss.

In every experience of trauma, there is also an experience of loss. These experiences of loss within trauma may come in the form of a death, a lost relationship, ambiguous loss, loss of parts of self, or loss of inner experiences such as innocence, safety, trust, or hope (Giacomucci, 2023). Many trauma survivors experience non-death-related losses that provoke a strong grief response. Psychodramatic grief work is not only focused on death but must also include helping clients grieve the losses described earlier. One of the other common losses that trauma survivors often grieve is the loss of what could have been if it had not been for the trauma and its impact on their life. These types of losses are often overlooked, which can lead to disenfranchised grief for clients who do not feel permission to grieve losses that did not include death.

DOI: 10.4324/9781003639497-11

In my ongoing line of trauma-focused psychodrama research in inpatient substance use treatment, we recently explored psychodrama's effectiveness in treating traumatic grief and prolonged grief disorder (Giacomucci et al., 2025). In a sample of 148 participants who averaged only 4.63 groups in our trauma-focused inpatient tract, we discovered a 31% decrease in traumatic grief and a 32% decrease in prolonged grief disorder symptoms. In more closely examining the sample of patients and utilizing the recommended cut-off score for probably prolonged grief disorder (Boelen & Smid, 2017), we found that of the portion of patients who were initially scoring high enough for diagnosis of prolonged grief disorder at pre-test, 91% of them were no longer scoring high enough to maintain the diagnosis at the completion of treatment just a few weeks later. Furthermore, all participants were asked to complete a series of Likert-scale-like questions, rating how much they agreed with various statements on a scale of 1–5. For the item, "Psychodrama helped me move towards resolution of my grief/loss," the agreement level was 4.46 out of 5, or an 89.2% agreement rate. This study seems to be the first larger study on psychodrama and grief, while offering very compelling outcomes, which were further supported by patients' qualitative survey responses.

Layers of Trauma, Loss, and Complicated Grief

Traumatic loss is unique in that it is a form of loss that includes a violent, sudden, and/or unexpected death, which is more likely to result in more intense or lasting reactions than other types of loss. Some of these lasting impacts can include complicated grief, traumatic stress, and prolonged grief disorder. When it comes to traumatic loss, there is not only a loss to grieve but also a trauma to try to make sense of at the same time. With traumatic loss, the trauma often prevents normal grieving, and the inhibited grief often mitigates one's capacity to process the trauma.

With traumatic loss, the trauma often prevents normal grieving, and the inhibited grief often mitigates one's capacity to process the trauma.

Complicated grief often results from traumatic loss. Complicated grief is characterized by its heightened intensity, duration, and impact compared to normal grief. Someone struggling with complicated grief may be experiencing profound sadness, anger, regret, self-blame, stuckness, longing and preoccupation with the lost relationship, disbelief, fragmented sense of identity, avoidance, numbness, and hopelessness. These characteristics tend to fade over time with normal grief, but do not decrease significantly when it comes to complicated grief. The DSM-5-TR (American Psychiatric Association, 2022) added a new diagnosis of prolonged grief disorder to label when complicated grief lasts for over 12 months and continues to cause significant impairment in an individual's life.

In my clinical experience, many of the clients I have worked with who are struggling with complicated grief are really stuck in anger for the injustice of their loved-one's death, self-blame for the death, and/or an existential crisis stemming from the death, which rattled their senses of self, relationships, the world, and meaninglessness. Many clients blame God for the traumatic loss, or believe the loss could have been prevented if it were not systemic injustices or failures, or have spiraled into shame and self-blame for their loved one's demise. The traumatic loss has shattered their identity, spirituality, or sense of safety in the world. Who am I without this person in my life? Was everything I thought I knew about God wrong? How can I continue to live in a world where horrific things like this can happen? Many clients struggle with the "what if's" and rumination on what they could have done or said to prevent the death. Others might get stuck on asking "why?" and trying to make sense of a senseless killing or unpreventable accident. The shock, suddenness, horror, and injustice of the traumatic death make it difficult to make sense of the experience or integrate the loss into any coherent narrative of one's experience.

The loss of safety and predictability that accompanies traumatic loss interferes with one's ability to feel the sense of security needed to engage in the vulnerability associated with grieving. For this reason, I find that the traumatic impact of the traumatic loss must often be addressed first before the grief can be focused on. This means oriented on the traumatic stress symptoms related to the death – intrusive images, nightmares, flashbacks, avoidance, dissociation, hypervigilance, reactivity, and distorted beliefs. Once the client has experienced some relief from these symptoms, then the grief will be much more naturally expressed and experienced (see Figure 11.1).

Figure 11.1 Depiction of traumatic stress symptoms blocking grief

Anger and Grief for Meaningless Death

Traumatic loss is quite different from other types of loss in that it is unexpected, sudden, and often violent. This often leaves survivors with a sense of grief that is infused with anger and helplessness. Sometimes, this anger is directed at others who were involved in the death, sometimes, it is expressed to God, and other times, it is turned inward upon oneself. As humans, we are constantly trying to make sense of our experience; but some experiences, especially traumatic loss, can pose quite a problem in trying to make meaning from them. How can there be meaning in the accidental death of a child, or the suicide of a college student, or the sudden heart attack of a parent, or even the death of a baby before it is born? Psychodrama provides us with an avenue of expressing this anger, grief, and exploring or creating new dimensions of meaning. The psychodrama example from Chapter 10 with Jerome speaking to the grim reaper about the loss of his hand depicts this in action. Jerome initially could not make sense of his loss, but the psychodramatic conversation with the grim reaper helped provide him with the opportunity to express his emotions and access new meaning, understanding, and perspective. This next case example depicts a psychodrama with a client who was pregnant and lost her baby.

> Jess is chosen as the protagonist of a psychodrama with the topic of grief around the death of her unborn child the year prior. She shares her self-blame wondering if she had done anything that contributed to the loss, as well as her overall sense of unfairness that other people have healthy babies and she didn't. She expressed feeling stuck in her grief and afraid to get pregnant again because of her loss and knew that she needed to grieve and heal in order to have another child. Her goal for the psychodrama was to allow herself to express emotions related to the loss and to try to find a way to move on with her family. We set up the psychodrama by enrolling supportive roles. She asked to have other women in the group join her for a sense of community. Multiple women shared about their own similar experiences of loss.
>
> Seeing that Jess had strong interpersonal support in the scene already, I asked her if a transpersonal role might be helpful in navigating her topic today; she agreed and enrolled God. I invited her to speak to God and ask God for help in her grief. She began, "Please help me, I'm so stuck after the loss that I'm afraid to move on. I don't get why I had to lose my baby. Why would you let this happen?" She continued speaking to God and it became clear that she had pent up anger towards God which we helped her access. "It's okay Jess, you can be angry at God, he can take it." With the help of the other group members, Jess tapped into her anger – "Its so unfair! How could you let this happen! What purpose could you have in letting an unborn child die!?" Jess broke down crying and was held by the other women. "I want to believe in you and trust you, but it is so hard after knowing that you let this

happen. Everything I thought I knew and believed has been tested. I want to trust in you but I'm not sure if I can." At this point, I asked Jess to reverse roles with God. I instructed her, as God, to respond to herself. She paused for a moment, struggling to get into the role while the auxiliary playing her role repeated her questions to God. As God, Jess took a more confident, nurturing posture as her eyes slowly filled with tears, she responded to herself – "Jess, I'm so sorry. I know it's not fair to see everyone else raising their kids while you are stuck in your pain and sorrow. It is a tragedy that you lost your baby and I grieve with you." I asked God to help Jess understand what the purpose of this was and how to move on. "Well Jess, I have a plan and there is a purpose for everything, but I can't reveal that to you right now. You will have to trust me on this. Your son is with me right now and you will meet him in heaven" I then asked God to tell Jess how she is supposed to trust him after this. "Jess, I know you are mad at me, and that is okay. I would be too. I'd rather you be mad at me than blame yourself, because you did absolutely nothing to cause this. I know you are hurting and grieving, as is your entire family. But this isn't the first time you and I have been through tragedy together. In the past, tragedy and suffering brought you closer to me. I supported you through those difficulties and I can support you through this too if you allow me." Next, I instructed Jess to reverse roles back to herself and to her these messages repeated back to her by the role player. With the support of her group members, Jess listened to God and softened.

Seeing that she had stabilized in her emotional expression, I invited her to next choose someone to play the role of her unborn baby who she had chosen the name of Brayden for. Brayden was enrolled in the scene and Jess began a discussion with him. "I waited for this moment to meet you, and it never came. I don't know what to say" – Jess begins to cry again. "Even though we never got to meet, I want you to know what I am your mother, and I love you no matter what. I think about you every day and I feel robbed in that you didn't even get a chance at life. I know you are with God, but I wish I could be with you too." Reverse roles (Jess now takes on the role of Brayden). I continue directing – "Brayden, you heard that your mom is devastated about your loss and was blaming herself even, what do you want her to know?" Jess, as Brayden, says, "mom I'm okay. I felt no pain and I'm in a good place now and forever. I'm watching over you." I prompt further – "Brayden, can you tell your mom what it's been like for you to see her struggle with grief, anger, and blame the past year?" Jess, as Brayden, responds – "it is heartbreaking for me to see you struggle because of me. I want you to stop being angry at yourself and at God for my death. I know sadness is normal, but I don't want you to be stuck in this grief forever. I want you to try again and be a good mom to other babies who are waiting

> for you in the future." I prompt deeper – "Brayden, tell mom exactly what you want for her going forward." Brayden says, "Mom, I want you to be happy and at peace. I want you to remember me and honor me by being the best mom you can be to your future kids." Jess reversed roles back to herself and took in these messages from Brayden with both tears in her eyes and a smile. She gave him a long hug and thanked him while promising to not give up on having kids in the future and to be a spectacular mom to them.

This example shows the power of psychodrama to help clients renegotiate their relationship to complicated grief and traumatic loss. Jess was able to gain support from other women, express her mixed emotions, and find new meaning and motivation in a single session. The scene allowed Jess to express her anger, self-blame, and sadness while receiving a sense of validation from the group and the other roles. Traumatic death makes it particularly difficult for survivors to have a sense of closure as there are often things left unsaid or undone in the relationship with the person who died. In the surplus reality of psychodrama, we can provide clients with an embodied experience of competing those actions and conversations that they might crave to experience – even though it would be impossible to do so in real life. A psychodrama about a loved one's death allows for closure that is impossible in life.

A psychodrama about a loved one's death allows for closure that is impossible in life.

Forgiveness and Self-Forgiveness

Another incredibly common theme in working with traumatic loss or complicated grief is addressing issues associated with forgiveness. The fueling factors of complicated grief sometimes include unresolved conflict or feelings in the relationship between the client and the individual who died. The client may have feelings of self-blame or guilt around their behavior with the individual who died (this is very common in my work with folks in addiction recovery). In these situations, the client often articulates craving forgiveness from the other person. However, more times than not, it is later realized that the other person does not hold them accountable for what happened, and really, they need to work on self-forgiveness. Sometimes, the client has been hurt by the individual who died and maintains resentment or anger toward them but wants help working toward forgiving them. In other cases, the forgiveness that the client craves is from a higher power or God. While the location and direction of the forgiveness may vary in traumatic grief work, it is quite often a central theme in the work.

The following is one of the more memorable psychodramas I have facilitated on traumatic loss and complicated grief:

> Charles is chosen as the protagonist with the goal of forgiveness related to the guilt around the death of his grandmother. Although Charles presents with a tough exterior, as soon as he begins to talk about his grandmother, he gets in touch with his emotions. He shared about his grandmother being the most supportive person in his life and growing up with his grandmother due to his own parents' absence in his life due to their addictions. He shares about how his own addiction resulted in drug dealing. When a conflict broke out between him and another drug dealer, it resulted in a shoot out at his grandmother's house and his grandmother was killed. As we began the psychodrama, Charles wasn't fully convinced that it would be helpful for him, which required a lot of encouragement from me as the director, as well as from his peers in the group.
>
> We set up a scene with supportive roles to provide him with some stabilization and validate the emotions he was experiencing. Many of the messages from the supportive roles included challenging old beliefs about masculinity and emotions. Once Charles was adequately supported and ready, we enrolled his grandmother into the scene, and I instructed him to tell his grandmother about the pain he has been experiencing since her death while asking for forgiveness. "Grandma, I can't stop getting high since you died. I blame myself for how you were killed, and the guilt is killing me. I thought about ending my life because the pain is too much when I'm sober. You were the only good thing in my life and because of me you are dead. I need forgiveness but I don't know if I deserve it." I invite him to role reverse with his grandmother. As his grandmother, he listens to his words repeated by the role player, after I prompt him to see himself through his grandmother's eyes and to respond. "Charles, its okay but you need to clean yourself up and stop using my death as a reason to get high." I prompt him, in the role of his grandmother, to tell himself what it has been like to watch him get high and blame himself. "Well, I don't blame you for what happen – you didn't shoot me. It was an accident, and I can't stand watching you kill yourself with drugs because of it." I say, "Grandma, your grandson Charles is dying for some forgiveness from you – do you think you can give it to him?" At the same time, I pick up a scarf and give it to him to represent forgiveness. As grandma, he looks at the scarf and then at himself; he appears uncertain. I encourage him – "grandma, you just said that you don't blame him for your death. Would you be willing to offer him this forgiveness that he has been craving? He really feels like he needs this from you." I also prompt the group member playing the role of Charles to repeat the request for forgiveness to grandma. As grandma, he looks at himself again and says, "Charles you know I forgive you. I love you no matter what. This wasn't

> your fault; but it is your responsibility to accept my forgiveness, get clean, and make me proud in your sobriety." He physically gives the forgiveness to himself. As soon as it leaves his hands, he pauses in introspection with a shocked look on his face. After a second or two, he turns to me, breaking role and says, "holy shit, something just happened inside of me. I felt something move when I gave the forgiveness. I can't believe it; this crazy psychodrama stuff actually works!" The group, previously on the verge of tears themselves, erupts in laughter with Charles as he savors the moment. I then invite him to reverse roles back to himself and experience receiving the forgiveness from his grandmother. The scene is replayed with Charles in his own role accepting forgiveness from his grandmother and making a commitment to honor her memory by getting sober and helping others in recovery.

After the psychodrama, Charles held onto the scarf that had represented forgiveness and shared how transformative the session had been for him. He refused to return the scarf back to my collection of psychodrama props. I initially thought he was joking but later realized he was not going to give it back to me when he refused to return it a second time. Realizing that the scarf meant much more to him than to me, I allowed him to take it as a reminder of his healing. Coincidentally, I happened to run into Charles at an alumni event several months later. He made a point to tell me that he had pinned the scarf on the wall of his recovery house as a daily reminder of his forgiveness and his commitment to his grandmother!

This psychodrama highlights the power of concretization and forgiveness in traumatic grief work. I suspect that, for Charles, the act of giving himself forgiveness while playing the role of his grandmother was synonymous with internally deciding that he deserved forgiveness and that he would accept it from his grandmother. I judged that his initial hesitation was related to internally trying to discern if he could accept it. The physical representation of forgiveness with a scarf provided a deepening of the experience and a symbolic representation of the movement of forgiveness from his grandmother to himself. Not only were the words of forgiveness spoken, but the visual representation of forgiveness was transferred. The act of physically opening one's hands and body to receive the physical representation of forgiveness parallels the emotional and psychological process of opening one's heart and mind to receive forgiveness. This is the integration piece that promotes lasting change after the feelings of grief, anger, guilt, or shame are released.

The act of physically opening one's hands and body to receive the physical representation of forgiveness parallels the emotional and psychological process of opening one's heart and mind to receive forgiveness.

Honoring the Ancestors

Another application of psychodrama adjacent to grief and loss is working with ancestors. Understanding our ancestors helps us understand ourselves. Psychodrama is a modality that can facilitate powerful experiences connecting with ancestors (Anderson & Carnabucci, 2011; Schutzenberger, 2013; Badis et al., 2025). Sometimes, ancestor work in psychodrama is oriented more toward relationships with ancestors as a supportive resource, and other times, this leans more toward exploring ancestral trauma. Occasionally, ancestor work is more complicated and includes a variety of feelings toward an ancestor. For example, in a recent psychodrama that I facilitated with a Chinese protagonist, there were mixed feelings toward ancestors. On one hand, there was a strong sense of family loyalty, respect, reverence, and gratitude. But on the other hand, there was also frustration or anger at the limiting beliefs about gender norms that had been handed down throughout the generations. Sometimes, in these situations, it is necessary to initially split the ancestor into two parts (such as "the good part" and "the bad part") so that the protagonist can differentiate and identify their mixed feelings while also holding space for the other feelings. I often find that, when working with someone from a cultural background that emphasizes family loyalty, this is a necessary step – otherwise, the protagonist is too conflicted to express negative feelings toward an ancestor or elder.

Understanding our ancestors helps us understand ourselves.

Ancestral trauma is another theme that often emerges in working with ancestors. I have yet to meet someone who has traced their ancestral lineages back and not discovered layers and layers of trauma that their ancestors have experienced – whether it be war, famine, poverty, disease, immigration, discrimination, slavery, genocide, racism, religious persecution, or other forms of individual or collective trauma. Exploring our ancestors' experiences of trauma can help us contextualize our experience and our families' experiences while developing a greater sense of empathy and gratitude for what our ancestors faced in order for us to be here. Sometimes getting in touch with our ancestors' traumas can elicit powerful emotions of sadness, grief, anger, fear, guilt, or shame. It can also help us to better understand some of our own experiences, which may be shaped by the experiences of our ancestors and passed down to us through generations of attachment styles, belief systems, norms, values, behaviors, and epigenetics. I have facilitated multiple psychodramas with a focus on exploring ancestral trauma related to slavery, immigration, discrimination, religious persecution, or war that resulted in powerful recognitions of the pain and suffering of one's ancestors. Through the exploration of ancestral trauma, the protagonist often emerges with a new connection to their ancestors that they can call upon for guidance and strength.

We can also directly approach ancestor work with the goal of connecting with the ancestors as sources of wisdom, knowledge, perspective, and resilience. Recently, I have facilitated a few psychodramas with clients who leveraged their connection to their ancestors to help them navigate the new injustices that they are facing due to Donald Trump's flurry of executive orders and the increased prevalence of racism and discrimination. In facing these political threats, clients are realizing that their ancestors have also faced many of the same threats and found their way, which makes the ancestors a potent resource for role modeling, inspiration, and strength.

Conclusion

The application of psychodramatic methods to the issues of grief, loss, and death provides meaningful entry ways into unrealized dimensions. Loss is at the heart of all experiences of trauma, including death, loss of relationships, ambiguous losses, parts of self, the loss of what could have been, and the loss of safety, trust, and innocence. The exploration of ancestors' experiences can provoke a deeper connection to one's self, family, and culture while initiating conscious contact to a new set of transpersonal resources. Traumatic loss and complicated grief are both incredibly difficult experiences to navigate. Psychodrama offers an effective and efficient tool for accessing unexpressed grief while renegotiating our connection to deceased loved ones and making sense of our experience.

The application of psychodramatic methods to the issues of grief, loss, and death provides meaningful entry ways into unrealized dimensions.

References

American Psychiatric Association. (2022). *Diagnostic and statistical manual of mental disorders (5th edition., text rev.)*. https://doi.org/10.1176/appi.books.9780890425787

Anderson, R., & Carnabucci, K. (2011). *Integrating psychodrama and systemic constellation work: New directions for action methods, mind-body therapies and energy healing*. Jessica Kingsley Publishers.

Badis, D., Hernandez, C. L., Nieto, L., Ruiz Esparza, M. P., & Tkachuck, C. (2025). A World with Many Worlds: Decolonizing Education with Action Methods. In S. Giacomucci, H. Fleury, & D. Altinay (Eds.), *Psychodrama in education: Creativity and experiential teaching around the world* (pp. 137–161). Springer Nature.

Boelen, P. A., & Smid, G. E. (2017). The traumatic grief inventory self-report version (TGI-SR): Introduction and preliminary psychometric evaluation. *Journal of Loss and Trauma, 22*(3), 196–212.

Giacomucci, S. (2020). Addiction, traumatic loss, and guilt: A case study resolving grief through psychodrama and sociometric connections. *The Arts in Psychotherapy*, *67*, 101627.

Giacomucci, S. (2023). *Trauma-informed principles in group therapy, psychodrama, and organizations: Action methods for leadership*. Routledge.

Giacomucci, S., Marquit, J., Briggs, H., & Gupta, R. (2025). Psychodrama's effects on PTSD, depression, anxiety, traumatic grief, prolonged grief disorder, and spontaneity: A mixed methods study in inpatient addiction treatment. *The Arts in Psychotherapy*, *93*, 102293.

Schutzenberger, A. A. (2013). Transgenerational analysis and psychodrama. In C. Baim, J. Burmeister, & M. Maciel (Eds.), *Psychodrama: Advances in theory and practice* (pp. 155–174). Taylor & Francis.

Chapter 12

Inner Child Work and Psychodrama

Carl Jung is often credited with initiating the idea of an inner child:

> In every adult there lurks a child – an eternal child, something that is always becoming, is never completed, and calls for unceasing care, attention, and education. That is the part of the human personality which wants to develop and become whole. But the man of today is far indeed from this wholeness.
>
> (1954)

Jung wrote of it as a primordial image of the child in our unconscious, or as a subpersonality, that is shaped by childhood experiences and influences adult behavior. Alice Miller (1981) and John Bradshaw (1990) popularized the concept of a "wounded child" to label the child-like part of self that carries the hurt from childhood trauma. Later, the concept of the "adapted child" was created by Eric Berne (as part of Transactional Analysis), further developed by Pia Mellody, and popularized by Terrence Real. The adapted child has been described as a child in adult clothes or a child's view on what it means to be an adult. This part of self has adapted to survive adversity in childhood, developing defenses and belief systems to sustain itself. The adaptive child is usually described in contrast to another role called the "functional adult" or "wise adult" – a more mature, grounded, and thoughtful part of self that can skillfully navigate relationships and emotions. These various terms and perspectives on the inner child offer different options for conceptualizing or presenting inner child work to clients.

Inner child work is one of the most common applications of psychodramatic methods. It would be hard to find a psychodramatist who has not directed multiple inner child psychodramas, as it is a theme that resurfaces often. The externalization of aspects of self in psychodrama lends itself very well to exploring one's relationship to themselves in the past or revisiting a moment in time in order to heal from it (Giacomucci, 2021). In psychodramatic inner child work, a protagonist engages in a conversation with their younger self, which provides an opportunity to explore their relationship to their self and their past.

DOI: 10.4324/9781003639497-12

This is most often suggested to promote self-compassion, self-understanding, and validation, address self-blame for past trauma, express previously suppressed emotions, challenge negative core beliefs from childhood, and work to meet previously unmet developmental needs related to nurturing or protection. Psychodrama's classic structure of "do-undo-redo" (see my suggested restructuring as "resource-undo-redo" in Chapter 4) often results in the witnessing and re-experiencing of a difficult memory in the past. It gives a protagonist the opportunity to see themselves in the past at a different age and to intervene in the memory as an adult today. Inner child work is not only about the inner child – I might argue that the healing is actually coming from the adult self, bringing new adaptive information to the past memory.

Inner child work is not only about the inner child – I might argue that the healing is actually coming from the adult self bringing new adaptive information to the past memory.

Younger Self as a Fragmented Part From Trauma

The overwhelming nature of trauma results in a fragmentation of the self – including disrupted memories, emotions, beliefs, and sensations. Inner child work with psychodrama could be understood as externalizing and working with these fragmented parts of self that were split off at the time of trauma. The "inner child" (or perhaps plural "inner children") within us represents dissociated states that are frozen in time, unprocessed, and unresolved. The language of an "inner child" is an endearing way to describe a psychological part of self that is connected by past hurt and continues to influence present-day beliefs, emotions, and actions. When one experiences a trigger that activates the old trauma within them, we could think of it as their younger self being activated and taking over their response to the situation. Only using the term "inner child" may be limiting, as most survivors of complex trauma have multiple fragmented memories and parts of self associated with various ages throughout childhood, adolescence, and maybe also adulthood. It may be helpful with some clients to conceptualize multiple inner children associated with different ages, traumas, or developmental stages. Bradshaw also spoke of this and highlighted multiple inner children, including an "inner infant," "inner toddler," "inner pre-schooler," and an "inner school age child." One of my clients found it helpful to differentiate their inner child from their inner teenager – for them the inner child held the hurt, pain, and fear, while the inner teenager was the keeper of the anger, rage, and defenses. The approach will have to be modified from client to client, but I would like to challenge us to go beyond simplifying inner child work to one templated version of an inner child for every client.

> Inner child work with psychodrama could be understood as externalizing and working with these fragmented parts of self that were split off at the time of trauma.

Trauma is essentially the past showing up in the present. Past memories, images, beliefs, emotions, and sensations are triggered and experienced in the here and now. Recent neuroscience findings further support that traumatic memories are experienced as if they are happening again in the moment (Perl et al., 2023). Inner child work with psychodrama allows us to make these fragmented parts conscious through externalization and role-playing, so that we can examine our relationship to them and reintegrate them into a more cohesive sense of self.

The Adaptive Information Processing Model (Shapiro, 2017), EMDR's theory of change, suggests that these traumatic memories exist within memory networks that are disconnected from all of the good, adaptive information that the client has gained through other unrelated experiences since the time of the trauma. The rationale for the effectiveness of trauma processing is multicausal, including multiple components that also relate to inner child work with psychodrama. The first is the presence of dual awareness, or the client's conscious awareness that they are in the here-and-now while also remembering and experiencing the traumatic content from the past. Being able to hold both at the same time helps the brain to process the fragmented memory and consolidate it into long-term memory like any other old memory. The visual presence of an inner child and an adult self in the psychodrama scene is an embodiment of dual awareness. In EMDR, the trauma processing happens through free association (with bilateral stimulation), which effectively helps the client connect adaptive information in one part of the brain to the previously fragmented traumatic memory. In psychodrama, the trauma processing occurs through the infusion of spontaneity to the past trauma through role-playing (which could be seen as a form of embodied free association). Remember that spontaneity means having a new response to an old situation in psychodrama. In trauma-focused psychodrama, the trauma processing is experienced by facing the trauma in a state of spontaneity. The spontaneity state allows the protagonist to channel new adaptive information to the traumatic memory – in this case, concretized in the role of the inner child.

> In trauma-focused psychodrama, the trauma processing is experienced by facing the trauma in a state of spontaneity.

In this example of psychodramatic inner child work, Layla is chosen as the protagonist of a group psychodrama with a focus on her experience of neglect and abandonment from her parents while addressing the resulting sense of worthlessness she has experienced throughout her life.

> She shares about her parents struggling with their own addiction and mental health issues and feeling unwanted since birth. She tells the story that was told to her of her mother rejecting and criticizing her the moment she was born. Our contract is to work towards developing a sense of worthiness. As I help Layla to integrate resources and strengths-based roles into the psychodrama, she references how she wished she had different parents. I take this opportunity to suggest that we enroll a different mother and father figure for her in this scene. Being very religious, Layla chooses Mary and Joseph, the parents of Jesus, to be her mother and father figures for today. She invites two group members to play their roles. I facilitate her role reversing with each of them to speak to herself about the preciousness of her life and their devotion to protecting and nurturing her. The messages from Mary and Joseph about worth, love, and protection were emotionally powerful for Layla to hear and quickly brought tears to her eyes. Next, we enrolled her infant self and created a rebirth scene where she could witness her infant self being born to Mary and Joseph as they respond with love and acceptance – a stark difference between what her actual experience had been. We replay this scene multiple times to provide Layla with the opportunity to experience the scene from the role of Mary, Joseph, her infant self, and her adult self. As her adult self, witnessing the scene for the final time, I ask her to embrace herself and speak to herself about her value and worth – "baby Layla, you are so precious and beautiful. You are an innocent and joyful baby girl, and nobody can take that from you. You deserve nothing but love." I instruct adult Layla to talk to baby Layla about moving forward in her adult life while nurturing this part of her that emerges within her and holding onto her newfound sense of worth. She says, "I realize now that I also abandon you when I believe that you are worthless – just like your parents. I'm so sorry that I haven't always been there for you. I promise you that I will be here for you now and going forward. I'll listen to you when you pop up and feel devalued or unseen. I've got you now."

Layla's psychodrama highlights one example of inner child work focused on infancy and birth stories. When engaging in inner child work, it is essential to consider the baby's relationship to their caregivers, as well as to the adult self. In this example, the initial source of the problems with worthlessness stems from the client's experience with their parents. In psychodramatic inner child work, it may sometimes be helpful (or necessary) to enroll "good-enough parent" roles. These good-enough parent roles provide the client with a template for what their experience should have been, or what they deserved in terms of parenting, in contrast to what they received. These good-enough parent roles become a model for the self-parenting work that is often necessary in healing from complex trauma (which will be discussed later in this chapter).

Old Unexpressed Emotions and Unmet Needs

One of the key components of inner child work with complex trauma is attuning to the unexpressed emotions and unmet needs from the time of the trauma. Many childhood trauma survivors are left to suppress their feelings or simply do not have a safe place or an adult that they could have expressed their emotions to. Sometimes, the amputation of emotion is fueled by cultural norms or gender stereotypes related to emotion (such as "men aren't supposed to cry"), while other times, the nature of the traumatic experience requires defenses that prevent emotional expression. The three common trauma response – fight, flight, and freeze (sorry, but I have yet to find any biological evidence in the research to include fawn or flop here) – which are biologically wired into our nervous systems, do not leave much room for emotional expression or only leave space for rudimentary expression of one emotion.

Inner child work with psychodrama provides an embodied avenue for expressing unresolved feelings or unmet needs from the past.

For example, a flight response is an embodied expression of fear, but does not allow for much emotional expression beyond fear. Similarly, a fight response could be experienced as an emotional expression of anger, but does not leave much more opportunity for the expression of varied feelings. A freeze response involves the immobilization of the nervous system and a shutting down that often does not permit much emotional expression at all. For many trauma survivors, the sharing of emotions at the time of the trauma would likely leave them even more vulnerable or targeted to experience more trauma or loss. For these reasons, it is quite common that old unexpressed emotions exist in relationship to past trauma.

Inner child work with psychodrama provides an embodied avenue for expressing unresolved feelings or unmet needs from the past. The container for these emotions and their expression is created by the validation of an attuned group and director, the safety and support from other roles in the scene, and especially the presence of the inner child and adult self dyad. In a psychodrama with an inner child role, I would first ensure that the protagonist can interact with the inner child in a state of spontaneity before role reversing them into that role. This would help to ensure safety and the integration of spontaneity and adaptive information. Once a protagonist has demonstrated this capacity, I would then role reverse them into the role of the inner child and coach them on expressing any unspoken feelings or unmet needs related to their experience (Giacomucci, 2023). This often includes a strong, healing abreactive catharsis of sadness, grief, shame, confusion, fear, anger, or rage. Sometimes, other emotions such as pleasure emerge – I see this occasionally related to sexual trauma when the protagonist experienced physical pleasure from the sexual abuse but also feels other negative feelings in relationship to it. Another occasional response I have seen from clients that would be important to be aware of is that some clients may not naturally respond to their inner child with love or acceptance. Their first reaction might be one of anger, self-blame, or to shame their younger self. These reactions suggest to me that the client may need more resourcing in order to interact with their younger self in a state of spontaneity rather than to reinforce the negative messages, neglect, and shame that were initially experienced because of the trauma. If the client is shaming their younger self for their feelings or behaviors, it will almost certainly be unhelpful to role reverse them into the inner child role, as they clearly have not given themselves permission yet to feel these emotions.

The catharsis and expression of these emotions is important in that it initiates an opportunity for emotional release and validation of the protagonist. Psychodramatic inner child work creates the safety necessary to feel what was unable to be felt at the time of the trauma. Furthermore, the validation from other roles in the scene, group members, the director, and from the adult self helps to renegotiate the intensity of the emotional valence of the memories. On another implicit level, the expression of emotions is also a form of exposure to the emotional content of the traumatic memory. Like other aspects of the memory, the emotions are often avoided or numbed (hence the PTSD symptom cluster of avoidance and numbing). The process of warming up to, approaching, and expressing the emotions includes a gradual exposure to the memory, which helps the protagonist experientially know that they are stronger than the memory.

Here is an example of a pretty typical inner child psychodrama from my trauma therapy group:

> Mateo is chosen by the group to be the protagonist with the topic of addressing the impacts of his experience of childhood sexual trauma, including struggles with self-blame and self-worth. His goal is to feel more confident in himself and his worth. When I ask him to identify a supportive role that could help him, he struggles to think of someone. I suggest it could be someone from a movie or story, to which he quickly responds – "Gandolf from Lord of the Rings." We enroll Gandolf into the psychodrama and he engages in a dialogue with Gandolf about his fear, self-blame, and struggles believing in himself. Through a series of role reversals and doubling statements, Gandolf powerfully affirms his worth while offering a sense of protection and strength.
>
> Next, I suggest that it may be helpful to have a conversation with younger Mateo at the time of the trauma. Mateo agrees that it feels like it would be

> helpful, so we bring Gandolf and the group with us to establish a scene. He identifies his childhood bedroom as a safe place (note that childhood bedrooms are often emotionally conflicted spaces, so be sure to assess and be thoughtful about setting up a scene in a childhood bedroom). He moves the furniture in the group room to simulate the positioning of his bed and desk in his childhood bedroom. He enrolls a group member as his 8-year-old self, from the time of the trauma. I guide him in initiating a dialogue with his younger self as he sits next to him on the bed. "Little Mateo, I know things have been hard and confusing for you and you blame yourself for the things that happened. But you need to know that it wasn't your fault, you are just a kid. You deserved love and attention, not abuse and neglect." Mateo offers himself comfort and validation while I instruct the other group member who is playing the role of his younger self to say things like "I must have deserved this" and "Nobody likes me and I'm not good enough." This helps to leverage the role reciprocity between the wounded inner child and Mateo as an adult. After he effectively consoles his younger self, I direct him to reverse roles and become his younger self. As his younger self, I encourage him to talk to older him and to articulate the emotions he feels about the abuse – "its not fair! I'm just a kid and have to deal with all of this. I just want to play with my toys and friends but instead he touched me and told me I had to keep the secret." As he expresses his anger and sadness, he begins to cry. We encourage him to continue expressing his feelings to his adult self and I offer him prompts such as "tell him about the secret – you don't have to keep it any longer," "can you talk to him about why you blame yourself for this?," and "tell him what you want or need from him." These prompts help Matteo drop deeper into his emotions and explore his anger, sadness, and shame. After he has his catharsis, I reverse him back into the role of his adult self and we replay the scene with Matteo as the adult comforting his younger self. Now that he has had the chance to express the emotions and be comforted and validated (as the younger self), he is more fully able to comfort and validate his younger self. The scene comes to a natural end as Matteo promises to take care of and protect his younger self going forward.

This psychodrama with Matteo's inner child shows how powerful the work can be and how the healing primarily comes from the adult self of the client. First, we resource the adult self, then bring in the inner child to be comforted by the adult self, next role reverse the client into the inner child, and always end with the client back in their adult self for integration. Next, we could move the psychodrama into a new scene where the client as an adult can stand up to the perpetrator and protect the inner child from the perpetrator (see Chapter 13 for more details). This is a natural follow-up scene to the scene described earlier, which could be enacted in the same session if there is time and the group is emotionally ready for it, or could be enacted in a follow-up session.

Inner child work with psychodrama allows the client to see the wounded child and negative core beliefs attached to the woundedness from childhood. Separating the wounded part from the adult ego state helps provide the containment, differentiation, and role reciprocity between the adult–child dyad that is often necessary for self-awareness and motivation to engage differently with the associated emotions and beliefs.

Cultivating a Relationship to Self

The use of psychodramatic inner child work is inherently a practice of cultivating a relationship with self – and/or a relationship between parts of self. Awareness and compassion for our inner child is awareness and compassion for the parts of ourselves that were wounded at the time of trauma and continue to be activated long after the trauma is over. Inner child work allows us to validate the defenses and survival mechanisms that we developed as children trying to find our way. It effectively provides a user-friendly avenue for bringing all of the new information we have learned as adults back to the younger selves who may still be frozen in time or in survival mode. Inner child work is almost like a firmware update for the parts of ourselves that we may have avoided or neglected for years because it was too scary or felt like too much work to address. Beyond the release and catharsis that often takes place during inner child work, there is an important integration of new information and self-compassion that occurs.

Inner child work helps us embrace our younger selves – and in doing so, we integrate the childlike qualities that we may have also lost contact with at the time of trauma or adversity. Connecting with our inner child can help foster a greater sense of playfulness, innocence, wonder, joy, trust, curiosity, creativity, and spontaneity. As we recognize the pain that our inner child has been carrying, we also come to know the strengths and positive qualities that our younger self had access to that we may have lost access to as adults.

Inner child work helps us embrace our younger selves – and in doing so, we integrate the childlike qualities that we may have also lost contact with at the time of trauma or adversity.

Perhaps one of the most important, and often overlooked, aspects of inner child work is that by recognizing an inner child within ourselves (or externalizing the inner child through concretization or role play), we are putting ourselves back into the adult role. From this adult place, we can more accurately observe and respond to the inner child rather than be stuck in the role of the inner child and acting from this place throughout our lives. When we are unaware of our inner child, we are more likely to be controlled by old emotions, beliefs, or defenses. Psychodramatic inner child work provides an opportunity to help provide internally what was originally missing externally in one's life as a child. The process of engaging in inner child work offers the possibility of growing up the inner child and reducing the intensity and frequency of past trauma being activated in the present. Inner child psychodramas are meant to be practice for the inner dialogue within ourselves during daily life. If one can nurture, validate, comfort, and protect their externalized inner child in a psychodrama, then they come to learn that they can also do the same internally in the moment-to-moment experiences of past memories or emotions being triggered. Inner child work is essentially a process of reparenting oneself.

Psychodramatic inner child work provides an opportunity to help provide internally what was originally missing externally in one's life as a child.

Conclusion

Psychodramatic inner child work provides a user-friendly way of conceptualizing and personifying the hurt parts of self. The wounded inner child carries the pain from early trauma and is activated by stimuli that might trigger past trauma. As the wounded child is activated, the beliefs, emotions, and behaviors associated with the younger self are also activated and hijack the individual. Just as the trauma exists fragmented within the individual, so too is the inner child – until we consciously develop a relationship with these parts of ourselves and work to meet them with empathy, understanding, and love. In psychodrama practice, inner child work often emerges as a dialogue between the adult self and the child self. This conversation creates the safety necessary to express what was unspoken and unfelt at the time of the trauma. The psychodramatic encounter with the inner child provides an external model for the ongoing day-to-day work of engaging in a supportive relationship with one's inner child on a regular basis.

The psychodramatic encounter with the inner child provides an external model for the ongoing day-to-day work of engaging in a supportive relationship with one's inner child on a regular basis.

References

Bradshaw, J. (1990). *Homecoming*. Random House.

Giacomucci, S. (2021). *Social work, sociometry, and psychodrama: Experiential approaches for group therapists, community leaders, and social workers*. Springer Nature.

Giacomucci, S. (2023). *Trauma-informed principles in group therapy, psychodrama, and organizations: Action methods for leadership*. Routledge.

Jung, C. G. (1954). *The collected words of C. G. Jung. Volume 17: The development of personality*. Princeton University Press.

Miller, A. (1981). *Prisoners of childhood: The drama of the gifted child and the search for the true self.* Basic Books.

Perl, O., Duek, O., Kulkarni, K. R., Gordon, C., Krystal, J. H., Levy, I.,. . .& Schiller, D. (2023). Neural patterns differentiate traumatic from sad autobiographical memories in PTSD. *Nature Neuroscience, 26*(12), 2226–2236.

Shapiro, F. (2017). *Eye movement desensitization and reprocessing (EMDR) therapy: Basic principles, protocols, and procedures*. Guilford Publications.

Chapter 13

Psychodramatic Anger Work, Empowerment, Antagonists, and Perpetrators

Empowerment is one of the most common goals and outcomes of psychodrama work with complex trauma. The experience of trauma and CPTSD leaves survivors with a sense of disempowerment, defeat, and stuckness. Trauma-focused psychodrama provides an avenue for getting unstuck and reconnecting to the power within ourselves and our community. The process of resourcing a protagonist (and the group) in psychodrama is often empowering by itself. When we shift from resourcing into the trauma-focused work of addressing perpetrator or antagonist roles in psychodrama, many protagonists experience a sense of empowerment that they have never felt in their life. Empowerment seems to be closely linked to other positive outcomes, including hope, motivation, self-esteem, self-worth, self-efficacy, and simply believing in one's self. Psychodrama has also developed a poor reputation in the past for the use of anger expression exercises without proper containment, safety, consent, preparation, or integration. Many psychodrama clients and trainees have experienced harm or retraumatization from anger work in psychodrama, so it needs to be approached thoughtfully and sensitively.

> Anger is one of the most common feelings resulting from trauma, especially complex trauma.

Anger is one of the most common feelings resulting from trauma, especially complex trauma. Yes, anger is a primary emotion. I cannot believe how many therapists I have heard tell their clients and groups that anger is a secondary emotion, covering up fear or sadness. I do not disagree that anger is used at times to cover up other emotions because feeling angry often feels powerful or in control – unlike feeling fear, shame, or sadness, which can feel scarier or more vulnerable to some. However, the neuroscience research is pretty clear that anger or rage is a primary emotion that all mammals experience when someone or something invades their space. This anger or rage response is also sometimes fueled by hunger, sleeplessness, fear, or frustration. One of the most important

DOI: 10.4324/9781003639497-13

aspects of empowering trauma survivors is to validate the anger that they feel, rather than devalue it and suggest that it is a secondary emotion.

Coincidentally, anger is also one of the most difficult emotions to work with and to navigate due to the risks of suppressing it and the risks of expressing it. Most of us have a complicated relationship with anger. Our sociocultural programming about anger does not help either, as it often leads to more distorted views of anger, often tangled up in our judgments about gender, race, or culture. However, when we learn how to tap into the anger within ourselves in healthy ways, anger becomes a newfound resource for recovery. Anger can help us set boundaries, protect ourselves and our loved-ones, feel empowered, preserve our sense of self-worth or dignity, protest injustice, and motivate us for positive change.

Risks of Suppressed or Expressed Anger

Many trauma survivors have experienced the harms of anger from multiple directions. Anger of other people often leads to trauma in the first place. Our own anger, when expressed in unhealthy ways, has often gotten us into trouble or resulted in hurting other people. Sometimes, we end up hurting ourselves when trying to navigate expressing our anger. Other times, we have suppressed our anger and/or judged ourselves for feeling anger, which only leads to other problems. We probably all have encountered someone who seems to be constantly angry and bitter, which is not too pleasant to be around either. The healthy expression of anger is not something that many people are taught, though most of us can identify plenty of examples of destructive expressions of anger. Many of those examples might include someone destroying property, punching holes in walls, throwing objects at others, fighting, unhelpful verbal altercations, or character assassinations through social media posts or gossip. We all probably have examples of trying to express our anger and overdoing it, causing harm to others or destruction of property, which results in us losing relationships and respect or having to apologize later and make amends. These experiences are likely to lead to more caution or fear of expressing our anger in the future.

Instead of expressing our anger, we might bottle it up. This approach might work in the short term to prevent some of the harmful examples of anger expression described earlier, but it is likely to lead to future problems. Someone who constantly suppresses their anger is likely to explode at other times and take their anger out on others. Or, we might have a tendency to take our anger out on ourselves through self-harm, suicidality, risk-taking behaviors, or develop addictions to block out the feelings. Many people have learned through social conditioning or culture to suppress their anger – there are plenty of examples of undesirable stereotypes that are used to prevent people from expressing their anger. I have heard people be labeled with all sorts of stereotypes for their anger, including being an immature man, a bitchy woman, an angry black or Latina woman, a violent black man, or a bitter old man. These stereotypes related to anger and identity may fuel much of the suppression of anger in our culture. Similarly, the experience of collective anger and injustice can fuel ongoing conflict between groups or communities. Regardless of the causes, the harms of suppressing anger can include increased stress, anxiety, depression, high blood pressure, heart problems, digestive issues, headaches, muscle tension, emotional numbness, isolation, lost relationships, and other mental health or medical problems. This leaves us in a bit of a dilemma, as both the expression of anger and the suppression of anger can cause problems in our lives.

Anger and Boundaries

> If anger is primarily a response to someone invading our space, it makes sense that anger could be used to help resolve the invasion of space.

Anger can serve a purpose and provide us with important information about ourselves and our experiences. If anger is primarily a response to someone invading our space (physically, emotionally, socially, etc.), it would make sense that anger could be used to help resolve the invasion of space (see Figure 13.1).

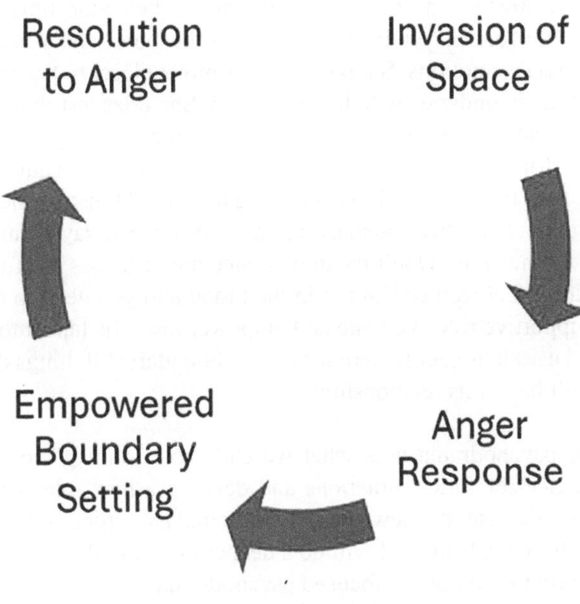

Figure 13.1 Cycle of anger and resolution through empowered boundary setting

This resolution comes in the form of boundary setting. For most trauma survivors, their experience of trauma involved the violation of a boundary; for many, it was the repeated violation of boundaries. This experience frequently leaves one with a sense of learned helplessness, that no matter what I do or say, it will not stop what is happening. This type of disempowerment seems to be quite common with childhood trauma or survivors of interpersonal violence. From what I can tell, most trauma survivors really struggle with either setting boundaries or respecting others' boundaries. Quite often, in my trauma-focused psychodrama work, the scene emerges as a boundary-setting scene with a part of self, another person, or an entity such as addiction or self-hate. These scenes, while emotionally intense, are often pretty straightforward in that they involve resourcing the protagonist with support and then moving to an expression of hurt and anger to another role while setting a boundary to renegotiate the relationship.

Here is a simple example of a pretty common and straightforward psychodrama on boundary setting:

> Mia is the protagonist of a psychodrama with the goal of setting boundaries with her boyfriend. She shares about her difficulty articulating her needs and limits due to past childhood trauma where her boundaries were not respected. After integrating supportive roles into the psychodrama scene, Mia chooses someone to play the role of her boyfriend. I direct the role player to produce in the boyfriend role using information Mia shared previously in the session about difficulties setting boundaries around his behavior, time with friends, and sex. The role player begins to defend the boyfriend's behavior which activates Mia's emotions. Supportive roles move closer to her and encourage her to set her boundaries with her boyfriend. She does just that – "you know, I told you that I want you to spend time with me Saturday night rather than going out drinking with your friends again. If you don't want to spend time with me, then this relationship isn't going to work." I instruct her to continue and talk about her other boundaries related to sex. She says, "and when I say no to sex, I mean no. Don't try to convince me or harass me for sex. Sometimes I don't feel well or I'm not in the mood and you need to respect that." As the supportive roles validate and empower her, Mia taps into more of her anger and uses it as energy to reinforce the boundary. "If things don't change, then I can't be in this relationship!"

This type of psychodrama uses what we call "role training" to help the protagonist practice for future situations and develop a new role with associated behaviors. In this case, the new behavior is boundary setting in her relationship with her boyfriend. Chapter 14 will do a deeper dive into the importance of role training as it relates to trauma-focused psychodrama.

Here is another example of a recent psychodrama with anger and boundary setting with a client who was struggling with a sense of worthlessness from his many experiences of trauma and addiction:

> Amir is chosen as the protagonist with the topic of addressing his lifelong sense of worthlessness and a goal of working towards self-love and self-worth. He shares about his experience as a mixed-race (black and Latino) man growing up in the United States and his experience of racism and sense of rejection for who he is. Beyond the trauma, he shares the feeling that he has done so many horrible things in his addiction that he has a core negative belief that he is simply a horrible person. First, we resource him with supportive roles – a double (I often call it a positive inner voice with clients), thoughtfulness, and caring. Initially, Amir struggles to repeat positive statements about himself from his double or to believe positive reflections from the strengths-based roles. The group wouldn't give up and kept doubling for him and reminding him of all the ways he had helped them, was thoughtful in his relationships, and how they valued his presence in the group. As the group became more and more involved, Amir began to believe the positive messages about himself from others. Once I saw that he had shifted from feeling worthless to feeling empowered and worthy, we enrolled this negative belief into the scene.
>
> Amir spoke to this negative belief about his relationship to it and how it has provided him with a sense of comfort, playfulness, pain, fear, anger, and a reason to continue drinking alcohol. I suggested that this negative voice may also contain some internalized racism. He agreed and consented to also include negative messages about race through the role. I coached the auxiliary role player to produce in this antagonist role and repeat some of the negative messages to Amir that Amir had identified. With the group's support, Amir stood up to this negative belief and affirmed his worth and goodness. He tapped into his anger and expressed his hurt to his negative belief – "I can't stand how sick our relationship has been. You bring me comfort, but you also lead me to do horrible things to people that I love. I almost killed myself with alcohol because of you! I don't need you anymore so fuck off! Leave and don't come back!" The group doubled for him to help him further express his anger. Next, I instructed him to role reverse and become his negative belief while we replayed the scene. This provided Amir with the experience of verbalizing all of the negative messages that he hears internally. I instructed him in the antagonist role to keep going strong with the negative messages until he is actually convinced by the boundary setting from the auxiliary playing his role (at this point I also remind the auxiliary in Amir's role to bring their own emotional content into the role and practice standing up to their own negative beliefs). After the scene was replayed and the negative belief leaves, I reversed Amir back into the role of himself for closure and integration. Amir

> reorganized the positioning of his support in the scene, and I directed each person to offer him affirmations related to his worth. Amir basked in the affirmations, and his entire body posture has shifted to a more confident and open stance. I asked him to check-in with his body and feelings and to discern what he would like to do or say to end his psychodrama. He looked around at the group, then gazed at the floor for a moment as he checked-in with himself, then he said "I haven't said this in a long time, but I actually feel grateful. I feel like a weight has come off my shoulders and I feel hopeful and valued for who I am."

Amir later shared that in playing the role of the negative belief, he could see just how distorted it was and that he would never say those things to anyone else, so it seemed unnatural to continue saying those messages to himself. He shared that from the role of the negative belief, seeing himself surrounded by support was intimidating and was the most convincing piece that led to the negative belief leaving. This provided Amir with important information about how to address this negative voice in the future when it reemerges internally. Amir's experience highlights how intertwined our sense of self can be with negative beliefs – which are often introjections from past perpetrators, bullies, or society. This happens quite frequently with identity-based trauma such as racism. Through the experience of trauma, abandonment, loss, discrimination, and oppression, we internalize negative messages from others and take them on as our own. Sometimes, these messages are explicit (such as someone saying "you are a loser"), while other times, these messages are implicit (such as someone concluding that they are a loser because they keep being ghosted or unchosen by men in their dating life). Amir's psychodrama depicts how important anger can be as an emotion that mobilizes us to set boundaries, stop tolerating unhealthy relationships, and create positive change within ourself or our lives.

As discussed in Chapter 2, the research evidence to support anger catharsis in therapy is quite limiting and actually seems to suggest that anger expressions increase anger, aggression, and hostility. Zerka Moreno's (1986) writing on anger urges us to tread carefully in how we engage in anger work with psychodrama:

> The wave of humanistic psychology, particularly certain forms of gestalt therapy, have invested much energy in getting clients to express anger. This became an end in itself and was supposed to be the aim of therapy. What often resulted was that patients could not get beyond the anger. They were not getting purged, which was assumed to be the positive outcome; they were merely learning to be angry. There are no rewards for this type of learning.
>
> (p. 145)

The most recent meta-analysis on the topic indicates that anger-reducing activities are most effective long term at reducing anger (Kjærvik & Bushman,

2024) – things such as deep breathing, mindfulness, and progressive muscle relaxation. This study, however, does not focus on anger from trauma, which is limiting. When I contrast these findings with my own experience, feedback from clients, and reflections from trusted colleagues, my conclusion is that anger catharsis can be helpful, but it needs to be followed up with anger-reducing activities and integration. Engaging in anger releases solely for the purpose of anger release seems to be ineffective and misguided – and the research shows that it increases anger long term. Instead, the anger release should be seen as a means to another end – an often necessary process of releasing pent-up anger so that something else can be absorbed and integrated in its place. This integration could come in many different forms. The most frequent that I see in my clients is integration in the form of forgiveness, empowerment, boundaries, new insight, and new beliefs about self. Another study on crying and catharsis (but not specifically on anger), reminds us that catharsis is helpful if certain conditions are met – (1) there is social support, (2) there is resolution or corrective experience related to the source of the emotions, and (3) a new understanding or insight into the source of the emotions is integrated (Bylsma et al., 2008).

Anger is an emotion that can be used constructively to set boundaries and promote healing. However, when anger evolves into rage, one is more likely to lose control, cause harm, and dissociate. The expression of rage is unlikely to involve body awareness or cognitive restructuring, both of which seem to be needed in the catharsis process to promote lasting change. For this reason, it can be helpful to assess the protagonist to discern if they can hold the boundary between expressing anger and expressing rage. If we can stick with the anger, without uncontrollably shifting into rage, the process will involve less risk and higher changes of effectiveness.

Completion of the Survival Response

Polyvagal theory (Porges, 2021) and Somatic Experiencing (Levine, 2010) offer us another conceptualization for anger work related to trauma healing. Porges' theory highlights three neural subsystems that underpin the nervous system's overall state, responses, and emotions – these evolutionary systems help to facilitate response to threat and safety (see Figure 13.2). The most primitive system is the dorsal vagal complex, which is associated with immobilization, freeze response. The next system that developed evolutionarily is the sympathetic nervous system, which supports mobilization responses of fight and flight. The final system to develop in humans is the ventral vagal complex (smart vagas), which is responsible for promoting social engagement. These three subsystems compose a map of human responses employed as physiological reactions to external threats – beginning with the social engagement system as a first adaptive response, preceding the mobilization responses (flight and fight), and finally calling upon the immobilization response as a last effort to survive. These responses

Figure 13.2 Polyvagal theory overview

were designed to be short adaptive behaviors to promote survival when faced with external threats, but, in the case of CPTSD, they can evolve into chronic responses to internal traumatic stress symptoms. Many of the clients that we work with in trauma-focused psychodrama sessions demonstrate these responses in relationship to others in the group, the group leader, psychodrama scenes, and even just the idea of joining a trauma group.

In the context of complex trauma and CPTSD, it seems that the freeze response is quite common because most children at the time of trauma do not have the option to fight or flee. Jumping from freeze into social engagement is usually not possible. Peter Levine, the developer of Somatic Experiencing, highlights the importance of becoming aware of the immobilization to move toward engaging the arousal (fight/flight) system (without overwhelming it) so that physiological activation can be discharged and the act of self-protection completed – thus allowing reengagement socially. If Polyvagal theory is approached as a map, this would mean that clients need to experience a fight or flight response to the trauma in order to move from freeze back to social engagement. We could also infer that clients who unsuccessfully attempted a fight or flight response at the time of the trauma may also benefit from revisiting this state of arousal and experiencing the successful completion of the sympathetic survival response.

Practically speaking, these theories from Polyvagal and Somatic Experiencing can guide us as psychodramatists in helping to create psychodramatic scenes where the protagonist can successfully complete a fight or flight response to the original trauma (Giacomucci, 2018). This often manifests as the protagonist gaining support in the scene to stand up to their perpetrator or another antagonist role while discharging anger (see Matteo's example below). Sometimes, the fight response is activated and expressed only through words, but other times, additional action is included in the scene, such as pushing, throwing scarves, ripping paper, hitting pillows, or similar (the necessary safety precautions should always be taken if any more intensive physical anger catharsis might be employed). The result is often a robust sense of empowerment and inner strength for the protagonist.

Internalized Perpetrators and Introjections From the Trauma

Psychodramatic work with perpetrator roles does not only include the role of the actual perpetrator but can also include working with the internalized version of the perpetrator. This can be defined and enrolled in different types of roles with varying degrees of closeness to the actual perpetrator of the trauma. For example, rather than enrolling the person who was the trauma perpetrator into a psychodrama, we could enroll the protagonist's internalized version of that person or the introjected negative messages from that person. These roles help provide more distance from the actual perpetrator and titrate the intensity of emotions in the process, which may be necessary to prevent retraumatization and help the protagonist (and the group) stay within their window of tolerance. A protagonist will have a very different level of arousal speaking to their perpetrator in a psychodrama compared to speaking to the negative messages from their perpetrator. If a client demonstrates the capacity to stand up to the negative messages or introjections from the perpetrator in the scene, then I would be more likely to next enroll the perpetrator as a role.

The role of the inner critic is often used as a less trauma-charged way of conceptualizing negative messages that have been internalized throughout life from unsupportive or traumatizing relationships. Many of my clients do not have the language of "inner critic" but instead use terms such as self-hate or self-sabotage, so I often enroll those as roles to accomplish the same objective as enrolling an inner critic or negative messages from the trauma (see Terry's psychodrama from Chapter 6 as an example). While the self-hate is definitely linked to the negative messages from the perpetrator, labeling the role as self-hate provides some distance from the trauma and lowers the potential intensity of the scene.

It is also important to consider that the perpetrator of trauma for an individual might not be another individual, but could be a group, a system, a government, or another entity.

In this discussion of internalized perpetrator roles, it is also important to consider that the perpetrator of trauma for an individual might not be another individual, but could be a group, a system, a government, or another entity. Working with collective roles as the perpetrator is often necessary and follows the same process as working with individual roles as the perpetrator in psychodrama. I would recommend using one role for the entire group/system to avoid the protagonist feeling outnumbered by perpetrator roles in their scene. Beyond an identified perpetrator, many trauma survivors feel equally harmed by the person who did not act and could have prevented or stopped the trauma from happening – sometimes referred to as the abandoning authority role (Hudgins & Toscani, 2013). It is not uncommon for anger work in psychodrama to shift toward an abandoning authority role, such as a parent or God (such as Jess's psychodrama in Chapter 11, which included anger toward God for her baby's death).

Practical Guidance for Working With Perpetrators, Antagonists, and Anger

When it comes to actually working with perpetrators, antagonists, and anger in psychodrama, it is essential to consider the importance of resourcing, safety, titration, and integration (Giacomucci, 2023). This type of psychodramatic work carries the highest risks of harm and retraumatization; thus, it should be the last type of psychodrama that a newer trainee learns to facilitate. The effectiveness of psychodrama work with perpetrators, antagonists, and anger is closely associated with the presence of resourcing beforehand and integration afterward. Anger work without resourcing is prone to retraumatization or harm for the protagonist or group, especially when there are complex trauma survivors in the group. Anger work without integration is likely to simply increase aggression and anger without lasting change.

The effectiveness of psychodrama work with perpetrators, antagonists, and anger is closely associated with the presence of resourcing beforehand and integration afterwards.

I frequently find that the clients who explicitly want to express anger are often the clients who do not need to do more anger work and would be better steered toward addressing the hurt and sadness related to their anger. At the same time, the clients who tend to avoid anger work are often the clients who would benefit the most from the empowerment that comes with owning and reintegrating their anger. With any psychodramatic anger work beyond boundary setting, it is important to inform clients that this is for expression and healing, not for practicing how to aggressively attack someone in real life.

As we approach anger with a protagonist, there are a few options to consider as the director – especially if there are concerns about the client/group's readiness. We must assess not only the protagonist's readiness but also the group's readiness for the anger work. Most often, the protagonist is more ready for it than the rest of the group. During the actual anger catharsis, we may need to direct the audience members to support each other or connect with some of their own resources to regulate their emotions associated with shouting or anger in the psychodrama scene. If we have a co-facilitator or assistant facilitator in the group, we could instruct them to attend to the audience members. We can also use surplus reality to resource the audience further – one simple example of this is to have each person choose a scarf to represent a strength that can help them ground themselves when there is anger in the room.

One option is to concretize the anger or enroll the anger into the scene as a role (see Amy's psychodrama in Chapter 4 for an example of concretizing anger). This often will shift the focus away from loud anger catharses toward exploring one's relationship and proximity to anger as a part of self. For clients who tend to resort to anger frequently, it may be more helpful to enroll anger as a role and initiate a psychodramatic dialogue with it to explore and renegotiate their relationship to it.

When we do choose to use perpetrator or antagonist roles in psychodrama, we have the choice of enrolling a role player to hold the role, using an empty chair to hold the role, or using an object to concretize the role. If I am concerned about the protagonist or group's ability to tolerate the intensity of enrolling a perpetrator or antagonist role, then I will often use an empty chair instead. This makes it easier for the protagonist to confront the role and reduces the risk of retraumatization. If I know that I am not going to role reverse the protagonist with the perpetrator role, then I often will opt to use an empty chair instead of a role player. Role reversing with a perpetrator role is something that should be done only with careful consideration and assessment. Before considering a role reversal, I am always assessing for the protagonist's capacity to be in a state of spontaneity in relationship to the perpetrator role – can they confront them, stand up to them, set boundaries, and maintain an adult ego state? If they have demonstrated this ability already, and I think there may be some clinical utility in role reversing with the perpetrator, then I will suggest a role reversal. I have had many protagonists gain significant insight, understanding, empathy, or stronger resolve after role reversing with a perpetrator role. The role reversal with antagonist roles also often creates new insight or perspective, which is an important piece of healing and change for the protagonist. If role reversal is utilized, it is important to ensure that the protagonist completes the role reversal back to self (not just physically in the scene, but also psychologically) and moves into an integrative experience related to the contract/goal of the psychodrama.

A reminder that the role reversal is the final stage of development in Moreno's theory can be useful here. Using the developmental theory as a guide, a director would consider the interventions of the double and the mirror before role reversing (or would assess if the functions of the double and mirror interventions are already embodied by the protagonist). Encountering a trauma role in a psychodrama with adequate doubling provides the protagonist with stability, support, expression, and the labeling of non-verbal traumatic content. Instructing the protagonist to first experience the trauma-based role interaction from the mirror position would provide distance, safety, and the ability to accurately label the experience while warming up to necessary changes in the scene. Once the functions of doubling (stabilization, expression, and labeling inner experience) and mirroring (differentiation and accurate sense of self) have been achieved, then it is safe to role reverse the protagonist into a trauma role. The role reversal with a trauma-based role, when used safely, provides further differentiation, understanding, catharsis, integration, and empowerment (Nolte, 2020; Roine, 2000; Hudgins & Toscani, 2013). In one memorable example of psychodrama work with a family member who was a sexual trauma perpetrator, a client engaged in the psychodrama to reclaim a sense of innocence that they felt had been taken from them at the moment of the trauma. The role reversal with the perpetrator role helped the client to develop a newfound understanding of the mind of the perpetrator and gain new curiosity, empathy, and insight into what may have been fueling their behavior. A year or so later after that psychodrama, the client was back at the treatment center as an alumni speaker and shared that they had later had a spontaneous encounter with that family member, which led to a vulnerable discussion about the trauma, where the perpetrator actually disclosed that they too had been sexually abused as a child and apologized for the trauma that they had caused. If it had not been for the work that the client did in the psychodrama, it is unlikely that they would have been able to engage in this healing conversation with their family member.

Furthermore, it is essential that we are attentive to de-rolling the group member who played the perpetrator or antagonist role. We are responsible for ensuring that they psychologically step out of the role, that the protagonist sees them as themselves and not as the role they played, and that the rest of the group has also psychologically de-rolled them. A lack of attention to de-rolling could result in an increase in transference within the group. When encountering a group member who needs extra attention to de-rolling, there are multiple avenues to further the de-rolling process. The auxiliary could be asked to use additional body movement to shake off the role with spontaneity or be asked to make statements about how they are different than the role they played in front of the group. For example, a group member after playing the role of an angry demanding mother might further de-role by stating, "I am not the angry demanding mother because: I don't have any children; I am loving and forgiving; and I am patient and understanding with others." Another playful way of de-rolling is to use surplus reality to set up a de-rolling station where role players are washed from their roles, unzipped from their roles, or transformed back into themselves with other creative and imaginary processes. One further method of de-rolling difficult roles is through the use of a mini empty chair dialogue between the role player and the role in front of the group. The role player is asked to separate themself from the role by putting it into the empty chair. Then, they are directed to speak to the role with a focus on differentiation. This provides the role player and the group with a visual, emotional, and cognitive experience of separating the group member from the role they played in the scene. When de-rolling in this way from an antagonist or trauma-based role, this also provides the role player with a chance to demonstrate safe, compassionate, insightful, and grounded statements or actions in front of the group after playing a role that may have been angry, dismissive, or antagonistic.

Anger catharsis can be done with or without physicality in the scene. As noted previously, sometimes, a physical element of pushing, stomping, hitting, ripping, or throwing can be utilized to provide a full-body catharsis beyond words. When using any physical expressions of anger, it is essential to have assessed for any medical conditions, physical injuries, or pregnancies before the group. Unless I have a thorough sense of each person's medical history and another trained, healthy, able-bodied professional to help facilitate the physicality of anger expression, then I will avoid any kind of pushing or pulling between roles. Hitting pillows or cushions reduces the risk of harm to others but may still carry some minor risk for the protagonist. Stomping, throwing, and ripping expressions of anger are less likely to carry the type of risk of physical harm that pushing, pulling, or hitting involve. While these types of physical expressions of anger may deepen experience, I often find that verbal expressions of anger are sufficient for most of my clients.

Integration After Anger Catharsis

Contracting with the protagonist before a psychodrama focused on anger catharsis is important. I would argue that it is limiting, and perhaps also problematic, to agree to a contract for the psychodrama that focuses solely on the expression of anger (or any other emotions). Catharsis, by itself, is not a good goal. A better contract for a psychodrama would be to connect with something after the catharsis. For example, instead of establishing a contract with the protagonist to "express my anger," set a contract to "express anger and find a sense of inner peace." When a protagonist expresses their goal of a psychodrama as expression of an emotion, I will simply ask them "what do you have to get by expressing your emotion?" – usually they are seeking peace, relief, closure, strength, or forgiveness. If I know what they are seeking to gain, I can better facilitate the expression of emotion toward the integration of their goal.

The integration after the catharsis is essential and should never be overlooked. An attendee at a recent training attributed the following quote to their trainer, Leticia Nieto, "Don't waste a single drop of catharsis without integration." Moreno differentiates abreactive catharsis from integrative catharsis and emphasizes integrative catharsis as the goal of psychodrama (Giacomucci, 2021). While the catharsis of abreaction provides the release, the catharsis of integration delivers something new within the self, thus solidifying an internal transformation.

While the catharsis of abreaction provides the release, the catharsis of integration delivers something new within the self, thus solidifying an internal transformation.

Integration often emerges on its own within a psychodrama scene. Sometimes, it is subtle and quiet. It may take the form of a new insight, perspective, or understanding of self or others. While catharsis is more emotionally oriented, integration is often more cognitive. Integration can also be facilitated through the introduction of new elements into the psychodrama, including concretizing something desired, enrolling a new role, practicing a behavior, emphasizing a new emotional state, or rehearsing a future projection. Integration can also be accessed through basic psychodrama interventions such as offering an integrative doubling statement, utilizing the mirror position for a new perspective, or engaging in role reversal with an integrative role.

To further depict this, we revisit Mateo's psychodrama from Chapter 12, where he engaged in an inner child scene to nurture himself. His goal was to reduce self-blame and increase self-worth. After the inner child scene with Mateo, we turn to confronting his sexual trauma perpetrator who was one of his older cousins.

He enrolls a group member into the scene as the perpetrator and repositions his inner child behind himself and Gandolf next to him. Mateo, supported by the group and Gandolf's protection, is fortified in his commitment to protect his inner child from the perpetrator. I direct him to talk to the perpetrator about what happened and tell him how it has impacted his life. Mateo starts, "what you did was so fucked up. Little Mateo deserved to be loved and to have a safe place to play, but you took his safety and innocence away." I encourage Mateo to express his anger at what happened. "I hate you for what you did! You are gross and pathetic, and I hope you die! I won't keep this a secret anymore, I'm done protecting you and I'm done blaming myself for this!" As Mateo stands up to his cousin, I instruct the role player to slowly back away as he starts to feel convinced by Mateo's resolve.

Next, in alignment with the contract, I invite Mateo to choose a scarf for blame and another for worth. I suggest that his cousin may have taken his sense of self-worth at the time of the trauma and that Mateo may be carrying around all of the blame for his cousin and that he can physically take back his self-worth and give back the blame. Mateo throws the scarf representing blame at his cousin and says "this is not mine and I'm done holding on to this. I was just a child and did nothing to deserve the abuse!" Next, I instruct him to take the scarf representing worth from the perpetrator but instruct the role player to only let go of it once he is convinced that Mateo believes in his own worth. This evolves into a short tug of war on the scarf representing worth.

> I invite group members to double for Mateo as he struggles to articulate his worth – "I deserve love, not abuse!," "I won't let the past define me!," and "I am worthy of recovery!" Mateo repeats each doubling statement and continues – "Because of you and what you did, I have had no sense of self-respect, self-love, or worth for years. I've come to realize that the sexual abuse had nothing to do with me and was all about you and your shit. I never deserved it and it was unfair. I deserved love, peace, and to feel valued for who I am!" As Mateo exclaims his worth, his cousin lets go of the scarf representing worth and steps away. Mateo yells, "get away from me! You are not welcome in my life or in my mind anymore!" At this point, the role player for the perpetrator steps out of the scene and I invite Mateo to take a moment to integrate his self-worth. I ask him to locate it within his body and feel the sensations and feelings of worthiness. To further integrate his sense of self-worth, I instruct Gandolf and the other group members to reaffirm his worth with short statements to him – "you are worthy," "you are a good man," "you are a valued member of our group," etc. Finally, I ask Mateo to tell the group what he plans to do with his self-worth going forward and how it will impact his behavior, beliefs, and relationships.

Mateo's psychodrama demonstrates a common psychodrama with a perpetrator in the scene. I often find that it helps to do the inner child work before the perpetrator work, as it seems to activate some natural self-protection instincts and further motivates the client for the tougher perpetrator work. Mateo's expression of anger could be conceptualized through polyvagal theory as a sympathetic activation of a fight response that allowed him to complete the survival response that he could not complete at the time of the sexual trauma – thus allowing his system to return to homeostasis and social engagement. The anger expression provided the release and abreactive catharsis. The reconnection with self-worth initiated the integrative catharsis and transformation. When it comes to integration, it can be helpful to facilitate the integration on multiple levels, including within the surplus reality of the scene, somatically within the body, emotionally within the self, relationally within the group dynamics, and further psychologically into one's plans for the future.

Mateo's psychodrama depicts the integration of self-worth after the catharsis. The exact nature of the integration will vary between psychodramas, clients, and topics. In my experience, the desired integration is often related to worth, forgiveness, peace, safety, willingness, love, or hope. If there is enough time, it is helpful to create a short future projection scene to help the protagonist directly practice integrating their newly integrated part of self into concrete situations in their life. Another suggested intervention that can be used after anger work to promote integration is the reformed auxiliary ego technique (Sacks, 1970). With this intervention, after the protagonist expresses their anger, the antagonist role returns for another scene having reformed. This can be explained within the scene in various ways, such as the person has taken a magic pill that cured them of all their shortcomings, or they went to therapy for several years and are now an empathetic, understanding, humble, and thoughtful person. As the reformed antagonist returns to the scene, they essentially offer the protagonist an amends and an apology for the harm they caused, which can help the protagonist let go of resentment and further humanize the person they are angry at. Chapter 14 will offer a comprehensive exploration of integration, future projection, role training, and posttraumatic growth through psychodrama.

Conclusion

Anger is a complicated emotion carrying risks when it is both suppressed and expressed. However, anger has an adaptive function in providing us with energy for protection and boundary setting in our lives. Psychodrama offers a powerful methodology for the expression of anger, boundary-setting practice, and the resolution of incomplete survival responses from the moment of the trauma. Psychodramatic anger work with perpetrator or antagonist roles should be approached with sensitivity and thoughtfulness due to the increased risk of harm that it involves. There are various modifications available for psychodramatic anger work that can help to prevent retraumatization. Anger catharsis by itself is insufficient for change without the subsequent integration afterward.

Psychodrama offers a powerful methodology for the expression of anger, boundary-setting practice, and the resolution of incomplete survival responses from the moment of the trauma.

References

Bylsma, L. M., Vingerhoets, A. J., & Rottenberg, J. (2008). When is crying cathartic? An international study. *Journal of Social and Clinical Psychology, 27*(10), 1165–1187.

Kjærvik, S. L., & Bushman, B. J. (2024). A meta-analytic review of anger management activities that increase or decrease arousal: What fuels or douses rage? *Clinical Psychology Review*, 102414.

Giacomucci, S. (2018). The trauma survivor's inner role atom: A clinical map for post-traumatic growth. *Journal of Psychodrama, Sociometry, and Group Psychotherapy, 66*(1), 115–129.

Giacomucci, S. (2021). *Social work, sociometry, and psychodrama: Experiential approaches for group therapists, community leaders, and social workers*. Springer Nature.

Giacomucci, S. (2023). *Trauma-informed principles in group therapy, psychodrama, and organizations: Action methods for leadership*. Routledge.

Hudgins, M. K., & Toscani, F. (2013). *Healing world trauma with the therapeutic spiral model: Stories from the frontlines*. Jessica Kingsley Publishers.

Levine, P. (2010). *In an unspoken voice: How the body releases trauma and restores goodness*. North Atlantic Books.

Moreno, Z. T. (1986). JL Moreno's concept of ethical anger. *Journal of Group Psychotherapy, Psychodrama & Sociometry*, *38*(4), 145–153.

Nolte, J. (2020). *JL Moreno and the psychodramatic method: On the practice of psychodrama*. Routledge.

Porges, S. W. (2021). *Polyvagal safety: Attachment, communication, self-regulation (Norton Series on Interpersonal Neurobiology)*. W.W. Norton & Company.

Roine, E. (2000). The use of psychodrama with trauma victims. In P. F. Kellermann & M. K. Hudgins (Eds.), *Psychodrama with trauma survivors: Acting out your pain* (pp. 83–96). Jessica Kingsley Publishers.

Sacks, J. M. (1970). The reformed auxiliary ego technique: A psychodramatic rekindling of hope. *Journal of Psychodrama, Sociometry, and Group Psychotherapy*, *23*(3–4), 118–121.

Chapter 14

Trauma Recovery Integration, Posttraumatic Growth, and Role Training for the Future With Psychodrama

Trauma work is not just about the trauma. Trauma recovery is about recovery from the trauma and growth after trauma. If we only focus on the trauma narrative and feelings, we may find temporary relief from validation and expression, but are unlikely to find lasting change. Phase 3 of trauma work is about integration and posttraumatic growth – it requires a conscious process of creating a vision of what trauma recovery could be like and taking steps toward that vision. Many clients reach a point in their trauma healing where they shift from being motivated by the pain of the trauma to being motivated by the possibility of goodness in the future. While it is important to engage in this recovery-oriented work with clients from the start of their trauma healing, it is also important that we do not use it to avoid the trauma work either. Some people refer to this as a "flight to wellness" or a "spiritual bypass," where there is a focus on wellness all of a sudden but not a reprocessing of the trauma or any deep work being done. The resourcing phase prepares us for the trauma work, the trauma processing removes the barriers to recovery, and the integration phase promotes the step-by-step incorporation of recovery within the self and life of the client.

As such, it makes sense that our trauma-focused psychodrama work should have a balanced focus on the trauma but also trauma recovery. My experience in addiction recovery communities and addiction treatment has really informed this aspect of the work for me. In addiction recovery, we often remind each other that we do not just focus on war stories of addiction but that our meetings and support groups must focus on what recovery looks like. I strongly believe that the same must be true for trauma recovery. In trauma-focused work with psychodrama, we have a unique opportunity to go beyond simply talking about what recovery could look like and move into embodying it in action. Psychodrama gives us the tools to envision trauma recovery and experience it in real time (Giacomucci, 2023). The technique of future projection allows us to become ourselves in the future in recovery or practice for future situations in recovery. The domains of posttraumatic growth can transform from dry research findings into practical

DOI: 10.4324/9781003639497-14

and concrete realities in psychodrama. The behaviors associated with trauma recovery and be practiced through role training and the role of a person in trauma recovery can be integrated within the self experientially.

The resourcing phase prepares us for the trauma work, the trauma processing removes the barriers to recovery, and the integration phase promotes the step-by-step incorporation of recovery within the self and life of the client.

Integration in Psychodrama

Prior chapters introduced the importance of integration in psychodrama scenes and the significance of the catharsis of integration after abreactive catharsis. Integration is important at each step of the process and can be integrated into each sociometry exercise, each psychodrama scene, each treatment episode, and every session closing. In my experience, I find that integration is much more important and needs much more time given in psychodrama sessions at lower levels of care (such as outpatient and intensive outpatient). In higher levels of care (such as residential or partial hospitalization programs, or even multi-day workshops), there is much more integration built into the treatment environment as participants are not usually going home after the psychodrama session but are attending other sessions and services where they have an opportunity to process and digest their psychodrama experience. In one of my prior psychodrama research studies (Giacomucci et al., 2022), we actually found that participants were continuing to experience changes in PTSD, posttraumatic growth, and spontaneity levels at our 30-day follow-up assessments, as compared to their follow-up within a few days of the 3-day workshop they attended. This suggests that psychodramas may take days or weeks (or even months) to fully integrate into one's self and into one's life.

One of the most beautifully articulated quotes about catharsis of integration in psychodrama comes from Kellermann (1984):

> To include not only release and relief of emotions, but also integration and ordering; not only intense reliving of the past, but also intense living in the here-and-now; not only a passive, verbal reflection, but also an active, nonverbal enactment; not only a private ritual, but also a communal, shared rite of healing; not only an intrapsychic tension reduction, but also an interpersonal conflict resolution; not only a medical purification, but also a religious and aesthetic experience.
>
> (1984, pp. 10–11)

This quote emphasizes that the integration takes place in the here-and-now and offers an experiential resolution and intake of something new after a release. The way that I like to simplify it is that the catharsis of abreaction is a release of something within us that creates an opening for change. The integration of something new into that same space is what creates change and prevents the unoccupied space from simply filling back up with more of the same. For example, when a client discharges anger through an emotional catharsis, there is an opening for a new insight, forgiveness, confidence, the reinstating of a boundary, or resolution to the source of the anger. If something new is not taken in by the client, they are likely to simply refill with anger over time. The integration prevents a return of the original problem, whether it be a negative emotion, belief, or behavior.

> The catharsis of abreaction is a release of something within us that creates an opening for change. The integration of something new into that same space is what creates change and prevents the unoccupied space from simply filling back up with the more of the same.

There are many different ways to incorporate integration into the end of psychodrama scenes including helping the protagonist locate the desired goal (such as hope, confidence, self-worth, love, etc.) within their body, taking a new posture or re-positioning the roles in the scene, using doubling to help the protagonist articulate a new belief or experience, role reversal or the mirror position for new perspective, concretization to bring awareness of something new, inviting the protagonist to make a commitment about how they will incorporate their new learning into their life, the use of music for internal digestion, or the directing of a future scene to put the new learning into action through a role training scene.

Similarly, there are many ways to facilitate integration after a psychodrama enactment before the session ends. The sharing phase of the psychodrama helps to promote integration naturally, but it can be helpful to build in more opportunities for integration, especially during longer and more involved sessions or multi-day workshops. This can be achieved through art-making (see Hudgins & Durost, 2022 or Nugent & Foster, 2025), verbal discussion, goal setting, or returning to sociometry exercises with prompts related to integration. A simple example of this comes from one of my recent five-day psychodrama training workshops, where, on the final day, I had everyone engage in a series of dyadic conversations with others about what they had learned throughout the week and would be integrating into their work:

- What is a new warm-up that you learned this week that you will use in your work?

- What is a new psychodrama intervention you learned that you will use in your work?
- What is one way you experienced personal growth that you will integrate into your life?
- What is one new idea or insight that you gained that will inform your work going forward?

These prompts could easily be modified for use at the end of a psychodrama client group:

- What is one new thing you learned about yourself throughout this group?
- What is one way that your experience in this group will impact how you show up in your relationships going forward?
- What is one thing you touched upon throughout this group that you know you need to revisit to do more work on?
- What is a personal strength that you feel you have cultivated or strengthened throughout your time in the group?

Regardless of how it is accomplished, it is important that we attend to the essential process of integration and meaning making in trauma-focused psychodrama enactments and sessions. One helpful framework for integration in trauma-focused psychodrama and trauma recovery is through the language of posttraumatic growth.

> Posttraumatic growth is the integration of healing and recovery in action.

Posttraumatic Growth Through Psychodrama

Posttraumatic growth is the integration of healing and recovery in action. It is a research-based framework for understanding the possibilities of trauma recovery. The five domains of posttraumatic growth were identified through tens of thousands of interviews with trauma survivors and stand as a testament to the real potential of trauma recovery. They represent the experience, strength, and hope of those who have walked the trauma healing journey. Chapter 1 introduced the five domains of posttraumatic growth, which are depicted again here in Figure 14.1.

These five domains of posttraumatic growth can be incorporated into every aspect of psychodrama practice, including assessment, treatment planning, goal setting, psychodrama contracting, sociometry prompts, psychodrama scenes, integration, sharing, and evaluation. In Chapter 16, I will also depict how these five areas of posttraumatic growth can emerge vicariously for the psychodrama practitioner through our work and training.

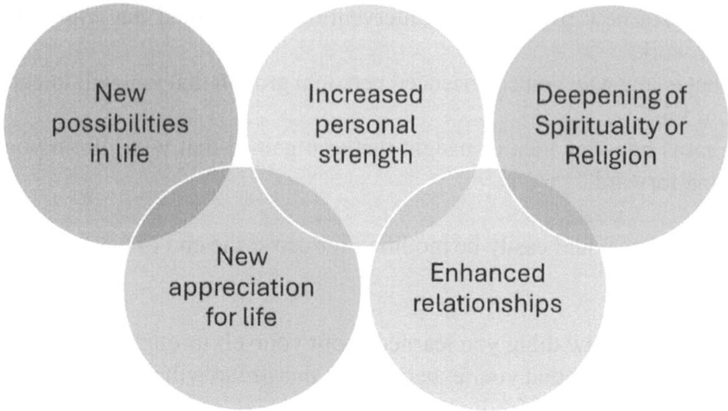

Figure 14.1 Five domains of posttraumatic growth

Psychodrama is unique in its capacity to cultivate posttraumatic growth through action. One of my research studies pointed to a positive relationship between spontaneity and posttraumatic growth for psychodrama participants (Giacomucci et al., 2022). Using psychodramatic techniques, especially role-playing, we are able to provide clients with avenues for exploring areas of posttraumatic growth experientially rather than simply talking about it. On the psychodrama stage, we can act out scenes embodying posttraumatic growth in the above domains while helping a client internalize these new roles, experiences, behaviors, perspectives, and beliefs. These domains of posttraumatic growth offer clients a template for future growth and the rewards of trauma recovery. Posttraumatic growth offers clients a vision of a future where their traumatic stress is transformed into growth. As such, these domains can be helpful for instilling hope, treatment planning, and guiding the progress of one's recovery.

Posttraumatic growth offers clients a vision of a future where their traumatic stress is transformed into growth.

For example, Nadine, a 35-year-old complex trauma survivor has been struggling with seeing a future for herself beyond her trauma. After adequate warming-up and resourcing Nadine in the scene, the facilitator asks her to choose someone to play the role of future Nadine living in posttraumatic growth. This initiates a dialogue between Nadine today and future Nadine. Throughout this interaction, Nadine envisions herself in the future having transformed her trauma into growth and gets to ask questions about the process of getting there. The facilitator instructs Nadine to reverse roles with herself in the future and respond to her own questions, now repeated by the other role player. Now embodying the role of herself in posttraumatic growth, Nadine speaks from this place to herself struggling today offering inspiration, advice, and insight. This exchange is entirely spontaneous. Nadine speaks from the role and experiencing multiple action insights through the process of validating, nurturing, and guiding herself. When stuck, the director or other group members offer Nadine support to help her stabilize in the role and continuing producing from the role. After some time, the director invites Nadine to role reverse back to the role of herself today receiving and taking in all the messages now being repeated to her from the role of her self in the future.

This deceptively simple role play provides Nadine (and the rest of the group) with a powerful experience of encountering a vision of self in the future, having transformed trauma into posttraumatic growth. In my clinical work, I find that most clients have not heard of this concept of posttraumatic growth before but that it provides a strong sense of hope. It concretizes and gives language to trauma recovery. Trauma-focused psychodrama allows us to bring trauma recovery to life and embody posttraumatic growth through role-playing.

My forthcoming research study from a trauma-focused psychodrama program in inpatient addiction treatment uncovered a 36.97% increase in posttraumatic growth (as well as 56.42% decrease in PTSD and 56.28% decrease in CPTSD) after just two or three weeks in treatment (Giacomucci, Marquit, Gupta, & Roldan, in preparation). This seems to be the largest study ($n = 175$) on psychodrama and posttraumatic growth to date and further establishes psychodrama's effectiveness at helping clients grow from trauma.

Connecting With Future Self and Hope

Future projection is one of the most common and helpful psychodrama techniques and interventions. It is a simple process, depicted earlier in Nadine's psychodrama example, where the client has an opportunity to speak to themselves in the future. In many ways, future projection is the opposite of inner child work, which involves traveling through time into the past to talk to a younger version of self. Psychodrama scenes that involve future projection help clients to orient to their trauma recovery goals and envision the potentials of growth in the future. The common piece of feedback I receive from clients after future projection psychodramas is that it helped them access an enormous amount of hope and excitement for the future. The future self, as a role in a psychodrama, is the embodiment of healing for the client and offers a taste of the rewards of continuing to engage in the tough work of trauma healing. This role can become a source of inspiration, insight, perspective, hope, and strength. The future self role in psychodrama can be employed as a resource early on in a psychodrama scene or as an integrative role at the end of a psychodrama scene.

One research study (King, 2001) explored outcomes between a group of participants journaling about their past trauma, another group journaling about their best possible future self, another group journaling about both, and a control group journaling about something mundane, which uncovered some interesting differences in outcomes. The group that journaled about the future self (future self only or future self and past trauma) experienced the larger reductions in physical illness, higher increases in happiness and positive mood, increased optimism, and reported feeling fewer upsetting feelings than those who wrote about trauma only. This particular study points to the healing potentials of connecting with a vision of ourselves in recovery from trauma rather than only focusing on the trauma experience itself.

While it might seem backward, I often find it helpful to start with future projection work with my clients so that we have a vision of where we are headed. Sometimes, in the first few initial sessions with an individual or group, I will have them reverse roles with themselves in the future to explore their treatment goals in action. I have found the future self role to be particularly helpful as a starting place for any type of trauma timeline work, in that it provides a built-in resource and stability for exploring the past adversity on the timeline. This is especially important when doing any type of trauma timeline exercises with complex trauma survivors, as asking them to write down or explore all their layers of trauma at once can be retraumatizing or destabilizing. I have also found it important to be thoughtful about how far in the future I am suggesting that clients begin to envision a future self. For someone struggling with CPTSD or depression, imagining a future can be quite difficult or feel inaccessible. In earlier stages of trauma recovery, I would recommend starting small with invitations to engage in future projections a few months in the future before suggesting future projections that are a year or more in the future.

Role Training and Practice Handling Trauma Triggers

Role training is another type of future-oriented psychodrama scene where a protagonist practices for a future situation that they expect to find themselves in (Giacomucci, 2021). Role training psychodramas are helpful for integration and preparing for future difficult interactions. In the context of trauma-focused work, role training psychodramas offer an opportunity to face trauma-related triggers and practice responding to them in new ways. I often think of role training psychodramas as similar to EMDR future templates, which are designed to help the client imagine facing trauma triggers and responding in new ways. Role training scenes can be created as a stand-alone psychodrama or as a final scene within a psychodrama with multiple scenes (such as after a scene doing inner child work or perpetrator work). Mia's psychodrama from Chapter 13 portrays a role training scene of practicing setting boundaries with a boyfriend. I most often utilize role training scenes to help clients practice setting boundaries related to trauma or addiction, to practice difficult conversations with loved ones, or to practice self-soothing while exposed to stimuli that reminds them of trauma (such as sounds of a siren, fireworks, arguments, perceived rejection, sexual attraction, anniversaries of events, or visiting certain places).

Here is an example of a role training psychodrama with a transgender client who has been struggling with bullying, rejection, and invalidation from others about their gender identity. Riley has begun to use they/them pronouns for the past few months and has been feeling helpless and fearful about having a direct conversation with their father about their pronouns. We set up a psychodrama scene where Riley can practice having this conversation with their father:

> Riley picks someone to play the role of their father and sets up the scene of their father's kitchen table where they expect to have this conversation. They face their father and begin to explain the purpose of the meeting – "I want to talk to you about me and my gender and I've been afraid to tell you this because I don't know how you will react." Riley goes on to tell their father about their sense of incongruence growing up as a girl and how they came to realize that they were non-binary. Riley shared about their feelings about gender and how they have decided to identify with they/them pronouns. After Riley said their piece to their father, I invited them to role reverse with their father and to respond with the best possible response they could hope for. After showing us what they want their father to say, I had them role reverse back and instructed the role player to repeat the response so Riley could experience it. Then, we replayed the scene from the beginning with Riley practicing their talking points again, but this time with Riley acting out their biggest fear of the worst possible response from their father. Experiencing this worst possible response gave Riley a chance to practice responding to their father back and forth if the conversation did not go well. We ended with another replay of the scene from the start with Riley acting out the most realistic response from their father (somewhere between the best possible and worst possible responses) and practicing responding.

Through this role training psychodrama, Riley was able to practice what they wanted to say to their father multiple times while also practicing replying to their father based on different responses. After the psychodrama, Riley shared that seeing themselves through their father's eyes helped them to develop a new understanding of how the conversation might impact their father and the sense of loss that he might feel about losing his daughter. This allowed Riley to have a newfound appreciation for the potential emotional impact of the conversation on their father. At the same time, Riley was reminded of the unconditional love that their father has toward them which helped to reduce their anxiety about the discussion.

When facilitating role training psychodramas, I often find it helpful to reenact the scene multiple times while exploring the best case, worst case, and most realistic responses from those involved. The format provides for multiple reruns of the scene to practice saying what needs to be said while also providing the protagonist with the experience that they crave for, the experience they are most afraid of, and the most realistic experience of the situation. In role training psychodramas, we can also employ doubling or other interventions to initiate the expression of emotions for the protagonist and a deepening of understanding for others involved.

As a side note, when doing psychodrama with transgender or non-binary clients, it is helpful to let them know ahead of time that the psychodrama process involves role reversals during which they are likely to be referred to with the pronouns associated with the role they are playing. For example, a non-binary client who uses they/them pronouns could play the role of a client's father, during which they may be referred to with he/him pronouns. I have had transgender and non-binary clients have an emotional reaction to this because it can activate or trigger trauma related to identity and being misgendered. I have found that mentioning this upfront tends to prevent any misunderstandings and limits the likelihood of clients being triggered.

Conclusion

Psychodrama interventions and enactments allow for an embodiment of trauma recovery, posttraumatic growth, and future goals. The three-dimensional experience of putting goals into action helps clients to envision and integration new behaviors, beliefs, and ways of being. Future projection in psychodrama creates an opportunity for clients to travel to the future and practice for future situations or to speak to themselves in the future to gain hope, inspiration, or clarity. Integration is essential to the process of change and must not be overlooked in trauma-focused psychodrama work. Integration helps clients to solidify trauma recovery within themselves and within their lives.

Psychodrama interventions and enactments allow for an embodiment of trauma recovery, posttraumatic growth, and future goals.

References

Giacomucci, S. (2021). *Social work, sociometry, and psychodrama: Experiential approaches for group therapists, community leaders, and social workers*. Springer Nature.

Giacomucci, S. (2023). *Trauma-informed principles in group therapy, psychodrama, and organizations: Action methods for leadership*. Routledge.

Giacomucci, S., Marquit, J., Gupta, R., & Roldan, N. (in preparation). *A mixed methods study on psychodrama in inpatient substance use treatment: Effects on CPTSD, PTSD, depression, anxiety, addiction recovery, resilience, posttraumatic growth, and spontaneity*.

Giacomucci, S., Marquit, J., & Miller Walsh, K. (2022). A controlled pilot study on the effects of a therapeutic spiral model trauma-focused psychodrama workshop on post-traumatic stress, spontaneity and post-traumatic growth. *Zeitschrift für Psychodrama und Soziometrie*, *21*(1), 171–188.

Hudgins, K., & Durost, S. W. (2022). *Experiential therapy from trauma to post-traumatic growth: Therapeutic spiral model psychodrama*. Springer Nature.

Kellermann, P. F. (1984). The place of catharsis in psychodrama. *Journal of Group Psychotherapy, Psychodrama, and Sociometry*, *37*(1), 1–13.

King, L. A. (2001). The health benefits of writing about life goals. *Personality and Social Psychology Bulletin*, *27*(7), 798–807.

Nugent, C. D., & Foster, C. (2025). After the psychodrama: The importance & process of integration. *Journal of Psychodrama, Sociometry, and Group Psychotherapy*, *71*(1), 1–13.

Chapter 15

Advanced Directing Techniques

The Group as the Protagonist

This chapter contains content from my previous book (Giacomucci, 2021) with updated material throughout. Reprinted with permission.

Directing a basic psychodrama is a complicated process to learn. Nevertheless, beyond the basics of directing, there are also various advanced interventions that can be employed in psychodrama to enhance the experience of the protagonist, the auxiliaries, the audience, and the group-as-a-whole. Essentially, we want the audience to internally experience everything that the protagonist is experiencing externally. In classical psychodrama, the focus tends to be mostly on the protagonist of the psychodrama, which can easily shift into an experience of individual therapy with a group audience if we are not careful. There is an even higher risk of this happening in settings where the protagonist is not chosen sociometrically by the group each session. In my experience as a psychodrama supervisor and trainer, the most common area of growth for my advanced trainees is learning how to involve the rest of the group in the protagonist's psychodrama. Moreno states in Psychodrama Volume One (1972) that

> The psychodrama director should see every member of the audience and thus establish, if not more, at least an illusion of direct communication with them. . . . A skillful psychodrama director should always create an illusion of communication by letting his eyes pass over everyone in the audience.
>
> (p. 325)

He reminds us that just as in traditional talk therapy groups, the facilitator needs to keep awareness of everyone in the group; the same is also true during psychodrama groups.

Essentially, we want the audience to internally experience everything that the protagonist is experiencing externally.

DOI: 10.4324/9781003639497-15

In this chapter, we will move beyond the basics of psychodrama directing and explore some advanced concepts for experienced psychodrama directors. Each subsection of this chapter will offer different methods for engaging the group-as-a-whole during the protagonist's psychodrama. The following advanced directing skills prevent the psychodrama process from becoming an individual therapy session within a group setting. The use of active sociometry within the psychodrama process will be outlined to keep the audience or group actively engaged and identified with the protagonist. The skillful weaving of group members' stories will be depicted through the use of surplus reality and clinical role assignments at the director's discretion. The use of clinical role assignments for both strengths-based roles and other roles will be explored. Complexities related to the multiple layers of object relations, role relations, and interpersonal relationships in a psychodrama group experience will be depicted. This section will also portray the use of projective identification in the psychodrama process in the service of the protagonist, the scene, and the group-as-a-whole. Brief interventions that explicitly expand the role of the protagonist from the individual to the group will also be demonstrated. The use of sociopsychodramatic and psychosociodramatic interventions will be explained. Furthermore, I will describe how to spontaneously incorporate whatever is happening in the real group room as a symbolic representation of what is happening in the surplus reality of the psychodrama scene.

Involving the Audience

One of the simplest ways to involve more group members in psychodrama directing is to use interventions that involve the audience throughout the process. For the experience to be therapeutic for observers, we want the audience to experience internally what the protagonist is experiencing externally. We want to remind the observers to look for similarities in their story and imagine what they would do or say if they were in the protagonist role at each step of the psychodrama enactment. Moreno (1972) states that "in a psychodramatic session the audience is always the patient" (p. 262). One of the simplest ways to involve the audience in a psychodrama is to invite group members to raise their hands if they identify with specific elements of the scene. This is something that I do multiple times throughout my directing to keep the audience engaged, looking for parallels to their life. Offering this simple sociometric intervention at various points in the psychodrama reminds the protagonist of the connection and peer support in the room while also showing the protagonist that their work is helping others. It enhances the sense of shared experience, universality, and group-as-a-whole experience while the protagonist's scene is enacted. Another simple sociometry intervention during the psychodrama process is to invite audience members to repeat significant statements from various roles when they relate to them (Blatner, 1996). This creates an echo of an important message and a sociometric connection through sound. Through this intervention, the protagonist becomes the double of the audience, who are repeating messages that they connect with from the protagonist's psychodrama.

Another use of the sociometry is to invite audience members to stand behind or put their hand on the shoulder of the role that they feel most identified with – or a role that they feel they need to speak to. Essentially, this is a locogram or hands-on-shoulder sociogram using the roles of the psychodrama as the options for choices. This can be used to cluster participants into a role – having multiple people play one role for more impact, to warm-up to psychodrama sub-scenes with the various roles, and/or to promote sharing. This process can be used in a simple, contained manner by inviting participants who identify with the protagonist's experience to stand behind the protagonist for support during the climax of the drama.

Sociometric Awareness Within a Psychodrama

Sociometry and psychodrama are different parts of Moreno's triadic system, albeit they have an intimate relationship to each other. As a director, it is important to maintain sociometric awareness throughout the psychodrama process (Gershoni, 2016). Each participant exists at the intersection of multiple systems, including their nervous system and other somatic systems, psychological systems, family systems, the group system, social systems, political system, cultural systems, and economic systems (Holmes, 2015). A psychodrama enactment and the roles within it interface with multiple systems and can only be fully understood through the lens of each of these systems. In social work, we describe this as person-in-environment or the biopsychosocial approach. This perspective of various systems intersecting offers insight into the overlapping systems of sociometry and psychodrama within a group psychotherapy session.

The sociometric warm-up is the first phase of a psychodrama group. Nevertheless, the sociometry of the group is useful to both be aware of and to actively utilize throughout the psychodrama enactment (Moreno, 1972). Although participants are being asked to play various psychodramatic roles in the scene, the interpersonal relationships between group members are inevitably still present during the process (Giacomucci, 2018; McVea, 2013). Knowing the nature of relationships between the group members may shed light on the nature of the role relationships in the scene. This often cultivates positive role relationships as the protagonist is likely to choose role players that they have positive relationships to. But the sociometry in the group can also be counter-productive to the psychodrama at times. For example, in the middle of a psychodrama, the protagonist might be asked to choose a group member to play the role of their younger self. If there is only one remaining audience member available for roles, they will not have a choice. If that remaining group member is someone who the protagonist has a negative relationship with, it could impact their ability to engage with the role of their younger self in a compassionate manner. Figure 15.1 depicts

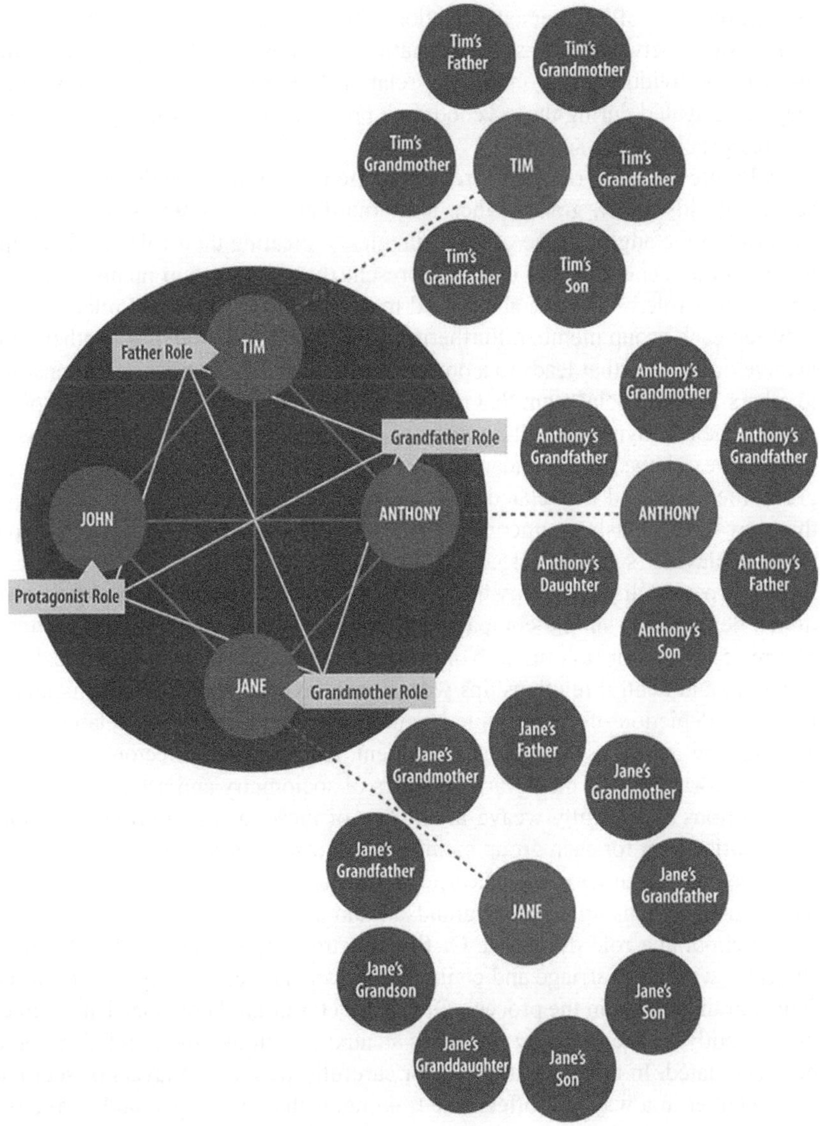

Figure 15.1 Multiple layers of object relations and role relations within a psychodrama enactment

Republished with permission from Giacomucci (2021)

the complexities of interpersonal relationships between group members, the role relationships between the psychodramatic roles they are playing in the scene, and each individual group member's relationships from their social atom that may be activated during the psychodrama process due to the role dynamics and role reciprocity of the scene.

In Figure 15.1, the rectangles represent the roles within John's psychodrama scene with his father, grandmother, and grandfather. Lines are used to connect each of the rectangles to the other rectangles, indicating their role relationships to each other. The adjacent circles represent the actual group member who is playing that role, with lines again used to depict the interpersonal relationships between each group member. Furthermore, each auxiliary role has another connective dotted line that leads to a portrayal of that group member's relationships to others in their social atom that may be activated due to the role they are playing and the role dynamics within the psychodrama scene. The larger square with dotted lines shows the boundary between the psychodrama being enacted by group members and the related roles from each group member's social atoms that may (consciously or unconsciously) influence their experience in the role they are playing (see Figure 15.1).

Many psychodrama groups involve more than four roles, so the aforementioned depiction is simple compared to most real psychodramas. Furthermore, Figure 15.1 only portrays the web of relationships without depicting the positive, negative, and neutral relationships within each layer of sociometry. This image is a good depiction of the multiple layers of sociometry or object relations that are engaged in any psychodrama enactment. An advanced director attempts to maintain awareness of these various layers of sociometry and use psychodrama interventions to skillfully weave in and out of these layers to provide optimal therapeutic effect for each group member – not just the protagonist.

In the role dynamics depicted earlier, a director might be aware of Jane's own conflictual relationship with her grandson and emphasize conflict resolution in the psychodrama role dynamics. Or the director might be aware that Anthony struggles with his marriage and could underscore the healthy marriage between John's grandparents in the process. Or the director might know that Tim's father died recently, so the directing of Tim as an auxiliary in the role of a father could be accentuated. In this way, the director carefully weaves the layers of sociometry together in a way that offers role training, catharsis, insight, and corrective experiences for each group member. A skillful director can facilitate a psychodrama for the protagonist where the other role players are also protagonists, doing their own work at the same time.

Clinical Role Assignments and Advanced Auxiliary Directing

While the protagonist usually is empowered to choose who they would like to play each role, there are times when the director might make use of clinical role assignments to enhance the experience for the group (Giacomucci, 2019). The practice of clinically assigning roles to participants based on the director's understanding of their personal/therapeutic goals or needs can be traced back to Moreno's original work around actor catharsis with the Theater of Spontaneity and Impromptu Theater (Garcia, 2010; Moreno, 2019). Clinical role assignments are most applicable when working with ongoing therapy groups where the director is familiar with each participant's stories. Although a director might be working with a group that they are not familiar with participants' back stories, information offered through the warm-up process and the protagonist selection can also be used to guide clinical role assignments. A simple way of using this is by incorporating the other group members who had volunteered as protagonists into the psychodrama in a role that allows them to do their own work in service of the protagonist's psychodrama. This is not always possible, but in most cases, it can be done without taking away from the protagonist's experience. An example of this is depicted as follows:

> Four group members volunteer as protagonist offering the following topics: worthlessness and self-worth by Lindsey; letting down defenses to trust others by Frank; hope for the future by Steven; and guilt, shame, and self-forgiveness offered by Jake. Jake's topic is sociometrically chosen by the group. As the psychodrama begins to unfold, Jake agrees when the director inquires if the role of a positive inner voice might be helpful for the scene. The director suggests Lindsey could play the role based on her proposed topic of self-worth. Through playing the role of Jake's inner supportive voice, Lindsey is able to achieve her own goals that she had hoped for as protagonist. Not only does she benefit from it, but because she is substantially invested in the role for her own gain, Jake benefits from having her as a strong auxiliary. Next in the psychodrama scene, Jake begins to share about his uncertainty about ever being able to forgive himself. Jake describes his negative beliefs about himself and his habit of pushing others away because he feels ashamed. At this point, the director suggests that Frank enter the role of the negative beliefs and behaviors that block Jake from self-forgiveness and connection. Frank is able to play the role without any role training based on his own warm-up to his topic. When role reversed with Jake, Frank (as Jake) gets to work on his topic through the interaction with Jake's negative beliefs/behaviors. As Jake renegotiates his relationship to these negative beliefs, he begins to warm-up to the potential of a future with self-forgiveness. Noticing the connection with Steven's topic of hope for the future, the director clinically assigns the role of future self to Steven after checking it out with Jake first. Steven steps into the role of Jake in the future having attained self-forgiveness and a positive relationship with himself. In the back and forth dialogue and role reversal between Jake and his future self, the director facilitates Steven's work at the same time.

Through the use of clinical role assignments related to the other volunteers for the protagonist, the director is able to provide a group-as-a-whole experience for participants while meeting the therapeutic goals and needs for the maximum number of group members (Buchanan & Dubbs-Siroka, 1980). While the role relationships in the protagonist's psychodrama are always given priority, each participant is seen as a protagonist just below the surface of the psychodrama roles. The director often reminds role players that as they are speaking to Jake, they are also speaking their messages to themselves – as they are playing the role for Jake, they are also playing the role for themselves (Giacomucci & Stone, 2019). In this process, it is also important to consider the sociometric relationships between the protagonist and the other group members before making a decision to assign a role. If Jake had a negative relationship with Steven playing the role of himself in the future, it could have jeopardized the success of his psychodrama. However, at the same time, a negative relationship between Jake and Frank playing the role of his negative beliefs and behaviors may have actually been helpful and even transformative for their interpersonal relationships, as it would have provided an opportunity for conflict, catharsis, anger, rejection, and change with the aesthetic distance of the roles. The skillful use of clinical role assignments makes for a more engaged, vulnerable, and fruitful psychodrama for everyone involved.

In a basic psychodrama enactment, the auxiliaries are simply playing roles for the protagonist's scene based on direction from the protagonist and/or director. An advanced director can encourage auxiliaries to bring themselves to the role they are playing using emotional content from their own connection to the topic or role dynamics (Blatner, 1996; McVea, 2013; Moreno, 1946). Drawing upon the awareness of the auxiliary role player's own social atom, the director can direct them to warm up to the role they are playing by accessing emotions related to their own lived experience of this role. This type of directing for auxiliaries can be used at any time and is especially relevant for auxiliaries who have been enrolled through clinical role assignments. It is also important to note that while clinical role assignments are one way to enhance the connection of participants to the psychodrama, the same group members are likely to be chosen for the roles based on the active tele between the protagonist and their peers (McVea, 2013).

Projective Identification

The here-and-now experience of group members is another source of information that can guide clinical role assignments. Using the same psychodrama example earlier, let us say that Tiffany is an audience member observing the psychodrama process with tears in her eyes, feeling vulnerable. Jake had referenced a desire to practice more vulnerability and be open with his emotions rather than defensive. With Jake's permission, Tiffany is integrated into the scene in the role of vulnerability, where she is encouraged to use the emotions she is experiencing in service of the psychodrama scene while representing the strength of vulnerability for Jake.

The example of Tiffany used earlier is conceptualized in the TSM as the use of projective identification in the group process (Hogenboom, 2020; Hudgins & Toscani, 2013). TSM teaches that the protagonist is projecting parts of self or emotions out upon group members who will at times identify with a projection and start to play out that role or emotion unconsciously. It is the role of the director and/or team members to be aware of the potential presence of projective identification and incorporate audience members who have identified with projections into the psychodrama scene so the protagonist can re-integrate the split-off part. The first instinct of a therapist might be to ignore Tiffany or allow her to leave the room to contain herself, but it is worth considering if her emotional experience might be one of projective identification and useful in the psychodrama scene. This process of projective identification in group therapy has also been described as it relates to group roles in traditional group work (Moxnes, 1999) and classical psychodrama groups (Holmes, 2015). The TSM uses projective identification in the service of this group-as-a-whole experience. Although we start with one protagonist, everyone becomes a protagonist. Although we start with one narrative, everyone's narrative joins into a collective narrative. And although on the surface we are concerned with the protagonist's inner role atom, each individual group member's role atoms begin to emerge in alignment with the drama. The layers of object relations form a symmetrical union – Moreno termed this as this *the organic unity of mankind* (Moreno, 1953). The group-mind emerges and accesses the autonomous healing center within (Giacomucci, 2019).

Holmes (2015) also describes the influence of projective identification on role players within classical psychodrama. He writes that the protagonist, in their interaction with a role on the psychodrama stage, is projecting that role and their experience of that role upon the role player who often identifies with the projections. It could be argued that projection and projective identification are the parallel mechanisms underlying the experience of role-reciprocity. Projective identification may also be underlying the process of doubling of the protagonist from other group members. In both cases, the projections from the protagonist are able to be held, articulated, and reintegrated by the protagonist in action.

Prescribing Roles

Another use of role assignments comes from the director's clinical judgment of roles that are missing in the psychodrama scene itself. A common use of this type of role assignment comes in the form of prescribing strengths-based roles or supportive roles when working with trauma or addiction (Dayton, 2005; Hudgins, 2002). The TSM offers a comprehensive clinical map that includes eight different prescriptive roles (see Section 7.8.1) with the functions of containment, strength/restoration, and accurate observation (Giacomucci, 2018). When working with trauma, these roles are prescribed by the psychodrama director into the scene to ensure safety. Some different examples might include prescribing the role of a *body double* to a protagonist struggling with body image; *interpersonal support* for a protagonist struggling to ask others for help; *courage* or *willingness* for a protagonist intimidated by the process; *self-love* for a protagonist struggling with self-hatred; *boundaries* for a protagonist struggling with healthy boundaries; a *manager of defenses* for a client struggling with maladaptive defense mechanisms; or a *compassionate witness* for a protagonist struggling with accurate labeling or self-judgment. As noted previously, the prescriptive roles enhance the sense of safety and spontaneity in the psychodrama scene, especially when working with traumatic material and trauma survivors. In many cases, without the presence of strengths-based roles, a protagonist risks repeating or re-enacting maladaptive behavior patterns or trauma in the actual psychodrama scene. If nothing changes, nothing changes. Regardless of the psychodrama enactment, it is also important to balance the use of clinical role assignments and prescribed roles with the protagonist's own choice of roles and role players. It can be helpful to think of the psychodrama process as a co-created scene between the protagonist, the director, and the group.

Moments of Multiple Protagonists

Traditionally, a psychodrama has one protagonist, and other group members play auxiliary roles needed for the scene enacted by the protagonist. An advanced psychodrama director begins to weave together the story lines of group members with both implicit and explicit interventions. One explicit intervention that accomplishes this is to direct moments where role players briefly step out of their psychodrama role and interact as themselves with another role in the psychodrama. Everyone is invited to become the protagonist for a moment and speak to whoever or whatever the roles represent for them in their life. This needs to be done in a way that is quick, contained, and does not interfere with the protagonist's scene or warm-up process. When done well, it can enhance the protagonist's experience by highlighting and enhancing group members' investment and identification with the psychodrama scene's roles, dynamics, and themes.

> Using the psychodrama scene from the image above as an example, let's say that John is revisiting a difficult, but meaningful moment with her grandparents sharing with him about their immigration story characterized by trauma, loss, and resilience. John's father was with him during the conversation for support. In the original, real-life scene John was overwhelmed hearing his grandparents' story for the first time and didn't know how to respond. Instead, he froze and shut down emotionally, unable to express his pain, sadness, shock, gratitude, love, and admiration for his grandparents after hearing the

details of their experience. His goal in this psychodrama was to revisit this moment in time, get unstuck, and be able to express the complex feelings that emerged for him. With the help of the group, he was able to do so in the psychodrama and had powerful catharsis letting out his sorrow for the trauma his grandparents experience and his anger towards those who discriminated against his ancestors. After releasing his anger and sadness, he was able to articulate his newfound appreciation, respect, and love directly to his grandparents. After John has thoroughly expressed his feelings, the director invites audience members to stand behind John, stepping briefly into the protagonist role and to state a sentence or two to the grandparent roles as if they were their grandparents (or whoever else they might represent for another group member). One at time, group members step forward next to John and offer statements of gratitude to their own grandparents or other grandparent-like figures from their own lives. As each group member takes their turn, John and the rest of the group drop into a deeper appreciation for each other and the shared experience of the psychodrama.

This moment of multiple protagonists provides John and the rest of the group with a concretization of the universality of the psychodrama topic and the role dynamics within. It reminds John that he has been a representative of the group while reminding participants of their own work related to the topic. This intervention allows the director to explicitly work with the group-as-a-whole and operationalizes the perspective of the group as the protagonist. In this way, group members not only see themselves in the protagonist but also get to step into the protagonist role briefly. Audience involvement is maximized, providing avenues for catharsis and integration to satisfy act hungers. In the aforementioned example, the intervention of a moment of multiple protagonists also served to cool down the protagonist after the scene climax and to move toward closure of the scene. This intervention can also be used in other phases of the psychodrama when deemed appropriate.

Psychosociodrama and Sociopsychodrama

Psychosociodrama interventions (as well as sociopsychodrama interventions) come from Brazil and Argentina psychodrama pioneers but also have their basis in Moreno's (1972) early work. Psychosociodrama involves the transition from psychodrama roles or scenes into sociodrama roles or scenes. Sociopsychodrama describes the opposite path, from sociodramatic, collective issues into more focused personal and psychodramatic work (Damjanov, 2021). In Psychodrama Volume 1, Moreno writes:

> The group approach in psychodrama deals with private problems. . . . But as soon as the individual are treated as collective representatives of community

> roles and role relations and not as to their private roles and role relations, the psychodrama turns into a "socio-psychodrama."
>
> (1972, p. 325)

I had read about these interventions for years but did not grasp it until I had seen it done while attending the Brazilian Psychodrama Conference. The director was facilitating a psychodrama with a protagonist who was confronting their parents about their internalized homophobia and their process of coming out as gay to their parents. This was a very emotional and difficult conversation for the protagonist, and it had become clear to the director that the audience (who had been very involved and rowdy during the scene) was very warmed up to the dynamics at place between the protagonist and their parents' beliefs about sexuality. The director permitted adequate time for the protagonist's catharsis and integration and, then with the protagonist's permission, redefined the roles of their father as "society" and their mother role as "culture" (this is actually quite accurate from a Jungian archetypal perspective). The director discussed how the closed-minded beliefs of the protagonist's parents were representative of the beliefs within our society and our culture – then invited the protagonist and other group members to step up to the new roles and speak their truth about sexuality to society and culture. This subtle but profound intervention turned the psychodrama into a psychosociodrama while deepening the process into an even more meaningful experience for the entire group.

After this experience, I was speaking to a colleague (Sérgio Guimarães) at the Brazilian Psychodrama Conference about psychosociodrama. He who provided a fitting metaphor suggesting that "there is a tunnel between psychodrama and sociodrama." He went on to suggest that most American psychodramatists have not yet seemed to find this tunnel entrance, but that once the tunnel entrance is found, one cannot continue to treat psychodrama and sociodrama as distinctly different approaches. Instead, they are intimately connected, and we can seamlessly transition between psychodramatic and sociodramatic elements in any given session. Moreno wrote that "Every role is a fusion of private and collective elements; it is composed of two parts – its collective denominators and its individual differentials" (1953, p. 75). Sociopsychodrama and psychosociodrama are defined by the transition between these private elements and collective elements of the roles in the scene.

Sociopsychodrama and psychosociodrama are defined by the transition between these private elements and collective elements of the roles in the scene.

In my experience facilitating psychodramas, the sharing phase of the group often helps to shift the focus from psychodramatic and personal elements of the protagonist toward more universal themes and sociodramatic elements of the group and society. This sometimes happens naturally as group members share how they relate to the protagonist. However, I often also find that the sharing phase maintains a very individualistic perspective, and psychodrama practice can become fragmented from larger social issues. This is where and how I see psychosociodramatic interventions to be of importance, in that they can help to transform our personal and individual psychodramas into scenes that also embody larger social issues. In my experience facilitating sociodramas, I find that the transition into psychodramatic content happens quite naturally in the sharing phase. After the sociodramatic enactment of collective roles, it seems easier for a group to share about their personal connection to those roles and themes. For me, I find the transition from sociodrama to psychodrama to be much easier, but this may be a result of my conditioning as an American psychodramatist primarily facilitating psychodrama in treatment settings with other Americans who have similar conditioning toward individualistic perspectives. In discussing this with Brazilian colleague Heloisa Fluery, she reminded me of the importance of contracting for sociopsychodrama as many sociodramas take place in public settings, organizations, or education, where the shift into personal and psychodramatic elements may not be as appropriate due to the different setting, goals, expectations, or dual roles.

Another example of psychosociodrama comes from a workshop I facilitated on resilience and trauma. This workshop took place at a very sensitive sociopolitical time, shortly after the election of Donald Trump and in the midst of escalating wars in Ukraine and Gaza. After a warm-up focused on the different aspects of resilience, we engaged in a sociodramatic scene, trying to connect a trauma survivor with these aspects of resilience. The sociodrama scene culminated with a powerful catharsis for the role player of the trauma survivor connecting with their resilience. As she played the role, I gently reminded her to integrate the supportive messages for herself as a trauma survivor. It seemed that the distance of the sociodramatic trauma survivor role had disintegrated and that she was in the role psychodramatically as herself. Noticing the appetite for more, and aware of the group's emotional connection to socio-political current events, I offered a psychosociodrama intervention – suggesting that we redefine the role of "the trauma survivor" to the role of "the world." This role transition re-energized the group's engagement and gave each person in their role more juice to engage with the role of the world that is suffering ongoing collective trauma. Although this was during a sociodrama scene, the role transition from an individual role (of trauma survivor) into a collective role (of the world) would be considered psychosociodramatic. One could also argue that the role player's internal transition from sociodramatically playing the trauma survivor role to bringing herself into the role and personalizing it would be considered a sociopsychodrama transition.

Baptista (2024) states that:

> A sociopsychodrama is characterized in which one does not lose sight of the fact that, even though it is a distinct feature, every protagonist is a representative of the group, and the dramatized personal theme is reflected in the other participants.
>
> (p. 46)

This quote seems to echo many of Moreno's own writings throughout the 1940s–1970s about the connection between sociodrama and psychodrama methods.

Whatever Happens in the Room Is Happening in the Surplus Reality

Another advanced intervention is to roll with whatever is happening in the group room, even the unexpected, and treating it as part of the surplus reality of the scene. This requires immense trust and spontaneity from the facilitator. Rather than interpreting things happening in the group room as separate from the psychodrama scene, we approach everything that happens during a psychodrama as part of the psychodrama. This means that if there is an interruption to the group from outside (or inside) the group, we treat it as part of the scene and find a way to integrate it into the scene. The director must act as if what is happening in the room is part of the scene; otherwise, we risk losing our warm-up and breaking from the surplus reality of the psychodrama.

Here are some examples of applying this in action to various degrees. A simple and common interruption during outpatient groups or training workshops is a cell phone ringing during the psychodrama. Rather than ignoring the phone or asking the group member to silence the phone, it can be incorporated into the scene by considering what is happening right now in the scene and considering if the phone call might literally or psychodramatically be part of the scene. A recent example of this was in one of my recent training workshops, where I was near the climax of a psychodrama scene where the protagonist was confronting an abusive family member with the support of various resources in their life, including their loving partner. Their phone rang at that moment in the scene, and it just so happened to be their partner who was calling them! We did not realize who had called them until after the session, but if we had checked mid-scene, we could have picked up the phone and enlisted their partner's support in real time into the scene rather than only psychodramatically. In other moments of phone calls during sessions, I might simply ask the protagonist who in their life might be reaching out to support them with the topic at hand. This would not involve actually answering the phone call, but instead treating the call as if it were part of the psychodrama and imagining who might be psychodramatically calling them. These responses to phone calls during psychodrama sessions are also applicable to situations where someone interrupts the group from outside of the group. In my inpatient group, I used to incorporate the staff member who interrupted the group into the scene by asking the protagonist – "who from your life has been missing and just showed up in our psychodrama scene?" or "who or what in your life often interrupts your progress towards this goal we are working on?" (the staff learned not to interrupt my groups pretty quickly!). This allows us to keep our momentum in the psychodrama scene even when there is an interruption.

Sometimes, there are things happening in the audience or with a group member that might be seen as disruptive by most facilitators but can be incorporated into the scene creatively – anything from group members leaving for the bathroom, returning to the group room, falling asleep, spilling a cup of water, and so on. If someone falls asleep in the session, we could enroll them as a part of the protagonist who went to sleep at the time of the trauma that is waiting to be reawakened (this is a fun and meaningful intervention I learned in my TSM training). Similarly, there are times when the protagonist might do something unexpected during the psychodrama, which may seem disruptive to the group but can be reframed within surplus reality as helpful to the psychodrama. One time I was directing a psychodrama with a client whose goal had to do with grief and anger toward their father. He shared about his fear that he was becoming his father, but that he wanted to be a different, better man than his father was. After resourcing the protagonist, we initiated a conversation with his deceased father so he could say what he needed to say to him. I then invited him to role reverse and become his father. Soon after taking the role of his father, he stood up from the chair, exclaimed, "I don't want to be my fucking father," and left the room angrily. It felt like everyone in the room was waiting to see what I was going to do as the director (including my supervisee and intern who were supporting the group that day). After pausing for a second, I smiled and said to the group that the protagonist had accomplished his goal today of not becoming his father. I sent the assistant leader to find the client, affirm his decision to leave the room at that moment, and invite him to return to the group, so we could celebrate him accomplishing his goal of not becoming his father.

Beyond interruptions from the group or other people, sometimes, there are other things happening in the building or outside the window that could distract the group. Over the years of facilitating psychodrama sessions, I have had various fire drills that take place during my group sessions. Sometimes, these are planned, and other times, they are unexpected. Of course, if there is a real fire alarm, we need to evacuate the building for safety purposes. However, there have been multiple times where I have been informed of a fire alarm test, not requiring evacuation, that is to take place during my psychodrama group. In these cases, I simply integrate it as part of the scene. The first time it happened, I was directing a scene with a protagonist whose goal was related to finding inner peace. By the time the alarm was set off, he had already been resourced in the scene, so I instructed him to practice connecting with inner peace right now as the piercing sound of the fire alarm echoed throughout the building. Another common use of this intervention relates to animals. One of the group rooms that I often lead psychodramas in has large windows that face a small, wooded area where there is often lots of bird activity. One time, I was directing a psychodrama, and there were two red cardinals sitting outside the window on a nearby fence. Once I noticed that they were there and that other group members were becoming distracted by them, I brought it to the attention of the protagonist and simply asked if the cardinals might represent two visitors coming to support their psychodrama. At this suggestion, the protagonist began to cry and stated that the cardinals may be their deceased mother and aunt who would be proud of them for the emotional work they are doing. I invited the protagonist to reverse roles with the new roles one at a time and simply incorporated them right into the scene.

My favorite story of using this intervention happened last year during a training workshop when a large spider appeared in the center of the group room during an inner child psychodrama scene. I stopped two group members who were about to kill the spider. I turned to the protagonist who had been talking to their inner child about fear, and I stated that their fear had just shown up in the room. We enrolled the spider in the role of fear. I asked the protagonist what they wanted to do with their fear to which they said – "I have let fear control me for too long. I need to stay with my inner child and not focus on the fear otherwise it will hold me back." For the remaining 45 minutes of the psychodrama, the spider ("fear") scurried throughout the group room, under people's chairs, and throughout the psychodrama scene. As the director, I narrated what the fear was doing to keep the protagonist and group aware. Eventually, the spider ("fear") disappeared and was nowhere to be found. This timing just so happened to coincide with a very meaningful integration scene in the psychodrama, where the protagonist met their goal for the psychodrama.

Conclusion

This chapter outlines various advanced psychodrama directing competencies and interventions focused on providing a group-as-a-whole therapeutic experience through the skillful interweaving of client stories and sociometric layers. The outlined interventions in this chapter are often too complex for one facilitator to track while also holding the other roles of director. It can be advantageous to work on a team of trained psychodrama professionals to share the responsibilities and directing functions. The use of active sociometry, clinical role assignments, and moments of multiple protagonists provide maximum emotional involvement for the audience and auxiliaries during the psychodrama process.

References

Baptista, T. T. (2024). Public psychodrama: More than a century valuing groups. In H. J. Fleury, M. M. Marra, & O. H. Hadler (Eds.), *Psychodrama in Brazil: Contemporary applications in mental health, education, and communities* (pp. 43–54). Springer Nature.

Blatner, A. (1996). *Acting-in: Practical applications of psychodramatic methods.* New York: Springer Publishing Company.

Buchanan, D. R., & Dubbs-Siroka, J. (1980). Psychodramatic treatment for psychiatric patients. *Journal of the National Association of Private Psychiatric Hospitals, 11*(2), 27–31.

Damjanov, J. (2021). Sociopsychodrama: Living sociometry, sociodrama and psychodrama. *In Sociodrama: The art and science of social change*. L'Harmattan.

Dayton, T. (2005). *The Living Stage: A step-by-step guide to psychodrama, sociometry, and experiential group therapy*. Health Communications Inc.

Garcia, A. (2010). Healing with action methods on the world stage. In E. Leveton (Ed.), *Healing collective trauma using sociodrama and drama therapy* (pp. 3–24). New York: Springer.

Gershoni, J. (2016). Highlighting sociometry in the psychodramatic process. *Zeitschrift für Psychodrama und Soziometrie, 15*, 353–357.

Giacomucci, S. (2018). The trauma survivor's inner role atom: A clinical map for post-traumatic growth. *Journal of Psychodrama, Sociometry, and Group Psychotherapy, 66*(1), 115–129.

Giacomucci, S. (2019). *Social group work in action: A sociometry, psychodrama, and experiential trauma therapy curriculum*. Doctorate in Social Work (DSW) Dissertations. 124. https://repository.upenn.edu/cgi/viewcontent.cgi?article=1128&context=edissertations_sp2

Giacomucci, S. (2021). *Social work, sociometry, and psychodrama: Experiential approaches for group therapists, community leaders, and social workers*. Springer Nature.

Giacomucci, S., & Stone, A. M. (2019). Being in two places at once: Renegotiating traumatic experience through the surplus reality of psychodrama. *Social Work with Groups, 42*(3), 184–196.

Hogenboom, I. (2020, April 9). *Working with projective identification in the Therapeutic Spiral Model (TSM)*. Retrieved from https://therapeuticspiralmodel.com/blog/working-with-projective-identification-in-the-therapeutic-spiral-model-tsm/

Holmes, P. (2015). *The inner world outside: Object relations theory and psychodrama.* London: Routledge.

Hudgins, M. K. (2002). *Experiential treatment of PTSD: The therapeutic spiral model.* New York: Springer Publishing.

Hudgins, M. K., & Toscani, F. (2013). *Healing world trauma with the therapeutic spiral model: Stories from the frontlines*. London: Jessica Kingsley Publishers.

McVea, C. (2013). The therapeutic alliance between the protagonist and auxiliaries. In M. K. Hudgins & F. Toscani (Eds.), *Healing world trauma with the therapeutic spiral model: Stories from the frontlines* (pp. 168–180). Philadelphia: Jessica Kingsley Publishers.

Moreno, J. L. (1946). *Psychodrama volume 1.* New York: Beacon House.

Moreno, J. L. (1953). *Who shall survive? Foundations of sociometry, group psychotherapy and sociodrama (2nd edition)*. Beacon, NY: Beacon House.
Moreno, J. L. (1972). *Psychodrama and group psychotherapy: First Volume (4th edition)*. Beacon House.
Moreno, J. L. (2019). *The autobiography of a genius* (E. Schreiber, S. Kelley, & S. Giacomucci, Eds.). United Kingdom: North West Psychodrama Association.
Moxnes, P. (1999). Understanding roles: A psychodynamic model for role differentiation in groups. *Group Dynamics: Theory, Research, and Practice*, *3*(2), 99–113.

Chapter 16

On Becoming a Psychodramatist

Spontaneity Training and VPTG

The process of becoming a psychodramatist takes more than certification, training, or supervision. Becoming a psychodramatist is also an internal process or integrating the role of psychodramatist into one's inner role repertoire. Chapter 3's subsection on role theory reminds us of the three phases of role development, which can be helpful to consider here. In the first phase, role taking, the professional is learning how to be a psychodramatist while addressing internal fears, insecurity, anxiety, and resistance to the role. Imposter syndrome is likely to emerge, and we can be left feeling like we will never be a good enough psychodramatist because of all of the complexities involved in learning the role. During role taking, we are often mimicking our role models (other psychodramatists) and trying to be like them. From this role-taking phase, we transition into a role-playing stage of development where we feel like we are a competent psychodramatist. The timing of this varies and may happen before certification, at certification, or after certification. It seems to me that honest feedback from clients, supervisors, peers, and trainers is essential in this transition. In the role-playing phase, the professional is able to hold the role of psychodramatist and facilitate psychodramas with spontaneity. The final phase of role development is role creating, which is when the psychodramatist brings their full self into the role and begins to hold the role in a way that it has not been held before. This phase of role development is not achieved by all but is evident through the integration of novel interventions, the combination of other professional training into one's psychodrama practice, and a differentiation from one's trainers.

In thinking about the development of the psychodramatist, it can be helpful to consider the four subroles of director (Kellermann, 1992). These four subroles together make up the role of what it means to be a psychodramatist – (1) sociometrist, (2) therapist, (3) analyst, and (4) producer (see Figure 16.1).

The sociometrist role is responsible for maintaining a group-as-a-whole perspective while tracking the sociodynamics and interpersonal nature of group dynamics. The therapist role is focused on developing therapeutic rapport, use of self, and empathy, while also being the agent of chance in the psychodrama. The

DOI: 10.4324/9781003639497-16

Figure 16.1 Four roles of the director

Reprinted with permission from Giacomucci (2021)

analyst role is devoted to applying theory to practice while considering clinical aspects and needs of the process, such as assessment, intervention, and treatment goals. The producer role is oriented on the aesthetic aspects of the psychodrama production, such as the use of props, space, roles, and the stage. Together, these four subroles make up the psychodramatist. Every psychodramatist has a unique blend of strengths and weaknesses related to these four roles, which allows us to use them as a framework for assessment (or self-assessment) in areas of growth as a psychodramatist. For example, in my work as a psychodramatist, I am aware that producer is my least developed subrole, but that I am skilled as an analyst and sociometrist. Consideration of these four subroles is essential for any developing psychodramatist and can offer insight into areas of growth.

Sociatry and Anti-Oppression

Learning how to become a psychodramatist also involves learning how to implement anti-oppressive interventions. Psychodrama grew within the idea of sociatry, which was Moreno's vision of healing for society. Becoming a psychodramatist means becoming a sociatrist. A hundred years ago, he wrote that society was sick and needed treatment. This sentiment still seems to ring true today. The famous opening words of Who Shall Survive? remind us that "A truly therapeutic procedure cannot have less an objective than the whole of mankind" (1953, p. 3). This means that, as psychodramatists, we must expand our therapeutic objectives to include everyone – especially those who have been historically marginalized and excluded.

Learning how to become a psychodramatist also involves learning how to implement anti-oppressive interventions.

In the same vein, I think it is important, though maybe unpopular, to also remind us that this means including everyone – even those that we disagree with, perpetrators of trauma, and political enemies. I firmly believe (and the research supports it) that those who cause harm through violence, discrimination, extremist religious or political beliefs, and close-mindedness are also trauma survivors. Without helping them also heal their trauma, there will be no end to white supremacy, gender violence, religious discrimination, political violence, and other forms of oppression. Of course, there are many nuances to this that I will not get into in detail here, but some considerations include how to navigate our own safety and grounding, protecting the group if a participant is unsafe, homogenous groups versus mixed groups, recognizing our limitations, checking our own bias, and learning to navigate conflict and disagreement in groups.

Making our methods accessible to those who are experiencing oppression or identity-based trauma means that we must first do our own inner work to make ourselves safer professionals for clients from diverse backgrounds. I do not believe that it is possible to be perfect in this regard; however, I do believe that this is an ongoing process for every professional. This requires doing the inner work to explore our own cultural biases, identify our own blind spots, develop a stance of cultural humility and responsiveness, and make amends when we make mistakes. Ongoing supervision, consultation, training, and self-reflection are key. I have found that it helps significantly to make a habit of asking for feedback and implementing changes to our facilitation style, group structures, and interventions.

The Trauma Therapist Is Also a Trauma Survivor

Most psychodramatists are both trauma therapists and trauma survivors at the same time. This dual role can be the source of tremendous empathy, insight, and passion but can also lead to increased risks of countertransference or vicarious trauma (Giacomucci, 2023). This phenomenon is common enough that some have labeled it the wounded healer archetype. Jungian psychology argues that the wounding can be a source of initiation for the healer (Farber, 2016). Many psychodramatists choose the path of psychodrama based on their own experience of healing from the method. Similarly, many trauma therapists are motivated to become trauma therapists based on their own experiences of healing through trauma therapy. This dynamic can promote a deeper sense of trust, peer support, and empathy in the therapeutic relationship.

Most psychodramatists are both trauma therapists and trauma survivors at the same time.

Herman (1992) also reminds us that traumatic countertransference is unavoidable in trauma therapy and will certainly have an impact on the therapeutic relationship. This happens when the unresolved trauma from the therapist and the unresolved trauma of the client become intertwined, which can lead to unintended consequences. This happens far more often than most of us are willing to admit. Addressing our own unresolved trauma as professionals is of the utmost importance. Traumatic countertransference is likely to increase risks of vicarious trauma and burnout (Giacomucci, 2023). This is an ongoing job that requires consistent personal growth, self-reflection, self-care, supervision, and training. The process of becoming a psychodramatist requires hundreds of hours of experiential training, which often includes therapeutic benefits of being able to engage in our own psychodramas during training. However, this cannot be a substitute for ongoing therapy. One thing I have noticed for myself and others is the over-reliance on these opportunities for personal growth and healing through training workshops, which often disappear as the trainee becomes certified, and especially when one becomes a psychodrama trainer themselves. The dual roles and conflicts of interest with other participants increase significantly, and it is not always appropriate to be doing our own trauma work as a participant in workshops where our trainees and students are also attending. I strongly urge all psychodramatists to find a therapeutic space outside of the psychodrama community to engage in ongoing therapy or personal growth work. In the same vein, it is important for all psychodramatists (and all trauma professionals) to continue to engage in our own supervision, self-reflection, and self-care practices. Ongoing self-care can help prevent traumatic countertransference, vicarious trauma, and burnout from running amok. Supervision and self-reflective practice can help us become more aware of countertransference while pointing us to areas of ongoing personal growth work.

Vicarious Trauma and VPTG

Vicarious traumatization or secondary traumatic stress is when the professional begins to experience traumatic stress symptoms in response to their work with trauma survivors. Vicarious trauma emerges similarly to PTSD with intrusions (flashbacks and nightmares), re-experiencing, avoidance, dissociation, arousal, reactivity, negative beliefs, and negative moods. The Professional Quality of Life self-assessment is a simple tool that can be used to measure one's levels of burnout, secondary traumatic stress, and work satisfaction (access it free at www.ProQol.org). Vicarious trauma is not only a risk for the professional but also a potential risk for all participants in a psychodrama group. Some examples of vicarious traumatization that I have seen include a psychodramatist working in addiction treatment losing hope in the effectiveness of treatment after seeing clients relapse and return to treatment frequently. Another example is a psychodramatist working with mass shooting survivors starting to feel unsafe in public places due to the stories of they have heard from shooting survivors. A further example is that of a psychodramatist with young kids becoming overprotective of their kids after working extensively with adult survivors of sexual abuse. The same argument that is often made about psychodrama being more effective due to its experiential nature could be applied to suggest that psychodrama carries higher risks of vicarious trauma due to its action methods.

Vicarious posttraumatic growth is the real possibility of the professional growing personally as a result of working with trauma survivors.

Anytime we are talking about vicarious trauma, I believe that it is also important to discuss VPTG. Psychodrama's experiential nature also accentuates its higher potential for VPTG. VPTG is the real possibility of the professional growing personally as a result of working with trauma survivors. Sometimes, it is referred to as Vicarious Resilience. VPTG is experienced in the same five domains as regular posttraumatic growth – (1) new sense of opportunity, (2) greater sense of appreciation, (3) personal strength, (4) enhanced relationships, and (5) stronger spiritual/religious connection. Any trauma professional who reflects closely on their work and their life is likely to find examples of VPTG. Here are some that I have become aware of in reflecting on my own work and growth it has caused: (1) through my work with trauma survivors, I came to see new possibilities in my career such as teaching others how to do trauma therapy; (2) in working with clients fighting terminal illness, I become more aware of how short life can be and developed a deeper sense of gratitude for life; (3) after working with some very difficult client cases and navigating complex ethical situations, I have become more aware of my own personal strengths; (4) after working with clients with tumultuous marriages, I became a lot more grateful for my marriage; and (5) through my work with deeply spiritual clients, I have seen how transformative spiritual roles are in psychodrama and deepened my own spirituality.

Like posttraumatic growth, VPTG is often something that happens spontaneously, but it is also something that we may need to actively work to cultivate. One meta-analysis (Manning et al., 2015) found that the four biggest predictors of VPTG for professionals were (1) supervision, (2) personal therapy, (3) self-care, and (4) supervision. These are four concrete activities that we can engage in and create routines to consistently stay engaged in. By doing so, we reduce our risks of vicarious trauma and increase our likelihood of experiencing VPTG.

Personal Growth Within Psychodrama Training

One of the most unique aspects of psychodrama training is that it inherently involves opportunities for personal growth. One cannot become a psychodramatist without experiencing the roles of protagonist, auxiliary ego, and audience member. Psychodrama training not only provides an intensive professional training in how to facilitate group therapy, sociometry, psychodrama, and sociodrama – but it also provides an intensive personal growth experience at the same time. It is quite common for psychodrama training groups to involve psychodrama enactments that are not much different from the types of psychodrama sessions with client groups. I have actually found that, in most cases, the depths and intensity of psychodrama experiences in training groups far exceed those of most client groups (and even exceed what would be appropriate or possible in most traditional treatment settings with real patients).

> Psychodrama trainees are challenged to not only thoroughly learn psychodrama, but to also thoroughly learn about themselves.

Psychodrama trainees are challenged to not only thoroughly learn psychodrama but also thoroughly learn about themselves. The experiential learning component of psychodrama training is not only educational but also therapeutic in most cases. Of course, the focus on personal growth needs to be secondary to the focus on professional learning in training environments. Additionally, the presence of one's colleagues or others with dual roles in the training group may impact one's ability to fully engage in personal work. For this reason, I notice that many trainees will join training groups outside of their geographical area, where they feel freer to dive into their own personal growth work during the training. I found this to be helpful in my own experience as a trainee.

Regardless, at the end of one's training, having completed 780 hours of training, a psychodramatist has inevitably also grown considerably as a human being and worked toward healing of their own traumas. While many other training programs also involve some secondary personal growth opportunities, I have not found any professional trainings that include the depth and frequency of personal growth opportunities encompassed in psychodrama training. As a participant in psychodrama sessions, I find it reassuring to know that the facilitator is someone who has engaged in their own healing work by the nature of their work as a psychodramatist.

Spontaneity Training

> The process of becoming a psychodramatist could be described as a process of spontaneity training and learning how to harness our own spontaneity to help others do the same.

The process of becoming a psychodramatist could be described as a process of spontaneity training and learning how to harness our own spontaneity to help others do the same. At its core, psychodrama itself is a process of spontaneity training for participants – learning how to have new responses to old situations or rehearsing for adequate responses in novel situations. It is often said that the psychodramatist must be the most spontaneous person in the room. After all, how can we help others warm up and access spontaneity if we have not already done so ourselves? Moreno writes in Who Shall Survive? (1978) that:

> A great deal of man's psycho- and sociopathology can be ascribed to the insufficient development of spontaneity. Spontaneity "training" is therefore the most auspicious skill to be taught to therapists in all our institutions of learning and it is his task to teach his clients how to be more spontaneous without becoming excessive.
>
> (p. 42)

All of the interventions within sociometry and psychodrama could be conceptualized as tools to promote spontaneity. Since spontaneity is the curative agent in psychodrama, it is one of the most important factors of a psychodramatist to attend to. While psychodrama sessions contain a basic structure, they also leave significant space for the unexpected. In most sessions, the director does not know in advance who will be the protagonist, what the theme will be, or what roles will emerge. The entire process is co-created in real time with the group. This unpredictability can create a sense of excitement and creative flow for a spontaneous facilitator but could result in a sense of anxiety and insecurity for a facilitator who has not accessed their own spontaneity yet.

The psychodrama training process is inherently a spontaneity training process. After hundreds of hours of psychodrama participation in training groups, practitioners learn to access spontaneity more readily. Many of the barriers to spontaneity are addressed in training (such as a fear of failure, inner critic, confidence, worth, etc.). Trainees develop an understanding and awareness of their own warming-up process, the common blocks to their spontaneity, and develop trust in the spontaneous process. On a general educational level, we could also argue that all education and supervision is an attempt at spontaneity training – literally trying to help the student or supervisee develop a new response to the reoccurring situations in their therapy sessions, or to have a good enough response to novel situations that emerge with their clients.

Perhaps spontaneity training is related to learning how to trust-the-process as the psychodramatist (Yaniv, 2018). Learning to trust-the-process is essential for any therapy modality but may be harder to do with psychodrama as the process looks different each time. I have come to think of it more as trusting in spontaneity rather than trusting the process in psychodrama. I learned to trust my own spontaneity as a psychodrama director, to trust the protagonist's spontaneity in the process, and to trust the group's spontaneity throughout the session. It is almost as if we come to trust that the spark of spontaneity will emerge through a warming-up process – and we come to trust in that.

In many ways, becoming a psychodramatist is not just about learning theory, techniques, or interventions. Becoming a psychodramatist is about cultivating a way of life that welcomes the unknown, embraces the here-and-now, and trusts in the collective wisdom of the group. Zerka Moreno writes, "Dr Moreno long wished his work to be identified as a way of life, instead of merely categorized as a therapeutic procedure" (Moreno, 2012). As we integrate this new professional role as psychodramatist into ourselves, we also learn to live more spontaneously beyond our offices and workplaces. Professional growth and learning in psychodrama are inseparable from our personal growth and learning. The spontaneity training never really ends. To become a psychodramatist is to become a vessel for spontaneity itself, trusting that within each moment, each client, each group, there is the potential for healing and growth.

To become a psychodramatist is to become a vessel for spontaneity itself, trusting that within each moment, each client, each group, there is the potential for healing and growth.

Conclusion

The process of becoming a psychodramatist requires a wholehearted commitment to professional and personal learning. Developing the role of psychodrama director involves a role-taking process to integrate the four subroles of psychodramatist – sociometrist, therapist, analyst, and producer. Most therapists and psychodramatists are also trauma survivors themselves. In this way, the role of psychodramatist is aligned with the wounded healer archetype. The past trauma of the professional can be a source of countertransference and bias, but it could also be the source of deep empathy and understanding. The experiential nature of psychodrama not only increases the risks of vicarious trauma for the professional (and the group) but also enhances the likelihood of VPTG. Psychodrama training is not just an educational and cognitive process but also a deep personal growth process teaching us to trust in the presence and possibility of spontaneity in every moment.

References

Farber, S. K. (2016). *Celebrating the wounded healer psychotherapist*. Routledge.

Giacomucci, S. (2021). *Social work, sociometry, and psychodrama: Experiential approaches for group therapists, community leaders, and social workers*. Springer Nature.

Giacomucci, S. (2023). *Trauma-informed principles in group therapy, psychodrama, and organizations: Action methods for leadership*. Routledge.

Herman, J. L. (1992). *Trauma and recovery: The aftermath of violence – from domestic abuse to political terror*. New York: Basic Books.

Kellermann, P. F. (1992). *Focus on psychodrama: The therapeutic aspects of psychodrama*. Jessica Kingsley.

Manning, S. F., de Terte, I., & Stephens, C. (2015). Vicarious posttraumatic growth: A systematic literature review. *International Journal of Wellbeing*, 5(2).

Moreno, J. L. (1953). *Who shall survive? Foundations of sociometry, group psychotherapy and sociodrama (2nd edition)*. Beacon, NY: Beacon House.

Moreno, J. L. (1978). *Who shall survive? Foundations of sociometry, group psychotherapy and psychodrama (3rd edition)*. Beacon House.

Moreno, Z. T. (2012). *To dream again: A memoir*. Mental Health Resources.

Yaniv, D. (2018). Trust the process: A new scientific outlook on psychodramatic spontaneity training. *Frontiers in Psychology*, *9*, 2083.

Index

For Product Safety Concerns and Information please contact our
EU representative GPSR@taylorandfrancis.com Taylor & Francis
Verlag GmbH, Kaufingerstraße 24, 80331 München, Germany